STRANGER THAN FICTION

THE LIFE AND TIMES OF SPLIT ENZ

MIKE CHUNN

COPYRIGHT

Published by Hurricane Press

PO Box 568, Cambridge, New Zealand 3450

www.hurricane-press.com

ISBN 978-0-9941359-4-0

Cover image: © Original painting Phil Judd

CONTENTS

1

BEGINNING OF THE ENZ

I know now I must leave Split Enz. The worst part will be telling the others. How will I tell them? And when?

Not tonight. Not when we're playing the last show of our American tour. It's here in Chicago, a frozen, drenched city. The sign outside the club where we will play says 'Spilt Enz'.

There was talk of cancelling the gig as so few tickets had sold. A night off wouldn't have been so bad. But it feels right that I 'know' when I'm on stage for the last time in the US of A with my band of merry pranksters.

Standing here on the shores of Lake Michigan with the city at my back, I'm lost in fleeting memories of the band. It's been four years since we performed in front of an audience for the first time. And it's been almost as long since we were first booed off a stage, beneath a shower of abuse.

Phil Judd must be thinking about this last show of the American tour too. He has already resigned; he has left the band. Tonight is his last show. He'll be relieved. I suspect we will have similar thoughts ... Reflections. On this tour, he's taken to walking off stage during sets, leaving the rest of us to hop, skip and jump around in our evolution of zany and wacky stagecraft. There has been drama of almost melodramatic proportions. Phil punched Tim. In the green room – dressing room? – locker room? – locked-up-room – in the state of Georgia. That was one for the books. This book.

Tim has already made plans. He's off to Baltimore to stay at his uncle's house with Eddie Rayner at his side. He knows what he has to do. They'll write songs together, mixing the new chemistry to replace the Judd-Finn partnership. Or will that now be remembered as Finn-Judd?

I look out over Lake Michigan some more. Canada lies beyond the horizon. I won't ever get there. Will Split Enz ever get there? It was always part of the plan, our plan – to conquer the world.

I face north. In the days of long hair and beards Tim and I used to face north on the Parnell Road in Auckland. We would buy *Melody Maker* magazines from the local stationer. Tim would peruse the articles on the new emerging acts planning one day to grace those pages as one of them. I would search the classified ads, dreaming of owning a cool bass guitar. We faced north because that's where England lay. The premier destination. Today I face north and the North Pole looks back.

I turn and face east. Europe is over there. The streets of London and the M1 and Liverpool and Bristol and Newcastle and the smog of cities and the fog of tired minds. Split Enz in a van rolling on through the night.

I look to the south-west. The United States lies there with its giant capability to grind you down and gently destroy you. It rolls in interminably from either side of Highway 61 like a turning tide. We're all exhausted, and trying to cope in our own ways, after weeks of stepping out at America's clubs and concert halls by night and sleepwalking through radio station visits and record company promotions by day.

We've endured a look-a-like contest, being booked as a support act for a comedian and played several shows to audiences that barely outnumbered us.

In Atlanta, we walked onstage to face an audience of two.

Tim called out: 'Are you having a good time?'

Silence.

'Well, we are' screamed Tim, ' ... and majority rule!'

Some nights we won. Those were the shows where the audience could see past the weird hairstyles, make-up and brightly-coloured suits and consider there might be alternatives, after all, to Fleetwood Mac and Al Stewart.

The breeze off the lake makes me shiver and brings my thoughts back to the present. I will complete my circle.

I turn to the south. New Zealand is way down there. I will be flying to New Zealand tomorrow. I am meant to be finding a replacement guitarist for the departing Judd. But I just need to get home. Fullstop.

I am unwell. I've been lost in a phobic maze and I need to find help.

I keep telling myself – tomorrow I go home. Tomorrow I go home.

I will look for a guitarist, even though I know the band will no longer be part mine. There will be another beginning, a new line-up for Enz. Another band of brothers will dream of big tours, epic albums and a decent night's sleep.

When I return to Auckland, I'll go to watch Neil Finn, Tim's younger brother. He has been rehearsing for a concert with my brother Geoffrey to be staged at the Maidment Theatre. Their band is called After Hours. I'll surprise them by turning up to the show unannounced.

Lake Michigan is serene in its icy stillness. A Lincoln car dented like a tin tea caddy arrives across the road. Out hop Bob Gillies, Noel Crombie and Eddie Rayner. They've no idea I'm going to leave. I will keep my decision in a shroud a while longer .... and I go to join them.

I walk into the bar, ready to put on makeup and change into my stage clothes. That's in two hours time. But now – sound check time – I climb on stage, put on my bass guitar and we play *Walking Down A Road*.

When all is said and done, we aren't a bad band really. We're pretty good.

A band with a weaving plot behind it.

And so it seems right for me now to tell you the story.

The formation of Split Enz occurred in a time that now seems very distant. A distance clocked by the changing world of technology. And mankind's propensity to be stupid and gargantuan at the same time.

Today the ambitious teenage rookies know it all. The music industry proffers seminars, booklets, courses, grants and publicity. And you can access everything instantly. The massive dosage of music spun out across New Zealand on mobile devices, car systems, headphones attached to anything you like (and that includes phones), the FM stations, the streaming, the downloads from server islands; all bringing to the novice a clear, concise picture that guides their 'next step'.

Images, songs, motion, technocracy – all is clear and nothing is left to guesswork. There aren't any trams to catch. And the creative brains at work must strive very hard to evolve a unique identity at the very least as the world is awash (at long last!) with a vast array of human beings making music.

In 1972, it was different. And let's talk New Zealand as there was no global connectivity. The music industry threw up middle-of-the-road nonsense on television and the AM stations were all the same. A muddy Top 40 mix of foreign (English and American) music that was, on the whole, insipid. Unlike the decade before. We rejected it all. It was perfect. We walked in a silent world with nothing but our dreams of a musical evolution; an evolution where all would be unique, individual and pioneering.

Only on a dark stage were we able to plan what was finally achieved under the bright lights. We collided at first because we couldn't see where we were going. But we got used to being blind. And then things shone!

This story is propelled by the songs of Phil Judd, Tim Finn and Neil Finn. For it was their extraordinary, singular talents that laid the foundation for the band's momentum. The book came to be on the suggestion of Ann Clifford.

I lost my mind writing it but – thanks to my wife Brigid – I found it again. Thank you B for your patience during that time.

Now let us away.

2

QUITE EARLY ONE MORNING

In the late 1950s, Auckland, New Zealand, was a sprawl of skinny roads, scrawny trees and short-back-and-sides. There was a sober pace and days rolled by. At the time, as the sixties loomed, New Zealand was in cultural isolation and still decades short on having some quantifiable presence on the global map.

There was a World War II hangover and an increasingly anachronistic reliance on the United Kingdom to sustain and provide. This was ironic considering Britain's frugal attitude at the time; England's slow recovery post-war was in sharp contrast to the boom in the United States where Elvis Presley, Marlon Brando and Jack Kerouac had merged from their divergent sources to forge an entertainment revolution, riding on the back of a massive commodity boom. Through huffing and puffing, the British Empire had staved off the inevitable economic realities of the twentieth century and was yet to implode; in New Zealand, we all stood for the national anthem before movies (not *God Defend New Zealand* but *God Save The Queen!*), the radios were full of royalty reports and shopping specials, and there was no television. We marched to a textbook beat and no one seemed to go off on a tangent.

The cinemas churned through British war movies in rapid succession, with John Mills on the bridge and moustaches on every lip. For a boy with grazed knees and grey socks, the fantasy of battle was re-lived in stacks of war comics and wooden guns made from fire-wood and suburban driftwood. Pieces of timber that surfaced out of nowhere to become Bren guns, sten guns and Lugers. I would attack the enemy in the undergrowth, under cover of the 20 fruit trees that dotted our half-acre backyard in the suburb of Otahuhu.

In moments of stealth and surprise I would pour red-hot bullets into the chest of my younger brother, Geoffrey. He was shorter than me but not by much and would eventually tower over me. In more ways than one. His sense of adventure was more inside his head and his original songs to be offered to the world many years later were a testament to that. His idea of playing war games was about survival. He tossed his skinny legs in the air and ran from the bullets. I shot him. He would refuse to die. I, on the other hand, tossed myself onto the rotting fruit and muddy earth all cadaver and carcass. Occasionally I would play alone and shoot myself. Then my mother would call me in and I would fade exhausted over a hot meal.

Each day as the sun set, the suburbs of Auckland shrank into themselves with only the lights of the odd bus, tram or Morris Oxford to indicate the life therein. A life of simplicity.

We would awake each dawn in clean, cold air often drenched in fog from the Tamaki Estuary. By midday it was gone and a blue sky would parade above us, if only for a short while. By mid-afternoon there were thunderclouds blacker than the night. These towering monoliths of water rolled in from the south and wiped the sun clean from the slate sky while sending my size-three feet scurrying down Hutton Street to number nine (now an old folk's home) in a (usually vain) attempt to beat the downpour. If I clambered the back steps five minutes too late it was thrilling; the cold water soaking slowly through the grey uniform and blue tie I wore every day to St Joseph's Convent.

St Joseph's Convent was old and packed with white women in

black habits through which poked sour faces telling us about Duck Luck and Chicken Licken and Janet and John. More often than not, though, they told us about heaven (should that be Heaven?) and just where we all stood with this invisible figment of fragmented fomentation. From my first day, these grim females instilled a tenacious fear couched in biblical references and social disciplines. The fear of God. The devil. (Should that be the Devil?).

Self-loathing seemed a cool thing to them. And I liked the perfect symmetry of 666. They were devilishly good at strapping us too. Thick professional leather straps. Some factory must have made them from really tough Otahuhu bulls. But there were paradoxes and holes in their arguments, and each year led to more confusions. One moment, God was turning water into wine. Presumably he could turn tap water into lemonade! Such bliss. The next he was splashing black across our souls because we missed mass on Sunday.

And black souls were a one-way ticket to hell.

I needed to know more about this variance, as the thought of a timelessness of scorched buttocks was more than I could bear. First, we were all told about the two categories of sin – venial and mortal. Each sin type was pegged to social and religious misdemeanours and was reflected in the soiling of the soul but was there a hierarchy of blackness?

Chunn: 'Sister Mary Carthage? How many venial sins does it take to earn one mortal sin?'

Carthage: 'No number of venial sins could ever equal a mortal sin.'

This was brilliant. All I had to do was make sure I got to mass each Sunday and eat macaroni cheese on Fridays, and I could dream all day about the breasts on those McAuley High girls, pinch my classmate's pocket money and let crackers off in the girls' toilets.

My punishment would only be a shortish period of flame-immersion in purgatory (should that be Purgatory?). Meanwhile my old mate Jim Skinner from over the hill, in a careless moment, would let the Communion Host touch his teeth and be guaranteed an infinite post-life in the fires of Satan. Poppycock.

With this clarity of purpose, I decided at the age of eight to be a petty thief and sneak into the movies for free. One day, I left Otahuhu at 5am and arrived in Queen Street six miles away at midday, totally and utterly devastated by starvation. I'd forgotten to swipe some pennies from my Dad's coin box in his underpants drawer. No mind. I snuck into the Civic Theatre in Queen Street at half time and watched *Toby Tyler* (Wikipedia will tell you all about it). That young man riding horses in the circus. What a perfect escape. I soooooo wanted to run somewhere. And then the movie finished. I walked out and made my way back home. As I staggered into Otahuhu at 5.00 pm I was met by my darling mother, Von, who was, in essence, understanding because my wanderlust comes from her side of the family. The local police however were deeply irritable, having spent all day trying to find me. I was on the radio 1ZB news. A lost child. I thought to myself, 'How can you lose anyone in New Zealand?' Shortly after that heady mix of fame and trouble, my father, Jerry (a closet literary gent), wrote a poem:

My name is Michael
I'm a sort of vicious cycle
In that normality
Seems to occur to me
Only as a possibility
Before (inevitably)
I recur to me

The only respite from the relentless classroom was the occasional visit to the dental clinic.

In the role of molar guinea-pigs, we could be found tilted back in huge chairs, our teeth drilled by student nurses while talk-host Aunt Daisy or the radio soap opera *Portia Faces Life* burbled on the valve radio in the corner of the room. Daisy would cry out to us as if to alleviate the horror of the drill: 'Good morning, Good morning, Good morning, Good morning. Good morning, Good morning, Good morning.'

Portia possessed a greater distraction. We imagined her as some dark, sultry Sophia Loren figure in a scarf and tight jumper. Her slacks were probably stirrup trousers and they would surely have been satin. But what was satin? It shone.

With a life of crime looking decidedly dodgy, I entered a talent quest at the Otahuhu Borough Council Hall and reached the finals with a spirited rendition of *The Longest Day* to a crowd of about 400 kids. With my continuing obsession with war movies, it was either that or *Sink the Bismarck*. I balanced my war fetish with a total obsession for Hayley Mills' movies. I had a scrapbook at home with photos, clippings and so on, and when *Whistle Down The Wind* came to town I was beside myself. Hayley BABY!!! I failed to win the talent quest, losing out to some twerp singing *Peanuts* in a high soprano voice. I was sensible enough to realise why I lost – I couldn't sing. So I took up the piano.

Our next-door neighbours, the Lyons, harboured two teenage girls, Janet and Margaret, who took a shine to Geoffrey and me. They had a cousin Harry who ended up in Hello Sailor. We would walk through the orchard, clamber over the corrugated-iron fence and spend time with them, listening to records and being shown basic songs on the piano. *Tammy* was one of them. It sank in. I had a go on their violin but it killed the goldfish, and Geoffrey was relegated to the ukulele ... later a guitar. I would listen to Margaret play *Robin's Return* on the piano and vow, in no uncertain terms, that one day I too would play that majestic piece. (I did by the way).

We balanced the creation of music with listening to records on their three-in-one record player. It was a particularly banal period in popular music but I was ignorant and became engrossed in the likes of *Move Over Darling* by Debbie Reynolds and *The Battle of New Orleans* by Johnny Horton. It wasn't long before the odd gem surfaced somehow and I became obsessed with *Fool # 1* by Brenda

Lee and *Tower of Strength* by Gene McDaniels. In fact the latter spurred me to have piano lessons proper and I found a wonderful, radical woman by the name of Mrs Beazley on the outskirts of Otahuhu who was an inspiration. Sidestepping (sideswiping more like it!) the whole Trinity School nonsense by avoiding exams she taught me the whole basis of what, in the end, would allow me a life in popular music – chords.

Instead of picking out and learning a Chopin ditty parrot-fashion, Mrs Beazley and I would tackle something like *What Shall We Do With A Drunken Sailor?* or the *Theme From Exodus*; it would take only a minute because the melody was simple and I would make up my own left-hand part by reading the guitar chord, thumping it out. I liked the left hand part. It had what we would much later call *balls*. *Heart And Soul* was another simple number that succeeded by virtue of its driving left-hand chords. I spent more and more time on the piano as the improvisational possibilities opened up. Chords were the magic key to the lock of composition and I dickered around on little homemade pieces. I also had a crash course in improvisation at the Scout Concert for parents.

As a scout I was less than satisfactory but when it came time for the annual Parents' Concert in the Otahuhu Church Hall, I was in. I chose the *Blue Danube* for some reason (this goes against my previous ramble on avoiding such classical pieces) and in front of 100 shuffling, shifting, fidgety adults I charged off with gusto. Rather typically, however, I started to daydream halfway through and suddenly had not a clue as to where I was on the page.

Instead of stopping and finding my place, I charged on making it up as I went. I took a sideways glance at the audience and they were all laughing. I brought the proceedings to a grinding halt with a dum-dum-dee-daa C major and walked off. While the other scouts relegated me to the blew-it bin, I was happy inside. I was going get more of this. I was going to fly by the seat of my shorts.

Not long after, I found myself in Wellington on a class trip. I was now at De La Salle College – an oppressive place. Compared to the nuns' wild and woolly mix of religion and discipline, the brothers were a vicious bunch. I was particularly in the firing line owing to my class-clown persona. There was one lay teacher however who had human qualities and it was he who chaperoned our sojourn south, the intention being to see the All Blacks play Australia. It was August 29, 1964, and they lost 20—5, as you rugby cognoscenti will know. However it wasn't the football that charged me. As well as the All Black match, we were treated to one and a half hours of the most exciting, uplifting and fresh bunch of songs I had ever heard in my life. The *Tammy*'s, *Terry*'s, *Bobby's Girls* and *Sad Movies* of the past few years dissolved in one quick rush as we sat goggle-eyed while all around us teenage girls screamed. We went to see *A Hard Day's Night*.

From then on The Beatles were a primary focus, a searing pinpoint for my pre-adolescent brain. Back in Auckland, my ma Von saw the light and would bring home sheet music of Beatles' songs. *From Me To You, Can't Buy Me Love* and *I Want to Hold Your Hand*. Songs that were the toppermost of the poppermost. The piano was working overtime. Then the big moment – I went down to the local record store to buy one of their records.

On the way I stopped outside Hannahs shoe shop and saw my first real Beatle-boots; zippered, Cuban-heeled seamed leather icons of Julian Bond fabness. Unfortunately never to be mine. I skipped on to the record store only to find that they had sold out of Beatle records! I spent my 2/6d on a single I'd never heard of called *Hang On Sloopy* by the McCoys. I took it home, took *Under Milkwood* by Richard Burton, Frank Sinatra's *In The Wee Small Hours* and Ella Fitzgerald *Sings Cole Porter* off my parents' stackable gramophone and played it. Oh boy … woweee … this was nothing less than splendiferous! They sang *Yeah, Yeah, Yeah* too. I started listening to the radio more and more but there was only one half-hour show a week that played good music. It was hosted by Peter Sinclair who said 'Gear' and 'Fab' and 'Groovy', and I was drawn in. It was on

Thursday nights and I heard Dusty Springfield and The Hollies one week, The Kinks, the Who, the Searchers and the Righteous Brothers the next ... and so on. This music was free, hooky, edgy, vibrant, driving and, while a lesser animal than the likes of *A Hard Day's Night*, certainly of the same ilk. The same thread of invention.

As 1964 closed off, I was brimming with the sense of the new. I was aware that over 'there' in the northern hemisphere there were demi-gods in Beatle boots with stove-pipe suits, Vox amplifiers and American guitars. Huge quantities of them, that presumably lived as fast as they played. One day I was going to be one. Maybe one day I would play a Hofner violin bass!

Twelve months later, I readied myself for departure from the De La Salle cage. My parents had scheduled my next five years as a boarder at Sacred Heart College, based on the premise that boarding school had seen my father right (I couldn't argue with that!). In early December I sat the school's scholarship exam but as January 1966 rolled around the news was bad. There were two scholarships awarded and I wasn't getting either. They had both gone to country boys. I wiled away the summer absorbing more pop music and readying myself for the mysterious lifestyle ahead. It could only be better than the two institutions I'd endured to date.

On January 30, 1966, Von and Jerry drove me to Sacred Heart College with a suitcase full of crisp new clothes and a bag of apples. Once there, we took in the grand, spacious surrounds of the college grounds and the long stretch of brick buildings swarming with the other 400 boarders. The three of us ended up in the office of the head brother; he spoke and then as we walked out, another scrawny keen-eyed boy accompanied by his parents walked in. I had five years ahead of me and the starter's gun had fired.

Brian Timothy Finn was born at Wharenoho Hospital in Te Awamutu, 30 minutes south of Hamilton in the Waikato. Contrary to his later discourse on the matter, he weighed in at a mere eight-and-a-half pounds, some ounces short of 10. He was the second child of Dick and Mary Finn who lived at 78 Teasdale Street (now an old folk's home).

Dick was a partner in a local accounting firm, danced well and had a passion for jazz music, especially Bunny Berrigan and his superlative trumpet playing. As a youth on his family farm in Te Rore he had spent many hours listening to the radio as accompaniment to his accountancy studies and his fascination for the big band era grew steadily. Mary was born in Ireland and left at the age of two when her father, Tim Mullane, a first class farmhand, came to work in New Zealand.

As a precursor to their marriage, Dick went through 12 intensive weeks of Catholic instruction to allay fears of theirs being a mixed, and unsuitable, marriage in the eyes of the Catholic Church. The corollary was that Dick's parents weren't enamoured of Mary's Catholic constitution and it took some time before she was able to lay claim to being the favourite Finn daughter-in-law.

It was in this house of strong Catholic faith and good quality jazz music that Brian grew into a boy. At the age of five he went to St Joseph's Convent, where the nuns with their keen discipline and powerful focus on traditional Catholic doctrine stood him to attention and set him on the straight and narrow and gave him a good thrashing now and then for good measure. As C.K. Stead put it, there was a 'crushing weight of propriety' in New Zealand society. The nation's education system was in regiment mode with gruff voices, the cane and a wary attitude to creative individuals. This, however, failed to stop young Brian keeping a keen eye out for the chance to be different.

At the age of seven, Sister Mary Aloysius asked him a question: 'Young Brian. What would you like to be when you are a grown-up?'

'A bodgie!'

'Hush your mouth, you brazen lad.'

Presumably he was a hair's breadth from being thrashed severely.

To counter the assembly line approach, Brian took to the stage as a writer and producer constructing vignettes and adaptations for other kids to act out. One of them was a loose translation of *My Fair Lady*, under the title *My Fair Laddy*. The night before the show, the lead actor went down with flu and Brian was obliged to step into the lead role that he had written but had no intention of performing. It was this moment that Brian realised he possessed an inherent, consuming disease – stage fright. Quite happy to concoct and produce these school plays, he shivered at the thought of performing them himself. However, there was no choice and he strode on with an opening soliloquy which, today, he has difficulty in recalling. There was somebody in the audience however who has remembered every word: his young brother Neil.

Cor, what a life
Sleepin' on other people's doorsteps
Pinchin' food to stay alive
Not knowin' where your next meal is coming from ...
[Woman walks past with a bag of apples – he steals one]
Wouldn't trade it for the world

Neil was born in 1958 and was only a minor interruption to the Finn household, weighing in a few ounces less than Brian. He would lie on the living-room floor, keeping a close ear on Brian's piano practice.

In Brian's eyes and ears, the piano was a powerful device. He had seen what it could do when Dick and Mary had friends over for parties. In sharp contrast to other more sedate soirees around Te Awamutu, parties at Teasdale Street would jump to a hefty dose of Dick's jazz music. Brian would listen closely, absorbing the melodic power and tight rhythms in his subconscious. As the beer and spirits flowed, the voices would grow louder; Colin O'Brien would sit himself at the piano, place his gin on the lid and roll his cigarette to the corner of his mouth. His fists would pump out rollicking swing numbers and his hearty voice would sing joy into everyone's ears. Young Brian would look around the room at the smiles, laughs, kneecaps, and legs, and would be pulled up to dance with one guest or another.

Brian's first piano teacher was Sister Mary Raymond and he wallowed in the chance to play music. After an initial period when the pieces were dull, he was presented with *Alley Cat*. He was immediately liberated as he shook off the former stiff musical ditties and imagined himself with a gin on the lid and a fag in his mouth. He countered this secular stuff by playing the organ at church. Up high in the loft, Brian would weave through chants, hymns and modal pieces with Mary conducting him, his thin legs pumping away. He would slip in diatonic, submediant and Phrygian scales occasionally to wake up the sleeping nuns.

At the same time, 1963, Neil started school. With the combined influences of his parents' noisy sing-alongs and Brian's piano lessons and stage activities, he confidently entered a school talent quest and won a dollar for his spirited rendition of *You Are My Sunshine*.

By now, Dick and Mary were ready to encourage a little party performance from their sons.

When Saturday night rolled around and the radiogram needle clogged up with beer and ash and Colin O'Brien took a well-earned rest, Dick and particularly Mary would encourage Brian and Neil to perform together. Brian would instinctively resist while Neil, sheltering in the shadow of his older brother, was at the ready. They would kick off with *Jamaican Farewell* or *Terry* or some song from the radio. In the early sixties, this would invariably be something middle of the road.

Radio was solely a government department then and Jackie Wilson, James Brown and other pioneers of the time were never heard. 'Funk' and 'Rhythm 'n' Blues' were an alien life form and 'Soul' was that mysterious part of the anatomy previously discussed. With this entertainment conservatism in place, those in the radio programming seat in New Zealand thought it best that teenagers didn't exist; *My Old Man's A Dustman* was about as radical as you should get. The only pocket of mayhem was the Sunday morning children's request show (broadcast through the nation) and this was effective in instilling into the young, impressionable New Zealand child a keen sense and appreciation of eccentricity.

The likes of *The Laughing Policeman*, *The Enchanted Trumpet* and *The Noisy Eater* were partly responsible for the virulent response to the call for 'adventure' both outside and inside the mind that flourished in the late sixties and early seventies. But we will talk more on that later.

It was the music of Bobby Darin, Eddie Hodges, Helen Shapiro and the like that was ingrained into the Finn boys' heads and moulded their sense of melody and structure.

Melodies they found easy to master, with Brian instinctively taking the high harmony and Neil the lower – as they still do today.

Brian was also obsessed with Hayley Mills.

Brian and Neil's adult-engineered performances were transposed to the family's Christmas holidays at Mount Maunganui. There, twin priests by the name of Father Durning and Father Durning would sing beautifully; Brian and Neil would join in. The wild abandon of these occasions – with flirtatious language, dancing and loud rapport – rubbed off on the boys.

In 1965, Dick suggested to Brian that he learn piano from a Te Awamutu jazz player, Chuck Fowler. The experience completely liberated the 13-year-old, as he learned chords and picked out melodies by ear. *Lara's Theme* from *Dr Zhivago* was one of them; when Neil heard it for the first time he resolved that that would be the first thing he learned on the piano when he was big enough to reach the keys.

This was also the year that the Dave Clark Five came to Hamilton. There, 15 rows from the front, sat Carolyn Finn, the eldest sibling; beside her, blissfully unaware of his uncool garb and spotty chin, sat Brian. When Dave and the boys walked onstage, the place erupted around him. Resplendent in suits and winkle-pickers with Cuban heels, long hair and god-like features, there stood the Dave Clark Five. They kicked off with *Bits and Pieces* and Carolyn surged off to the front of the stage, leaving Brian wide-eyed. This hysterical moment was a revelation. Here it was ... the answer to the adolescent question ... the hidden source of female attention with a guarantee. It was rock 'n' roll music not jazz. He notched that one onto his belt for future reference.

All of a sudden, as in Otahuhu, the British beat boom hit Te Awamutu. The Beatles were on the airwaves (now and then) and in their wake came that plethora of quality music. Brian latched on quickly, absorbing the likes of The Beatles and The Kinks. He relished the brash cocky style, the hooky three-minute songs and the guitar-driven melodies. He met up with a Maori family, the Papesches, who were also excited by this new music and they would form bands to mimic the hits, with plastic Beatle wigs crowning the occasion. In his logical mind he never considered this mysterious, musical explosion filtering through from England as a possible career although something inside of him was stirring.

The world of the rock star, whatever it might be, seemed at odds to his ambitions of gaining mass approval and utilising his competitive nature to achieve recognisable goals. He felt the need to dwell in the context of society as it stood and his increasing love of music was the fail; an almost fantasy distraction steeped in mystery. A mystery compounded by the complete lack of music on television, which left the young Finn wondering what these musicians looked like ... how they acted and what they wore. He had to build his own interpretations, devise and project his own persona.

Parallel to this world of music and performance, Brian excelled academically and in November 1965 sat an examination for a boarding scholarship to Sacred Heart College in Auckland. From a field of over 100 hopefuls, there were two successful applicants from the countryside and Brian was one of them. So, on a clear Sunday night on January 30, 1966, Brian drove with Dick and Mary to Sacred Heart College with a suitcase of crisp clothes and a bag of apples.

On arrival they took in the grand, spacious surrounds of the college grounds and the long stretch of brick buildings swarming with the other 400 boarders. They sat themselves outside the head brother's office to wait for the introductory interview with Brother Urban. It wasn't long before the scrawny boy ahead of them emerged from the head's office wearing a jittery look of expectation-suspecting years of bad food, discipline with strap and cane, cultural starvation, and religious fervour – and as the Finns walked past him into the room, I looked at Brian for the first time ... and he looked at me.

3

THE BLUE OF THE HEAVENS

In 1966, while the northern hemisphere embraced the revolution of youth culture, the process of change in New Zealand lagged considerably. To a 13-year-old in a boarding school, there was none. Permission to leave the school grounds was restricted to the odd 'free' Sunday; the sense of confinement was very real with the school gate a symbol of freedom that boys would glance at longingly, imagining they were out there somewhere eating proper food and wearing civilian clothes.

The whole evocation of the female half of society became quickly warped and the one attractive member of the kitchen staff became the obsessive daydream of every boarder: the wafting, sweet smells of incense at Sunday benediction titillated the imagination, allowing the pleasure of a passionate love affair with her behind the locker rooms. This would be quickly followed by confession to allay that familiar blackening of the soul: 'Forgive me Father for I have sinned. It has been two days since my last confession and since then I have had 700 impure thoughts.'

Amongst the third formers, social groups formed in mercurial fashion. Brian first spoke to me on the banks of the 1st XV field. I don't know why we were there. Dreaming as usual? His short hair looked like it would explode if he let it grow and his eyes fixed you. You sensed they went back a long long way into his head. And he spoke with a clarity. Each word counted. And his legs were very thin. He and I joined a group of lads who quickly came to grips with the lie of the land, conforming to a satisfactory standard while keeping an eye over our shoulders for the Master of Discipline with his worn dowel cane. We balanced night-time study sessions by writing poetry steeped in morbid imagery and naive adolescence.

Brian sent his home:

... Casting my thoughts upon life's spoken steed
Emitting a train of flexible thoughts
My voice does its best to portray my emotions
But fails in a destitute condition of knowledge

I sent mine home too:

To give a sickening cry that sends
a chill of fear to spine and nerves
Fatigue that transmits to the brain a sin,
but bliss will soon emerge.

This failed to ignite much response from anywhere so we set about the ritual of nicknames.

By virtue of my unusual surname having oriental connotations I became 'Chang'. Brian became 'Fang' on a sympathetic vibration although he was generally called 'Hound-dog' via the Huckleberry Finn/Huckleberry Hound connection. There was a multitude of others:

Martian, Bounce, Buck, Chopper, Tank, Tub and so on.

And then there was mass on Sundays. In the pews, we all put our heads on our folded arms and fantasised about being free. Whatever that was. What about sex? None of us had seen a naked woman so there wasn't much to hold on to.

With the onset of winter, however, we shifted our focus to the central core of the school's raison d'etre – rugby. On the dot of 2.30 pm every wintry Saturday, 15 tall muscle-bound and grim-faced youths would take to the pitch to battle it out with strangers from another school.

On the banks of the number one field, the huddled boarders would scream out the school song:

The blue of the heavens ... the blue of the seas
Comrades, oh comrades, our colours are these.

We third formers were particularly enthralled with this mob encouragement and would go hoarse for the cause. We all harboured the same dream: one day we too would run onto that field wearing the special colours of the 1st XV.

Towards the end of the year a huge change came over our lives. From living day to day in the often fruitless pursuit of catching the odd pop song on the radio, the first New Zealand pirate radio station arrived – Radio Hauraki – and from that day on we were immersed in a glut of outstanding music. From The Kinks to Unit Four + 2, the Four Tops to Every Mother's Son, the Small Faces to the Rolling Stones, Dusty Springfield to The Mamas and The Papas, the Strawberry Alarm Clock to Crispian St Peters, the La De Das to Larry's Rebels and not forgetting the Vanilla Fudge – all bowing in reverence to the extraordinary Beatles – it poured out of our tinny trannies and we were obsessed, lying awake at night with our heads under pillows, one ear glued to the mono AM sound. The sound of the future. I found myself being more and more focused on New Zealand bands and during the August holidays I bought my second record, *On Top Of The World* by the La De Das. I played it 300 or 400 times and got inside it rather well. I was particularly impressed by the bass guitar dive bombs.(Perhaps Google that).

At the end of the year, Brian's conscientious dedication to success took him to the top of the class. My conscientious dedication only placed me fifth, and I resolved to give the country boy more run for his money the next year. As well, Brian scored the more notable achievement of receiving the most canes in our particular dormitory. With a sense of satisfaction, he threw his smelly clothes in the suitcase and headed off to Mount Maunganui for a summer of surfing and singing with Neil and the Fathers Durning.

I scarpered home to Otahuhu, where my brother Geoffrey and I spent an entire eight weeks listening to his new birthday present – the Beatles' album *Revolver*. Von and Jerry had displayed an acute sense of 'being *with it*' by buying this album. It 'blew our minds' and we dissected every note, word, drum beat, and image that flowed from the songs, until they were coming out our ears as opposed to going in. Never again in my life did I saturate myself with a record as I did that one. We ferreted around on the family piano trying to work the songs out. Not easy.

As far as other pursuits went, I was into surfing – but our family holiday place was on Auckland's west coast at Bethells Beach, where the waves thundered and rolled mercilessly. During the year Brian had come out now and then, and been appalled at the bad surf which contrasted with the elegant waves at Mt Maunganui. As far as he was concerned, I was a 'West Coast Sucker'.

The following February we all gathered back at college, this time ready for a little action.

Having acclimatised to the school routine, immunised ourselves to the sour mashed potatoes and strangely coloured corn beef, and shaken off the stigma of being 'turd formers', we found ourselves taller, more hairy and united. This was the fourth form and first up was the caning record. Two years previously, a particularly enterprising 4A class had achieved a total of 644 canes off the form master Brother Stephen. It became our ambition to better this and we quickly set about talking in class, arriving late, cutting up his cane, flicking ink, farting, clicking Biro pens, and failing to complete homework. Things started slowly and by mid-March we had only amassed 23 canes from the man. But there was time on our hands. And music in our heads.

I had come to school in an extreme state of enthusiasm over *Revolver* and quickly made it clear to Brian that there was something radical happening in the world of Beatle music. The Mop-tops' 'yeah

yeah yeah' songs about 'holding hands' and 'no reply' had been replaced by songs about death, the taxman and sleeping; there were backwards guitars and pumping rhythm sections. (It would be some time before we learned how they recorded tracks while playing fast and then slowed them down so they were at their proper pitch but deep and languorous and just – well – too much! Perhaps Google that too).

By now, I was learning the piano from one Miss Curtis, a spinster in horn-rimmed spectacles who fell asleep as I plodded through sonatas and the odd polonaise which I thought sounded like a spaghetti dish. I would wake her by breaking wind loudly, bringing her to consciousness in a shuddering torment. (Where was my Mrs Beazley!!). The only reason I suffered this woman was it gave me uninhibited access to the music rooms, ostensibly for practising the current Mussorgsky piece. As the rest of the school grappled with trigonometry and Latin, I would grab Brian by the scruff of his neck and we would retreat to the music rooms where we tackled the latest Top 40 hits and a stash of Beatles' songs. Down below in the concrete cloisters, the empty tuck shop and the brick toilets, our purposeful piano notes clanged around and around.

The *Sgt Peppers* album was now on the street; Geoffrey had poured colour on our home during the August holidays when he went up to the Otahuhu shopping centre one Friday night and bought a copy. As with *Revolver*, we couldn't turn it off. I was particularly excited by Paul McCartney's bass tracks. His melodic command was something I'd never heard before and producer George Martin had mixed him VERY LOUD. Very soon everyone was talking about the bass guitar on *Sgt Pepper*.

On returning to school, I was standing outside the tuck shop when a kid with a trannie walked past; the *Sgt Peppers* track was playing, and I stopped him. We stood there listening intently. As the song finished, the track segued into *With A Little Help From My Friends* and all around us the crowd built up. By the time Ringo had sung his last note there were 15 kids surrounding that transistor radio

– stationary, silent and enthralled. The Beatles had us all by the nuts and we couldn't move!

Back in the music rooms we tackled new songs and it seemed to fall into place. I believed we should get up on a stage as soon as possible so we approached our music teacher, Brother Ivan, for permission to hold a concert during music period.

Brother Ivan was enigmatic and influential and we called him 'Guff' – no one knows why. Had we been aware of the term at the time, he would have been 'cool'. He never caned anyone. He had a gentle sense of detachment and unlike the brothers such as Rat and Boof, he seemed to know the world was changing and that it was poised to be a more exciting place. He was a beatnik in disguise and we would hear him at nights, off in the distance, playing Dave Brubeck on the assembly hall piano. When he coached the school choir we could hear them singing through the coloured walls. He played guitar as well and would bring Bob Dylan records to music class.

'Morning boys. We're going to listen to Bob Dylan's new album *Nashville Skyline* this morning.'

I'd pipe up. 'Brother, I've got the new Cream album *Wheels of Fire*, how about that?'

Guff: 'I'll give you three Cream tracks for three Bob Dylans.' And we would sit and listen to records and it was beautiful.

But his crowning achievement came in 1967 during school assembly. Ivan led the school singing, which was a regular feature following the head brother's speech. There had been signs of a willingness to stretch things a little by having the school sing Dylan's *When The Ship Comes In* as opposed to *The Lord Is My Shepherd*. But this wintry day in 1967 as 650 teenage males of ascending sizes, assorted shapes and varying degrees of acne, skinniness and greasiness, stood to attention in their navy-blue shorts and jerseys, Ivan presented them with his coup de grace – The Beatles' *Strawberry Fields Forever*. We sang it out. The psychedelic moment of a momentary dream ... steadfast. It wasn't lost on our hungry imaginations. We saw the eccentricity. The surreal situation. Brother Ivan was holding a torch for us all and a few of us took the opportunity to follow the beam. Consequently, it was no surprise when he okayed our request for a class concert and allowed us to haul the pump organ over from the chapel into the assembly hall, so we could faithfully reproduce our Beatle and Procul Harum numbers. We roped in a couple of classmates, Buck and Tank (Philip Buckelton and Gene Paul), on bongos and guitar, and on September 28, 1967, Brian and I walked onto a stage together for the first time. In rapid nervous succession we played spirited renditions of *Homburg, Ticket To Ride, To Love Somebody, With A Little Help From My Friends* and *Homeward Bound*. A veritable roundup from the toppermost of the poppermost. Brian hid behind my piano in fright but did his duty at the microphone and stunned the class. He sang like a bird and froze the lot of them.

Brian had felt his voice fill the assembly hall and it was a peak moment. For a few seconds we dared to think that IT might be possible. That there might be something there that could break through the rigid goals we had in our heads and the restrictions surrounding us. But as we shuffled off to maths, the spark of hope dulled. Brother Ivan in his wise way was careful to avoid inflating egos and his reaction was more bemused than enthusiastic.

A few days later we dragged out the school tape recorder and recorded seven songs in the school assembly hall. I was certain we had something extraordinary here, and the more I could do to spread our music around the harder I worked at it. After laying the songs to tape we played it back. It was this listening session that was the moment for Brian. The revelation.

Here, for the first time in his life, he could hear himself as did others. He knew then that there was a chance. The tape was dutifully sent off to Te Awamutu, where all and sundry gathered around to marvel at Brian's vocal grace and ease. Neil in particular was most impressed. He recalls this moment as his realisation, also, of Brian's obvious vocal talents.

Meanwhile, back at Sacred Heart, there was one more task to be completed. In a moment of massed effort and sustained mischief, the entire 4A class, including the outcasts – and the downtrodden, the rogue elephants and the isolationists, the gregarious and the plebs, pushed Brother Stephen to the limit. In a semi-delirious state of authoritative panic, he mass-caned the entire class and we took our yearly total to 825. The rest of the school cheered and applauded as we smashed the previous caning record with a figure that has never been beaten and never will. Brother Stephen has now passed away.

A week later, we were on holiday and I dived back into musical pursuits with Geoffrey. By now I had scored a guitar for my birthday (which I still play) and thrashed the living daylights out of it and Geoffrey got a snare drum for Christmas. We could be a band! Geoffrey had continued his foraging for radical records and brought home Hendrix' *Are You Experienced?* We marvelled at the gut-wrenching lead solos. Geoffrey furthered his reputation as a contemporary by introducing Iron Butterfly's *In-A-Gadda-Da-Vida* to the house.

Down south, Brian was off to Mount Maunganui. The Mount was a haven for teenagers worn down by the rigours of school life. (Still is). In an idyllic setting of white sand, even surf held aloft by off-shore breezes, a vivid array of cool surfers, teenage girls, quart bottles of Lion Red, high-waisted cords and Rothmans cigarettes, the social focus was nothing less than pure romanticism. Once again, Tim and Neil took to the boards at social gatherings – Neil jumping at the chance, and both turning on increasingly competent performances. They too took in the odd gathering around the old record player, watching the 45s drop like cowpats onto the grooved rubber turntable. Then it was back to school.

With the arrival of 1968, there was a sense of purpose in our heads. We took up where we left off, working in the music rooms and periodically putting stuff down on tape. By now, we were dabbling in original songs with as many psychedelic notions we could muster. *Sgt Peppers Lonely Heart Club Band* had wiped the music industry slate, obliterating all the rules and regulations of commercial pop music and we adopted the stance. Geoffrey was now at Sacred Heart so we utilised him on drums (or should that be drum?).

During the May holidays. Geoffrey and I borrowed a couple of tape recorders and using the most primitive tape to tape multi-track process imaginable, we recorded 10 of our own songs.

We took the tape to Stebbing Recording Studios where they made an album out of it. We called ourselves Astley Shrine. The album was made of thick shellac and, of course, there is only one in existence – safe in my bottom drawer. The songs were all a natural extension of the morbid nonsense we had thrown up as poetry a couple of years before, although Geoffrey had a better way with words. I played all the dinky, naive bass parts on my nylon 6-string guitar and realised something in the process – I loved playing bass.

Back at Sacred Heart, we put together various concerts through the year – all following the same pattern. Drag the organ over from the church and put the word out that we were going to play. A crowd would turn up, happy to be missing study periods, and we would dish up a platter of recently rehearsed pop songs. Brian's soaring vocals always killed them in the aisles despite his ever-present stage fright; we would return to the dormitory and our shorty pyjamas, charged with adrenalin and clean our teeth.

By the end of the year we were ready for the real thing: the Walter Kirby music competitions, an established part of the College's extra-curricular activities. There was a group section, which we entered with the help of Geoffrey on drums and a seventh former (who was younger than us), Stephen Streat, on piano. Stephen was an academic genius who had scored a University Scholarship in his sixth form year at the age of 15. Aside from this, he had a strong creative, musical streak and we would bash away in the music rooms with him. He adored The Beatles, of course! The competition rules did not permit the use of amplified equipment, which we felt hindered our chances of 'letting rip', but it was a moot point as we didn't own any anyway.

We rehearsed one number solidly – *Yesterday* by The Beatles, of course, and when the night came, we gave it all we had. Which wasn't enough. We were beaten by a duo on guitar and piano accordion who played *A Man And A Suitcase*. We steeled ourselves in readiness and vowed that the next year and the year after that, we would take the winner's prize. We also pondered another matter – who was Walter Kirby?

The year ended with a rash of school certificate exams, which distracted us from music.

Brian scored a creditable 335 marks out of 400, which wasn't good enough because I scored 342. After years of trying, I'd finally beaten the bastard!

Back in Te Awamutu, things were much the same. Geoffrey and I turned up near Christmas at the time the Finns were holding a party for a boarder, Marsha Strait, who had been living with them and was returning home to the States. We threw some instruments together; the Beatles' *White Album* was hot off the press and we proceeded to learn the easiest track off it – *Ob li De Ob Li Da*. (Yes, I know the actual title of the album is *The Beatles* but no one calls it that).

During rehearsals, Geoffrey hopped off his snare drum and let Neil play along. He kept pretty good time for a nine-year-old and that night he joined in. In contrast to crooning *Jamaican Farewell* at his parents' parties, this group-in-a-rock-idiom appealed to him. At the same time, Neil had gotten hold of an acoustic guitar that Brian had brought home from school.

Neil had been taking piano lessons but found the guitar easier to master, picking out chords to accompany himself. The first song he shaped up was The Monkees' *Daydream Believer*.

1969 found Brian and I in 6th form tackling scholarship exams and the volume of calculus and T.S.Eliot was extraordinary. We balanced this academic overload with drinking as much beer as we could on the odd times we managed to get outside the grounds, the odd concert and many hours in the music rooms.

As well, we had an interesting English teacher, Brother Richard, whose dexterous mannerisms quickly had him dubbed Fingers. He seemed to have a focus on all things international so we asked him about 'hippies'. He said: 'They'll go inside come the winter.' We liked that. There was indeed something – *unsure* – about the hippie thang.

Fingers' crowning glory, however, was when he took the entire class to the *Easy Rider* movie. Presumably he knew full well that in that one-and-a-half hour whirlwind of peace, love, sex, drugs, and rock 'n' roll, we were formulating our plans to have it all. We felt we were halfway there: there was plenty of peace and love in our lives and we were forging ahead with rock 'n' roll. It was just the sex and drugs that were a problem. Aspirin and watching the kooks in the kitchen didn't add to much. As usual there was always mass on Sunday mornings to savour. As Father Wood repeated himself over and over, we all put our heads on our folded arms and fantasised about scoring for the 1st XV, riding in the green room at Waimea Bay or playing through double Marshall stacks at the Auckland Town Hall. Me? I dreamed of being free. I made a quiet vow sitting there in my pew. I would forge a life where I could walk down a suburban street any day of the week and no one could stop me.

And then after mass? Back to the music rooms.

The real excitement came mid-year when my particularly insightful Uncle John presented me with a birthday present of one hour's studio time at Stebbing Recording Studios. This was a real opportunity. We had been content to foster our musical life within the walls of the college and the concept of recording in a proper studio had seemed impossible, principally because of our naivety. And no money of course. But here it was – a whole hour! So on a wet August night in 1969 we set off to Herne Bay with a carload of cheap gear. By this time we had recruited another Sacred Heart lad, Paul Fitzgerald, on drums; as we had never managed to find a guitar player, we had yanked Geoffrey off the kit and thrust a six string in his hands. He took to it rather well. I had recently purchased a Tiesco bass for $35 from Sydney Eady's in Queen Street and I was ready to rip. The lead track was an old melody of mine rejuvenated with a Brian lyric. He called it *Near Hosts*. That night, with Eldred Stebbing at the helm, we put down three songs: two originals, *Near Hosts* and *Take It Green*, and a weird version of The Beatles' *Got To Get You Into My Life*.

With a good balance and loads of reverb etc. from Eldred's deft fingers, we savoured the results. The night was blissful and Brian and I both felt that our musical quest was progressing, albeit within the parameters of our own ignorance. Today we look back – ignorance was bliss. We put the tape in a bag and went out into the rain. When I got home I put that tape in my bottom drawer.

A short while later, The Beatles' *Abbey Road* was released. Instead of a crowd of 15 hovering around a trannie, the arrival of the album into the school grounds found virtually every boy resident in Leonard House (the single room dorm for seventh formers and groovy sixth formers) seated around the common room record player. There would have been 30 of us waiting in anticipation that Friday afternoon. The needle was put on at the start of side one; it was taken off at the end of side two – and not one boy spoke for the entire duration of that record. Tell me something, dear reader. Does that happen today?

As the end of the year drew near, so too did the Walter Kirby. We had received our first major knockback when we held a concert one Saturday night in the school assembly hall and foolishly invited the other school band to support us. They were led by Wally Wilkinson who was a dayboy, which we held against him; we had short hair, which he held against us.

When the big day came, Wally arrived with a wild array of professional equipment which he wouldn't share. They blew us away, particularly when they played The Beatles *Come Together* from the *Abbey Road* album. We had planned to do *She's So Heavy* from the same album but couldn't work it out, so we started with something else instead. And our equipment was tacky.

Consequently, with this trough experience fresh in our minds, we entered the Walter Kirby intent on success. We rehearsed the Bee Gees' song *Words*, which was a Finn showpiece providing him with ample opportunity to slide and glide over the romantic lyrics with tons of hefty vibrato. On the night we gave no mercy and it was a magic moment when we strode to the stage to take the first prize.

The next year, 1970, was our last at Sacred Heart and we were seniority. Brian now held a true leadership role and was held in high esteem by many of his peers for his varied talents in the academic and musical fields. It was, however, on the rugby field that his ability to motivate had been visibly realised.

The previous year, Brian had made it into the 2A rugby team where he was chosen as captain. Having had a fairly lacklustre three years up to this point, the general consensus was that Finn was out of his depth with this horde who were essentially the reserves for the 1st XV. Twelve weeks later, however, the doubts were allayed when with a magnificent victory over Auckland Grammar School, they took the championship honours.

Perhaps a quote from the school magazine is in order here:

'... the team must record its debt to the captain, Brian Finn, who was always an inspiration. He was at his best at practice, always so important, but a sound, not brilliant half-back in the games. He played the thoughtful rugby, to his backs, where a more individually talented player may have upset the balance of the team.'

The second term of 1970 brought with it another rugby season. It was with a wild sense of achievement and an adrenalin rush that both of us ran onto the field to take on St Pauls as members of the Sacred Heart 1st XV. We heard the roar from the banks.

Here they come – here they come
Blue red blue!

Brian had a great season, playing in all matches, and the team was placed third in the competition. I had both bones in my skinny right leg broken during the second half of our first game and never played again. There was an upside – the school doctor and my father (also a doctor) ran onto the field, and I was injected with a few grains of morphine. They were searching for my mainline. They found it alright. As they straightened my useless leg into a splint I felt nothing but a sweet puffy exaltation and I perused the crowd for a familiar face. The head brother, Stubbs, was standing on the field and I waved at him. His look was interesting. I sensed that he knew I had crossed the great divide and I was lost to his catholic world. My wave – a sincere gesture indeed, a quick moment to allay his fears that I might be wincing and squirming in pain. I was as happy as Larry. As the St John's Ambulance attendant laid me to rest on my stretcher, I gazed into the heavens and saw God.

His deep, resonant booming voice came down through the clouds to my zinging eardrums:

'Chunn?'

'Yes?'

'Sins don't matter.'

I knew it!

This shattered leg also put paid to my athletic career and I would watch from the side as the myriad hordes whizzed around the track. There was one kid who had legs like large thick stumps of kauri and he was a mean high-jumper. He was apparently a bit of a whizz piano player as well but we were prevented from having anything to do with him because he was a dayboy. His name was Tony Rayner.

Off the field, the focus was girls. While being a member of the first XV brought major social status, it failed to transpose to the female sex. Brian still had the Dave Clark Five concert at the back of his mind, so we put ourselves up for a slot at the Baradene College folk night in the hope of attracting female attention. The evening was a sedate affair, with nylon string guitars twanging away and Joan Baez sound-alikes. Once we'd done our obligatory Simon and Garfunkel song, we decided to break the mould and did a blues version of *God Save The Queen*. This allowed Brian the chance to do his glissando minor thirds, which had me in fits, and I tried a little Hendrix-like licking, which had Brian in fits; there was disapproving silence from the audience. Afterwards, shrouded in shyness, we failed to socialise and drove back to school where we cleaned our teeth again and went to bed.

By now we were in our Woodstock phase when we dreamed of having long hair, smoking weed and owning large amplifiers. We had to be content with mass on Sundays followed by porridge for breakfast. The Woodstock movie had shown clearly the cohesiveness of the youth revolution and, much to our satisfaction, it seemed to revolve around songs. Words and Music! The new American wave of youth fixation was following on from the British invasion, clearly inspired by The Beatles and their LSD admissions and exploratory musical directions – directions that never stayed still for a moment. From a distance, we were fascinated at the pure hedonism we deemed it to be. A world of invention and joy that was out of reach and outside the paths along which we found ourselves travelling. Somehow we would cross that great divide.

But there were still the music rooms and we saved up some money and returned to Stebbing Studios, where we recorded another four originals. This time Geoffrey was on drums.

He provided an original song that Brian breathed life into and Stephen Streat played piano on. After the session we listened back and deemed the results to be satisfactory. Geoffrey and I drove home to Otahuhu, and I put that tape in my bottom drawer where it still is.

The third term brought with it various school music and drama productions and Brian auditioned with gusto. He played the lead role in Gilbert and Sullivan's *Trial By Jury* and did particularly well.

When first my old true love I knew
My bosom welled with joy.

As well, he played Edmund in Shakespeare's *King Lear*, which satisfied his literary leanings (in 1970, strongly focused). I auditioned for the part of one of the daughters but was rejected. At year's end, Brian took the Old Boy's Essay Prize, the Brother Stephen Prize for English Literature and the English Prize. With the 1st XV, singing at girls' schools and the ability to handle beer out of the way, there was one last shot before leaving school. The Walter Kirby.

By the end of the year, we were full of Simon and Garfunkel's *Bridge Over Troubled Water* album and we decided to tackle *Frank*

Lloyd Wright, if only because it gave me the chance to play the new flute I'd bought. Those that know the song well will be aware that it is Paul Simon's farewell to Art Garfunkel (Have a listen. At 2' 57" producer Roy Halee shouts out in the background, 'So long, Artie') and so too with us: this was our farewell to the brick buildings, quadrangles, locker rooms, common rooms, dining rooms and rugby fields that had locked in our bodies while we freed our minds. From the empty heads we had brought in to the packed, kaleidoscopic banks of information, memories, hopes, fears and ambition that we took away with us five years later, much had been achieved. Our constitutions were ready for the wild years ahead.

So with a flourish of concentration, superb vocals, competent guitar playing, and passable flute, we took the first prize (we were first equal actually) and the applause was rather good, particularly with our parents in the audience and young Neil Finn to boot. Neil was due to start boarding at Sacred Heart the next year and he formulated his conquest of the Walter Kirby in the glory of Brian's success.

One week later we were gone.

Inspired by Brian's musical conquest, Neil, on holiday at Mount Maunganui, entered the Soundshell talent quest. In sharp contrast to Brian's prevalent stage fright, Neil was ready for the task at hand and strode on purposefully. He sang Arlo Guthrie's *Comin' Into Los Angeles* but the irony of this 12-year-old singing about importing two kilograms of hash through customs failed to ignite the judges and he was pipped by a yodeller from Hamilton.

Undaunted, he resolved to return and conquer.

It was at this time that Neil bought his first record, Donovan's *Hurdy Gurdy Man*. The cover featured a kaftan-clad Donovan surrounded by swirling colours and trippy notions. On the back of the cover was a poem:

Precious little do we kiss the sun
drink the rain.
We will find out that good can be bad
and bad can be good.

The sentiments appealed to the impressionable youngster, so he grabbed a guitar and put the words to music. And there it was. His first composition.

Brian meanwhile had immersed himself in the surfing sphere at the Mount. The focus was on the Aussie surfers who were winning world championships and being held in high esteem. Surfers such as Nat Young. This whole scene was at its most intense in the summer of 1970, and the Mount Maunganui teenagers were steeped in the Australian surfing culture that crossed the Tasman by way of magazines and word of mouth. Their clothes, deformed knees, motorcycles, girls, and grace in the water epitomised 'cool'. It was all part of the natural progression of Brian's shifting attention span. First the bodgies, followed by The Beatles. Now the Aussie surfers. What would be next?

Sean Fitzpatrick, All Black Captain

'During my time at Sacred Heart when Split Enz were in their prime, the boys had a special affinity to the group as we felt they were our own; old boys of Sacred Heart College. They dared to be different and yet their music was easy to relate to. As you would walk past the music rooms down on the lower levels of the school block, you would always think of Tim Finn, Mike Chunn and Split Enz.'

4

OUT FLEW THE WEB AND FLOATED WIDE

COME 1971, I enrolled at the Auckland University Engineering School for a degree in Theoretical and Applied Mechanics. I don't recall what came over me. The Chunn family had left Otahuhu and were now squashed into a townhouse on Parnell Road a stone's throw from the main drag – Queen Street.

Brian had returned to Auckland from Te Awamutu in late February to his new home, O'Rorke Hall, which was one of the hostels on the University campus; a rambling labyrinth of dark hallways and patched wallpaper reminiscent of Ghormenghast. He searched out his room, eyed his roommate, Nigel Hooper, and scurried off to classes where he was studying various philosophical and political papers towards a Bachelor of Arts degree.

Very soon it dawned on him that O'Rorke Hall was a place of madness where, just as at Sacred Heart, there was a head authority surrounded by minions, ordered meal times, dormitories, music rooms, and shared bathrooms; the difference was that this boarding school was anarchic and free movement, drugs, sex, and mischief were part of the curriculum. Water bombs rained down on visitors and rockets flew down the corridors. Nigel Hooper had an ice-pick, which he kept on the wall; one night, he drove it into the floor beside Brian's sleeping head. Just why Tim was sleeping on the floor is unclear. Another time Hooper invited a junkie back, allowing Brian a close scrutiny of heroin on two legs. Watching him shoot up, Brian thought the devil had walked into the room.

There was, however, a small group of individuals that immediately caught Brian's attention. All Elam Fine Arts students and as thick as thieves, they were the coolest guys in the place. In room 129 was Rob Gillies. I first spied him on the O'Rorke roof playing the flute. He maintained an effortless and subtle smile and his knowing eyes seemed to be telling you that 'all is nonsense so just enjoy.' Rob rode a Suzuki 50 scooter and his legs were of medium build. He was from Wanganui and possessed a quick wit, a swift sketching talent and was a more than proficient saxophone and trumpet player (the flute was just a doodle and a doddle). Rob had been blowing trumpet from an early age, initially in quasi-military regimental concerns such as the Queen Alexandra's Own Brass Band. He progressed from there to a cocktail-lounge outfit called the Blue Serenaders who played such auspicious Wanganui venues as the Palm Lounge, Aramohoe Boating Club and the Savage Club Hall. Rob then hit the big time (in Wanganui) as trumpet player in the Dick Le Forte Quartet, which headlined at the Palmerston North Jazz Festival and occasional 2ZW radio broadcasts. By then he had sat the preliminary exams for entry to the Elam Fine Arts course at Auckland University and been accepted. He drove the 300 miles north to Auckland on his Norton motorbike, settled into O'Rorke Hall and sold the bike because he was broke. Rob Gillies had a keen appreciation of the absurd.

He would be the one to buy *Zap* and *Yellow Dog* comics.

Then there was a tall one from Wellington called Geoffrey Crombie. Mr Crombie was enigmatic with his unique presence and deeply temperate voice cajoling you to listen carefully. He had grown up in Paekakariki, then moved to Karehana Bay on the Paremata

Harbour when he was 12. He attended Mana College in Porirua, near Wellington, and developed a taste for surfing.

He and others of his ilk would drive to White Rock or Ning Nong Bay to paddle out and ride the waves. By the time he was in sixth form, Geoffrey was floundering. With the end of school nigh, he had nary a clue as to what the future might hold for him. Fortuitously, the renowned artist Robin White came to Mana College to teach art and she quickly realised the creative bent that Geoffrey possessed. She guided his artistic talents and he returned for his seventh form year solely to sit the prelim exams to the Elam Fine Arts diploma course in Auckland. His attention to other subjects was so minimal it is quite possible the school authorities didn't know he was there.

He was also inspired by the poet Sam Hunt, who spent time as a relieving teacher at the college.

Sam Hunt, poet

It was 1967. I'd just recently moved to a place I named Bottle Creek, an inlet on the Cook Strait coast. I got a job sort of babysitting a couple of English classes at Mana College. Wasn't long before I became aware of a rather unusual and gifted young man, name was Geoffrey Crombie. A friend of mine, Robin White, also of Bottle Creek, was Geoffrey's art teacher. He was a star pupil. (Head prefect at the time was Gary McCormick.)

The following February, 1971, having being accepted for Elam, Geoffrey travelled to Auckland where he found accommodation as a boarder in an elderly woman's home. He quickly befriended the Elam art students who were resident at O'Rorke, and spent more and more time there. In the end he would stay over most nights in Room 129, where Rob had constructed mezzanine beds in a DIY flurry of nails and wood. He was quickly noticed by the mob. He used to make his own clothes: capes and wide gingham suits in pink and white checks. Friday nights down Queen Street, with his lips painted red, his long hair and ginger beard floating behind him, he would carry a silver bolt of lightning in his hand. The public parted before him muttering under their breath: 'He must be queer!'

The third was a dark-haired lad who had set tongues wagging at Elam with his superb painting talent. Phil Judd. Juddsy as we called him stood outside the circles and hub-bub. He carried himself with a surety and his eyes fixed you but you didn't know what he was thinking. But you knew he was thinking something – at some speed. The less the number of people in the room the more animated he became. He was at his most communicative when it was just you and him. And he had a jack-of-all-trades aura about him where anything might be possible. Give him a kazoo and he might play you *Flight of the Bumblebee*. He came from Napier, where he had reacted to his older brothers' love of The Beatles by listening to the Vienna Boys Choir. It wasn't until he heard Led Zeppelin's *Whole Lotta Love* that he felt he had heard anything sensational. He had arrived at O'Rorke Hall with an acoustic guitar. He would jam with Rob and another Napier friend, John Hadwin, on stuff like the Bee Gees' *Lonely Days Lonely Nights*. Phil too was in Room 129.

In the company of these people, Brian was excited. Dying to throw off the shackles and go out as far as he could, he immersed himself in their sphere and was drawn to change. Their view of the world, particularly Phil Judd's, flew in the face of all that Brian had assimilated through his sheltered years at Sacred Heart College. While we had created our own adventures on a musical level, we had had little exposure to the artistic world of which the likes of Judd, Gillies and Crombie had so much awareness. From Rembrandt to *Yellow Dog* comix, Dali to Robert Crumb to the MC5 and S Clay Wilson – the variety seemed endless and he absorbed as much as he could. At the same time, he was handed his first joint and, having looked forward to this moment for years, inhaled deeply. I joined the fray a while later. We got the stuff off a chap who has since departed this mortal coil on a horse ride, and we found the music we were listening to a sight more detailed and richer. Our sensory perceptions glowed more brightly. We also found a desire to eat a lot.

I made a habit of dropping in on this colourful crowd in either 129 or Brian's room, and Brian and I would mosey along to the O'Rorke music rooms to jam with Rob Gillies. Phil would drop in occasionally and whack away on the drums as would brother Geoffrey, now a gopher in a television studio. As usual, I thought we should take on a public performance so we somehow secured support for a group performing at a university hostel party. They were called 'Pwick' so we went by the name of 'Qwunt'.

Rob. Brian. Geoffrey and I; with our Bethells beach friend Graeme Gash on guitar, did the best we could considering we were drunk. Phil Judd had brought along a roll of theatre tickets that matched those being used to buy drinks so we had unlimited beer. By now resplendent in shoulder-length hair and beards, we played Neil Young and Buddy Miles numbers. The three minute pop songs of our youth were fading into the past to be replaced by progressive rock, as it is now called. To us it was just the music of the day; different from yesterday's, as it had to be. The emphasis was on exploration and riffs and melodic arrangements. The acoustic guitar was taking on the electric guitar, and they were neck and neck. The better units as far as we were concerned merged the two: Led Zeppelin, Family, Jethro Tull.

Midyear, Jethro Tull came to town and set the standard for our musical drive. Starting with a 45-minute version of *Thick As A Brick* with a power never thought possible, led by the manic frontman Ian Anderson, their extraordinary performance drilled into Brian's head the value of stagecraft and presentation in fulfilling the musical promise. Rob, Noel and Phil were all equally enthused by the show.

Unfortunately, the next few rehearsals failed to provide any solutions to our problem of sounding less than satisfactory. Deciding that our musical ditherings were logged in a rut, I answered an ad in the paper for a bass player and joined a three piece hard rock band called

Moses. The name Moses made Brian laugh. The unit was led coincidentally by guitarist Wally Wilkinson, which made me laugh. We
were finally in the same band together. Wally grinned a lot and saw
the humour in things even when things weren't humourous. He, in
his own way, loved life. And music was a cool contrast to his day-time
job as someone who changed huge reels of magnetic tape in an air-
conditioned computer room. Wally had a moustache and flailing long
hair; Indian shirts hung off him and his jeans were so flared you
couldn't tell how big his legs were. And he played a Gibson SG
cherry red. That was cool.

On material by Hendrix, Cream and Alice Cooper I soon got to
grips with my Fender Mustang bass guitar as we played suburban
dances and the like to a smattering of people. Occasionally we played
to an empty hall.

Over on the other side of town, young Neil Finn was settling into
the rigours of life at Sacred Heart College. The first term was spent
establishing slots in various sporting teams and at this the young 'turd'
did rather well. He played rugby for the 6As and the school magazine
applauded his efforts:

An adventurous and well drilled set of backs set the stage for
many good wins. Neil Finn and Owen Cooney formed a very good
inside combination.

It wasn't rugby however that was the principal focus – it was a
time-honoured tradition that has been an important part of boys'
boarding schools since their inception in 1288. The swish of the
cane. While the strict disciplines of the sixties were now draining
away, with long hair, uniforms optional for some and travel outside
the school more free, life as a third former still presented a
subservient existence. Consequently, without a caning record to
better, the whole third form devised a competition whereby the recip-
ient of the most blows in the year would be the victor.

The initial enthusiasm was spectacular. One night, as a member
of a horde of pillow-bearing mutineers, Neil took to the other lads in
his dormitory for a spot of pillow fighting.

They were sent scurrying by the brother on duty. A second time they lashed out, only to be ordered back to bed. Then, for a third time, in a true display of foolhardiness, they charged off with pillows aloft only to be met by the Master of Discipline. The whole dormitory was herded into the gymnasium where interrogations commenced. Finn was deemed to be guilty along with various others and brother Michael looked him in the eye and declared: 'Finn! You are a water rat undermining the foundations of the school!' Amongst various punishments was a good caning and it was then, staring at the pink, blue and purple welts on his arse, that the novelty of the caning prize wore thin. To his credit however, when the individual scores were tallied at the end of the year, Neil came third.

Through all this, Neil continued to spend hours and hours in the music rooms fashioning by ear, on guitar and piano, a mix of current favourites. They were songs from the albums he was listening to at the time, from artists like Elton John.

In the city, life on campus was hotting up. The collective ethic was more and more left-wing and the University Quadrangle would host forums that packed them in. Tim Shadbolt would lead the fray, spurring on the students with solid anti-establishment rhetoric. The youth focus had arrived and with it, Sue Kedgley and the feminist movement, blues clubs, political awareness, arts festivals, pub crawls, abortion issues, pollution issues, and Vietnam. The latter served as the ideal focus for the campus activist and one Friday night 17,000 people marched through Queen Street chanting 'HO, HO, HO Chi Minh'. Dutifully, Brian and I painted a banner on the floor of his hostel room which read: 'The Cong, the Cong, the lusty Cong Is Not A Thing To Laugh Or Scorn.' But then, perhaps it didn't. No matter. That we had a banner is indeed true and we carried it aloft much as teenagers today hold flags at rugby matches. It didn't matter to us, the radical mob, that the US marines had virtually vanished from Vietnam by then.

As 1971 drew to a close, and with it the end of institutionalised life for the O'Rorke Hall inmates, there was one more parting gesture.

The vagrants gathered outside the house of the head warden, a Doctor Packer, and in a ritualistic, cathartic gesture fired a sky rocket through his window, setting fire to the curtain. Just the start. They then dropped a smoke bomb down his chimney. He gathered his family and left for good the next day. The ultimate boarding school fantasy came true.

By the end of the year, the core friendships were solidly in place. On the night before his last exam, Brian looked out his window and noticed Phil Judd sitting on the O'Rorke chimney, riding it through the stars. And the next morning he found Crombie, Judd and others standing outside his window draped in blankets, smoking cigars and perfecting a cackling laughter. They had been up all night on an acid debut and had tales of serendipity, fata morgana and trance.

Later that day, after the exam, Brian and Paul Pattie, another Elam student and frequent visitor to 129, went to the Auckland Domain. Exams were over and their blood was charged and their laughter liquid. With the sun on their faces and California Sunshine on their tongues, slowly seeping into their brains, they strolled through Alice's Wonderland and allusions fell neatly into place. The next day I had my last exam and the whole fantastic circus started all over again. Purple Hearts were popped into our mouths and we skated away, following whatever took our fancy. One hour it would be a row of trees, the next it would be a page in a comic book. *Ivanhoe* to be precise. He looked like Liberace in chain mail as I recall. Later that night, around midnight, we went outside to sense the night air. I had an acoustic guitar in my hand; as I picked out a note, it would scoot off around the world and come back an octave higher. We finally went our separate ways around 10 the next morning – the intrepid explorers, home to bed.

It was a fitting end to what had been the year of transition. For while nothing was different, everything had changed – particularly from Brian's perspective. As O'Rorke closed down, the lads slowly sloped off to their respective territories. Phil returned to Napier to work in the freezing works; Brian packed up, hopped on a bus and returned to Te Awamutu for a summer of haymaking. It was there that he heard about Neil's success.

During his time in the confines of Sacred Heart, Neil spent many hours in the music rooms. He had secured a copy of Elton John's Tumbleweed Connection album and played it to death.

He then proceeded to master as many songs from it as he could, piecing them together by ear. It was during a thumping rendition of *Burn Down The Mission* that 6th former, Bernard McHardy, attracted by this clever display, dropped in with his guitar. The two of them struck up a musical rapport that lasted through the year.

As the close of 1971 approached, so did the Walter Kirby competition. Bernard and Neil put together a four piece for the group section, chose James Taylor's *Carolina On My Mind* as their entry and rehearsed conscientiously. Neil brought in a spectacular intro and outro solo piano piece that dressed the song up particularly well. Full of bravado, they took to the stage and, singing in full harmony, took first place. (First equal actually!)

Flushed with this sweet victory, the 13-year-old Neil went home for the holidays and immediately put his name up for the Mount Maunganui Soundshell talent quest. He had something to prove this time and, on another warm East Coast night, walked onto the Soundshell stage sure-footed and confident. Seated at the organ, he broke into Carole King's *You've Got A Friend*. Up on the back seats, the Finn family, wrapped in blankets, enjoyed the young man's adventures. Brian didn't know how he could do it alone.

When the votes were counted, Neil was the clear winner. He put the $100 cheque into his back pocket and, with a sense of vindication, left the stadium. It would be many years before he would be back on that stage.

Come 1972, Brian rang me about a talent quest being held at the racecourse in Te Awamutu. We decided to put together a group and enter. With Rob on flute, brother Geoffrey on drums, Brian on piano, friend Ben Miller on bongos, and me and my bass we took to the stage dressed in tie-dyed Indian shirts and denim overalls. Bare feet too.

Up against an assortment of locals, we played the old *Take It Green*
(which we'd recorded in 1969 at Stebbings) and the hippie connotations somehow seemed to suit the smell of grass and horse dung:

> *Taking it green*
> *On a raft floating down in a stream*
> *Nothing to see but the flies*
> *And the heat of a dream (take it green)*

We won $500; because there were five of us, we raked in $100
each. Rich!! We celebrated back at a hotel in the Te Awamutu town-
ship and drank it all.

A short time after, Neil returned to Auckland to Sacred Heart.
Brian followed a few weeks later, this time to a flat in Patterson Ave,
Mission Bay, that Dick Finn had purchased as an investment and was
happy to see Brian and Rob Gillies rent for $5 a week each. They
settled into the first floor unit near the beach, drove into varsity every
day in Brian's Morrie Thou, and soon reacquainted themselves with
the various O'Rorke personnel who had gathered from the four
corners of New Zealand for another intense year 'en campus'.

Phil was back from his time in the slaughterhouse and quickly
decided he'd had enough of Elam Fine Arts School. While generally
regarded by his peers as an extraordinary painter, it had become clear
to him throughout the previous year that those with lesser talents
were reaping rewards by virtue of better verbal skills and rapport
with the tutors. His shortcomings in that area edged him out, as far as
he was concerned, and he wanted out for good. This lack of spontaneous communication plagued Phil to a degree. In the small group
that he had immersed himself in, he was able to be one of the boys;
play practical jokes and be comfortable. But in the presence of
strangers, his first instinct was to avoid direct dialogue. This quickly
led to a reputation of aloofness which was not the whole story. Phil
was incapable of the social, gregarious behaviour that came so easily
to people like Brian.

To some extent influenced by Phil's exit, Brian found himself
yearning to be free of the academic life with its structures and formal-

ities. He quit late in the first term. Dick and Mary weren't enamoured of his departure and asked the obvious questions: 'Why? What now?'

Brian didn't really have the answers but he knew academic life wasn't for him. By 1972 we had all grasped the reality of the changing social norms. In contrast to a past dominated by the older generation and the strict systems that they had felt obliged to perpetrate, the seventies were all about social conscience, free speech and freedom of choice; the media attention on young people allowed them, in the public eye, to make impressions previously impossible. This new era of opportunity, blissfully unaware of the rampant inflation, oil shocks and retrenchment just a few years away, was a foundation on which Brian and the rest of us thought we could challenge the goals we had felt obliged to set for ourselves, knowing that we had only been trying to please other people not ourselves.

It was into this new climate in Mission Bay that Neil would arrive on his 'free' Sundays from Sacred Heart. Brian, Rob, and the others, with long hair, beards and greatcoats, would fill the boy's head with the challenge of change. Brian suggested the painting of obscenities on the school walls and handed Neil a copy of *The Little Red Schoolbook*, which talked a new language. He said Neil should stand up to his teachers and question authority and, as a consequence, Neil's form master, Brother Christopher, found the young Finn sticking up for himself. As well, Neil would go to Mission Bay with others from the college, drink beer and make a racket while his classmates were back at school playing tennis.

Brian was now gone from university and Neil's commitment to Sacred Heart waned in parallel. It was near the end of the first term and the rugby trials had just been completed.

Team announcements were made and Neil had failed to secure a place in the 5As. This setback convinced the young boy that he was in the wrong place; boarding no longer held the opportunities he was seeking. He had made a commitment to himself two years earlier that he was going to make a life as a musician or performer of one sort or another; the sooner he left boarding school, the sooner this might be realised. On Friday May 5, 1972, he drove out of the Sacred Heart grounds for good.

Enrolling at Te Awamutu College, Neil found the freedom of life as a dayboy much more to his liking. Religion became a civilized option within the confines of the family home and he actively pursued musical activities. The only place there were any, however, was at the 'All 'n Some Folk Club', which was run by one Felicity Saxby. Neil found Felicity to be a warm, encouraging woman with hippie tendencies of which Neil approved; but she wasn't overly appreciated by many of the townsfolk because of her pro-abortion stance, amongst other things.

Neil would visit her at home and be invited along to the folk club where he was able to perform his Donovan and Beatle covers. As well there were public performances of sorts when the club arranged shows at Tokanui Psychiatric Hospital, Waikeria Prison and the Plunket Society. It was at the folk club that Neil met Rod Murdoch. A fair few years his senior, Rod saw in the youngster a fiery ambition and a definite musical talent, and they played together often.

At Mission Bay in Auckland, the thirst for adventure and mind expansion was at a peak. In an intense, almost serious and methodical way, the 'group' would search out locations and with the help of some traffic lights fly toy aeroplanes, sit on the beach wall and devise new ways of looking at the old. The acid trips were magic wands that they waved over their heads. As time wore on, Brian spent more and more time with Phil Judd. He found Phil's view of the world kaleidoscopic and Phil's artistic perceptions pervaded their conversations. Whether it was Phil lying on his back staring at the sky and talking about the Sistine Chapel or doodling on the piano, slowly piecing together some sequence of chords, the man's presence enveloped Brian. In fact, Phil was immersing himself more and more in all things musical.

One particular weekend, six of them drove off to Whitianga and in the middle of winter, in the middle of the day, they found them-selves on the shoreline tripping merrily. They stared long and hard at the wild sky and discovered a perfectly square cloud above their heads. Phil and Brian stood at the water's edge staring out to sea. Phil was calling out, 'The Venetians are coming!', and Brian looked out to find the horizon flooding back through his eyes. He rushed naked into the water as if to clamber over the edge of the breaking waves and slide off the side of the earth. Later they found a washed-up 40 gallon drum and started to beat it with driftwood until the clanging turned into a frenzy of white noise mirrored in the crashing surf. A huge wave engulfed them and they revelled in their power to summon the sea.

On returning to the beach house, Phil was playing a mellodrone and birds were flying in the macrocarpas. This image etched into Brian's mind, with the phrase 'charming the birds out of the trees.' That night Phil picked up a guitar and Brian sat next to him, his foot resting against Phil's. Usually uncomfortable with any affectionate contact with other males, this seemed perfectly natural to Brian. As Phil picked out notes on the guitar, Brian would concoct melodies that seemed to merge perfectly. It was this moment, as they weaved and searched, that Brian solidified in his head the notion of Phil Judd as a true artist; a unique person who could give Brian the courage to believe he had a place in the world of creativity and imagination that Phil possessed. A notion bathed in romanticism. He returned to Auckland from a weekend he would never forget.

In August, the Students' Arts Festival loomed, and Brian and I thought we should perform.

I had already booked Moses in for a thrashy set and Graham Nesbitt, the Festival coordinator, was happy to include Brian and Phil's combo which was going by the name Mellodrone. They pieced together a 20-minute epic, a montage of pieces written individually.

Phil had brought an album by the English duo McDonald and Giles to our attention, and it was the basis on which the Mellodrone work was put together.

On the night, the theatrical stance was supreme. Brian sat at the piano in his long coat, Phil was on drums with blue checks painted on his face, and Rob stood to attention, his flugelhorn at the ready. I cradled my bass and, well, I realised I looked like an engineering student in a Swanndri that had wandered onto the stage. In some way that was true. The stage was littered with a gruesome assembly to boot; Geoffrey Crombie stood expressionless the entire performance while his partner, Raewyn Turner, sat in a chair knitting; friend Roger Brookfield wandered around, his face painted blue (blue-boy); Paul Pattie and Jenny Harland completed the line-up of non-performing performers. I think Jenny wore gumboots. Brian shut his eyes, couched his stage fright in steely reserve (for 20 minutes) and sang loud and clear. While the reaction to this first-time performance with Phil was more messy than magnificent and it garnered little praise, Brian felt that it was just a matter of time.

I went along to the Festival the following night to peruse the other bands. One, called Orb, played an assortment of progressive English music from the likes of Yes and Bowie. Their best tracks were from the current Yes album *Fragile*, and their keyboard player was absolutely brilliant. He had thick legs and long, blond hair; it was – you guessed it – Tony Rayner. The lead singer was a tall charismatic lad by the name of Alistair Riddell; the drummer, well-schooled in the Bill Bruford way, was Paul Crowther.

By now, Rob had moved out of Mission Bay to a flat in Kohimarama called Malmsbury Villa; Phil moved in with Brian at Patterson Ave. In the post-Mellodrone rush, Phil was motivated and would spend hours at the piano concocting chord sequences and accompanying lyrics, with Brian fleshing out melodies and contributing the odd line, Phil had brought with him a variety of tangents for Brian to fly off on, Herman Hesse novels, including *Beneath The Wheel*, the Mervyn Peake *Titus Groan* trilogy, and Led Zeppelin and Traffic albums. Phil was excited with the new musical adventure. In late October, Brian rang me and told me that he and Phil had written some songs and were going to form a band. He'd thought of a name, which he'd culled from a page of scribbles he had in a book – it was to be 'Split Ends'. He then jokingly said that their first performance would be at the Great Ngaruawahia Music Festival scheduled for the first week of the New Year 1973. I said nothing and thought, 'You'll be lucky!' But was he joking?

He rang three weeks later. He and Phil had met a brilliant violinist by the name of Miles Golding and their material was really coming together. Phil and Brian had written two songs in one night: Split Ends and another called *For You*. But they needed a place to practise.

'Can we come and rehearse in your bedroom?'

'Sure.'

So they came round; Miles looked like a boy with a swathe of curls all over his head. There was something innocent about him. Had he never crashed a car? He didn't direct proceedings or even say much. I guess that's what violinists in orchestras do. Wait for the conductor to bring his (her?) baton down on them. And then he put his string to his bow and we all stood still. We stared at him when he played. Brian sat at the piano, Phil set up his drum kit and they proceeded to bash away. As an ensemble it was a mess. I didn't say anything. Geoffrey and Graeme Gash were there, watching curiously. (They had a band called Rosewood). Then, Phil hopped off the drums and picked up an acoustic guitar; Brian picked up a tambourine. Brian explained that their intention was to break up their rock set with an acoustic bracket and they had written three songs for that purpose. Phil and Brian proceeded to sing them. Sitting side by side, Phil strummed out these weird-shaped chords and the two of them sang in a strong, spirited fashion. The songs were unique ... unlike anything I'd heard before and we all listened intently.

For You, Wise Men and *Split Ends*.

At the end there was silence in the room.

I was stunned, floundering in this discovery. I walked over to Brian while trying to look noncommittal. 'Brian,' I said. 'If you're looking for a bass player, I'd be keen to play.'

He looked at me. 'Well, actually ... that's why we're here.'

5

WRITING LETTERS TO MY FRIENDS

I took Brian aside and said that the concept of a rock band format with Phil on drums wouldn't work and that we should be solely acoustic. He agreed. Phil stuck to his acoustic guitar, Brian clutched his tambourine and Miles brought in an acquaintance, Mike Howard, on flute to further the acoustic concept.

In a spurt of furious activity, Split Ends commenced rehearsals in my bedroom. It became immediately apparent that Phil had found some way to forge his wild imaginings onto the acoustic guitar. He had devised strange string tunings to make his fingerings easier and consequently no one knew what chord he was playing. This gave us the opportunity to explore our fret boards for whatever notes sounded most interesting. The results were multi-layered, harmonic hybrids. And Miles quickly showed himself to be a violinist of extraordinary capability, weaving and soaring with prodigious effect. Coupled with this was the great leap forward in lyrical style from the previous 'Mellodrone' piece. I was itching to give the public a taste and, aware that brother Geoffrey's Rosewood were soon to play at a blues night at the Wynyard Tavern in Symonds Street, I asked him to see if we could come along also and play our three songs. He secured a slot for us and also managed to have us included in the Sunday folk night that was running on the same night at Levys Saloon in Customs Street.

Brian and Phil were buzzing at the chance to play and we rehearsed in a frenzy until the day came. At 7.30 pm on Sunday December 10, 1972, Split Ends gave its first performance to 30 people in the Wynyard Tavern. We dressed in wild, loose clothes: Phil in his spencer top and Miles with his bow tie, a pseudo-mockery of the classical violinist; three of us wore op-shop waist-coats with two-headed eagles painted by Phil on the reverse; I also wore jackboots painted gold by Phil. In a flash it was over. I don't recall the reaction. It was all too fast. Besides, that was just the warm-up.

Elated, we clambered into our car and drove off down the road to Levys Saloon where we found a sedate audience savouring some Neil Young covers. We waited in the corner of the dank, smoke-stained room, revelling in our pocket of isolation and ready for the charge. We took the stage and kicked off with *Split Ends*, followed by *For You* and *Wise Men*.

The response was enthusiastic and the promoter of the evening, Barry Coburn, came up to us and suggested we play some more. Brian told him we only knew three songs so we went back and played *For You* again.

On leaving the stage, Coburn took us aside and started to ask questions: 'Your own songs? How long have you been together?' He heard the answers he wanted to hear, such as 'Yes' and 'Three weeks'. Coburn was thin, in his late twenties, and had previously been a florist in Christchurch. Presumably this meant he was adept at arranging things. He wore country music shirts and may have even worn cowboy boots. He started talking about recording sessions and records, and how he was putting on this huge music festival in the New Year with his partner Robert Raymond. Black Sabbath were coming down for it, and it was going to be called the Great Ngaru-awahia Music Festival. If we wanted to, we could play at it. I looked across at Brian who pretended not to notice my glance. I sensed the corners of his mouth holding back a smile.

The next day we had a confirmed slot at the Festival, directly before the La De Das on the Saturday night, and we planned rehearsals to learn new material. By now, Rob Gillies had moved out of Malmsbury Villa to Bankside Cottage in the inner city so Brian and Phil moved in. Malmsbury Villa was perched precariously on the slopes of 17 Kohimarama Road, and Brian and Phil were on the first floor-peering out over the sweep of houses that fronted the sea. The floors rolled this way and that; the ceiling dipped towards the ocean as if acknowledging the aloof, itinerant tides. The rooms were draped in multi-coloured cloth to hide the bare scrim long left naked by peeling wallpaper, and Wagner's *Tristan und Isolde* or *Led Zeppelin IV* would echo through the house. There wasn't a poster of Che Guevara anywhere.

Phil set up an easel and his painting activities continued although the focal point of the summer days and warm nights was his guitar. He and Brian embarked on a writing spree that would prove nothing less than stunning. On the back lawn under the sun, in altered states, Phil would pick out chords as building blocks for his lyrics; Brian would find melodies, and the flow ran unchecked – a continuous outpouring. Brian had now obtained a Yamaha acoustic guitar (the same model as Phil's FG300), and Phil painted them both in black and white checks with the twin-headed eagle resplendent on each.

At each rehearsal we gathered together on the leaning balcony of Malmsbury Villa, where Brian and Phil would present a new song. As we pieced it together we glowed. Songs such as *Lovey Dovey*, *Malmsbury Villa* and *No Bother To Me*. Gazing out across Kohimarama we were playing to the whole world. There was pure magic at play; an unreal rarefied atmosphere that completely enveloped us. By now my Mustang bass had been painted gold by Phil.

At the time, with no practical experience behind us and a music industry coughing and spluttering in its infancy, the creative flow and the rapid evolving of concepts seemed perfectly natural. In hindsight, albeit through my rose-coloured spectacles, I was witness to an extraordinary experience that happens very rarely in a lifetime ... if at all!

In 1972, in our private world, we flew in the face of naivety. Instead of a pragmatic approach, we were trying to enact a dream, working very hard in the hope that it might come true. There was a logical momentum to what we were doing, and the vast output of incredible material from Judd and Finn was almost taken for granted – although we were all amazed at where exactly this sudden rush was springing from, considering the measly volume of work composed over the previous 18 months.

Judd was unlocked by the LSD, there's no doubting that. His reticence and introverted nature had previously been channelled into his work on canvas but, after that weekend at Whitianga, his direction shifted and the world of musical composition enveloped him. With Brian's concentrated assistance, he found this well of music waiting inside him. Miles Golding played a pivotal role as well. Brian and Phil were aware of his vast musical knowledge particularly in the realms of classical music, and his encouragement and approval was a real spur to them. He provided us all with our first lessons in the importance of arrangements and we relished his constructive approach.

In parallel with this internal rush was the sloping off of all things external. Phil and Brian, in particular, became so absorbed in their writing and, perhaps subconsciously, keen to avoid external influences that they stopped listening to the music of the time. In the realm of commercial music that made a lot of sense. In the history books, the early 1970s will be remembered as a particularly banal period as far as the singles market went. The world's Top 40s were plagued with the likes of The Bay City Rollers, The Osmonds and The Partridge Family. They were all toppermost of the poppermost.

In New Zealand, there was a flourishing television focus on pop music as this was the pre-video clip era and music shows were produced locally. On Saturday evenings, the *Happen Inn* show would feature resident pop performers with minimal credibility. And once a year the record industry would celebrate local successes with the RATA Awards which received a prime-time television slot. Various local performers who achieved notoriety through middle of the road weekly variety shows and resident status on the *Happen Inn* pop show would come forward as finalists. They all wore suits with flared bottoms, bow ties and ruffled shirts. Their hair was long, combed perfectly, lacquered and stiff, and they projected negligible personalities. Brother Geoffrey and I would watch the proceedings, envious of the publicity they were receiving and appalled at the songs.

On the contemporary front, albums were the thing and it was not uncommon for major rock acts to never release singles. Led Zeppelin, Yes, Jethro Tull, Family and so on were virtually never heard on radio and that medium suddenly ceased to feature in our lives.

Word quickly got back via Brian to the Finn household about the first performances and curiosity was aroused. When the family learned that we were to be playing again at Levys Saloon, Neil and sisters, Judy and Carolyn, drove to Auckland for the show.

Seven years later, on the sleeve of the album *The Beginning Of The Enz*, Neil recalled the event: 'I first saw Split Ends in 1972 at Levys Saloon in Auckland. Back then I was still a pimply schoolboy but that performance and those first songs made a lasting impression on me. I went back to Te Awamutu and wrote Split Ends on my pencil case.'

It was at that second Levys show that Phil debuted *Time For A Change*, which was performed by himself on guitar and vocal and Miles on violin. We had never heard it before and were floored at the intricacy of the guitar arrangement and the extraordinary beauty of Miles' violin solo. In recalling that moment, Brian now believes that the song should have been recorded with just that arrangement. But it was not to be.

In the meantime, however, were more mundane matters such as the New Year and the Great Ngaruawahia Music Festival. New

Zealand had never seen a multi-day music festival apart from a quasi-affair three years before in Auckland, where Robin Gibb of the Bee Gees was the headline act and he ran from the stage when people started throwing beer cans at him. But Ngaruawahia was the real thing, just like we'd seen all those years before in the Woodstock movie.

My first impression was of two heads sticking out of a tent. One, a male cranium, was furrowed and concentrated in the act of copulation. It was poised above a female head squizzing curiously at the blue sky, seemingly oblivious to the passing footloose traffic. Dust flew around their entwined bodies as the hordes wormed their way to communal showers and food stalls.

We set up a tent near backstage on the Saturday morning and waited nervously. There were 18,000 people on the site and 17,896 had never heard of us. Neil had arrived from Te Awamutu and watched the tuning up, fidgeting, strategic planning, and nervous yawning with keen interest. He then took up a spot out in the crowd as the dusk settled in. All around him young men poured beer down their throats as a precursor to their big moment: the return of Kevin Borich and the La De Das.

Split Ends walked on stage at 8.00 pm to a restless crowd that failed to acknowledge its arrival. Brian was spinning and started talking to the crowd in an Irish accent. Committed to this strange pretence, he was obliged to stick with it. We kicked off with *Split Ends*, which sounded weedy by virtue of my plugging my bass guitar into the wrong amplifier. For half the song I was playing away in silence. We followed this with *Under The Wheel* which we had just learned that week. It was delivered at a rapid-fire speed fuelled by intense adrenalin, each of us incapable of any rational control. The crowd failed to respond. We played *For You*, followed by *Lovey Dovey*. Brian opened his eyes briefly and looked across at Miles, who was playing so hard his bow was shredding fibres in the harsh spotlight. There was a grim determination on his face, and Brian and Phil sang maniacally.

By now Neil was aware of a certain feeling in the crowd, epitomised by the young man who was sitting across from him screaming 'Piss off ... Get off' at the top of his lungs. In the vast expanse of the night sky, our acoustic display was drifting away in the breeze and Neil started to feel alone.

After *Spellbound*, halfway through the set, the stage MC, Adrian Rawlins, came up to Brian and said that we had to get off. They had the Maori Concert Party ready to go on as a ruse to quieten the restless mob.

Brian reacted instinctively by going up to the microphone and asking a question: 'We've just been told we have to get off. Do YOU want us to finish?'

There was little need for the crowd to discuss this amongst themselves. In a roar of unanimous approval they screamed, 'YES!!'

Shocked and confused, we charged off into 129, our last chance to prove ourselves. Brian sang as if he was staring into the eyes of every drunk who wanted him out of there. He filled his lungs and made an extraordinary effort, as he spat it out.

We walked off as the Maori Concert Party shuffled on, and drove home. The grand moment, the big opportunity, had crumbled before our very eyes and the inexorable rise to fame and glory seemed dented.

Brian bounced back quickly though and back in Auckland looked forward to more Levys shows and the impending recording sessions. Phil was less sure, having found the whole Festival experience disturbing. His natural psychology was towards the euphoric moment; the setback left him with a crisis of faith, his trust in the public to react positively to the band shattered.

However, Barry Coburn was still with us and he scheduled time at Stebbing Studios in the first week of February to record the single. At this stage we had no formal written recording contract with Coburn. In fact, we never would. On the morning of February 4, 1973, we drove off to the studio, all crammed into my father's Morrie 1800 with Richard Burton's rendition of *Under Milk Wood* blaring on the car stereo for inspiration. We had decided to have drums on *For You*, and a Hamilton chap, Div Vercoe, was brought in. He was obsessed with Motown and in particular The Temptations. This meant nothing to us.

Raised on New Zealand radio, we heard the distilled versions of black American music via The Beatles doing Smokey Robinson and The Stones and Animals with their r'n'b covers such as *Little Red Rooster*. We weren't aware of their roots and the whole concept of 'groove' was alien to us. However, that didn't stop Vercoe showing interest in our music. We set up, taught Div the song and after half an hour it was in the can. I had borrowed Wally Wilkinson's Gibson guitar so took the opportunity to play a five-note lead solo on the tail of the solos. We then threw down *Split Ends* as a B-side. Brian and Phil put down the vocals, changing the line about Geoffrey Crombie in *For You* to 'Blue-boy's on the stage' to avoid any negative response from the line that followed: 'People think he's queer.' Changing the direct reference from Crombie to Roger Brookfield made sense at the time. Uncommon sense.

We listened back and it felt very, very good. We found the use of drums gave *For You* some oomph so we decided to ask Div to play with us on a semi-permanent basis and he agreed. We then took some time off and Miles returned to Wellington, his home town, to a holiday job. While he was there he met up with Coburn and they mixed the two songs at HMV studios. He returned to Auckland two weeks later and rehearsals kicked off again. By now, the unit was finely tuned and the new songs were given intense, wild arrangements, and they kept on coming, from the confines of Malmsbury Villa. *Spellbound* was one of them.

Back in Te Awamutu, Neil had decided that Split Ends were incredible. He spent more and more time composing with Rod Murdoch. First there was an untitled instrumental, which was included in some shows they performed at in early 1973 at the Kon Tiki folk club in Hamilton and a country folk festival outside Te Awamutu. Then a couple of other songs came into the repertoire:

Mother Of Five and *Late In Rome*. At Teasdale Street, he kept practising the piano, working his original pieces until he was satisfied with them.

In late February, Miles, Brian, and Phil got together at Malmsbury Villa for an afternoon out on the rim. Miles had his violin and wandered around playing a riff he had written ... over and over it went – climbing and descending. Climbing and descending. In the kitchen of Malmsbury Villa, it was resolved to pursue this embryonic creation at rehearsal.

A few days later, the three of them, Div Vercoe and myself gathered in my bedroom at Parnell Road and proceeded to piece this thing together, with Vercoe's contribution quite productive. Miles' opening riff set the majestic feel and there was a grandness to the melodies. A spoken piece, culled from the flyleaf of a Mervyn Peake novel held the title: check the back cover of the 1974 edition of *Titus Groan*.

Stranger Than Fiction started to take shape before our very eyes. It seemed different somehow. I recall thinking to myself, 'This is serious stuff!' Miles' riff was nothing less than mesmerising as it climbed then spun. Climbed and spun.

Unfortunately, while Div's drumming was in our favour, his increasingly cantankerous traits were not and it was decided to let him go. This coincided with the appearance of Coburn on the scene to tell us that *For You* was going to be released on the Vertigo label which was an imprint of Polygram Records, and that we had a tour of New Zealand campuses ahead of us as support for an Australian hard rock unit by the name of Itambu. 'Progress!' we thought.

We abandoned the drummer concept, shelved *Stranger Than Fiction* and, in late February, took off in a van with three long-haired Australians, folk singer Lindsay Marks (a Coburn protege) and Coburn. It was our first tour and we quickly revelled in the spirit of the road, lucky to have a gig. Live work in New Zealand had yet to achieve the virile state it reached in the late seventies, when the pub circuit was extensive and lucrative.

Pubs in 1973 stuck with resident showbands performing John Rowles and Engelbert Humperdinck covers and the only avenue for original music was on the university campuses. Luckily, Coburn knew this, worked hard on it and secured us the tour.

The first concert was in the Otago University Union Hall to a full house and the reaction was excellent. The campus paper, *Critic*, ran a review by Roy Colbert, which was encouraging: 'Their music – delicate and tinklingly intricate – demands that each guy plays just about perfectly if the effect is to be total. The violinist did some arrestingly abrasive things.' (That was Miles in *Spellbound*).

The joy of finally playing to an attentive crowd outside of Levys Saloon was tempered by the reality of touring. Miles and I spent the night on a double mattress under a scratchy blanket. Still, it was better than Brian and Phil who were on a kitchen floor. From there, we played cafeterias where the smell of sausages and hot fat would penetrate our nostrils as we spun out our tales and tunes. By the time we reached Auckland, the novelty of driving the length and breadth of the country had worn thin and we were glad to be back home. None of the latter concerts had reached the height of the Dunedin show but we felt we had accomplished something – and the word was spreading.

Brian was developing a stage persona; he had realised that he would be the ringmaster and that he was going to have to learn his craft the hard way. He was delightfully free of vanity; his inward focus being on the unit not the self. He took a natural leadership role in front of the public where his diplomacy and ability to communicate made him the obvious focal point. Phi's natural inclination was to remain tight-lipped, which belied the fact that he was, in fact, enjoying himself; revelling in the new experience of taking his music to the people.

Brian was still, however, a reluctant performer and would spend most shows with his eyes jammed shut, staying in a womb of darkness; but, charged with his subconscious desire for success, he would act out a wild, energetic and spirited role almost as if it were a disguise.

The result was fooling everybody as he was soon regarded as a natural frontman. The best in the land.

The tour also gave us the chance to live on the road. This was our first time together and we had a chance to check each other out. Phil would play the prankster, quick to trick an unsuspecting cohort. As far as our travelling companions, Itambu went, we couldn't relate to them in the slightest.

The proof of their stature in the scheme of things came in Palmerston North, when the local sheep-shearer students walked on stage during their set and brown-eyed the crowd. They didn't do it to us!

Coburn, in his entrepreneurial state, was now bringing in overseas tours and he scheduled Split Ends to support John Mayall's tour for Auckland, Wellington and Christchurch. His announcement to us was followed by a more sobering phone call. Miles rang to say he was leaving the band. Principally a classical player, Miles had no option in his quest as an orchestral violinist than to go to London and further his studies. Which he did ... and Brian and Phil were shattered. As far as Phil was concerned, Miles was the cornerstone of Split Ends, particularly since his fiery success on the NZ tour and his writing contribution to *Stranger Than Fiction*.

Brian was similarly inclined. He had no solution and he too seemed resigned to the group's demise. So after a final farewell bash in my bedroom, Miles drove off to pack his bags for London. Brian and Phil headed to Malmsbury Villa.

I rang Brian thirty minutes later.

'Brian?'

'Yeah?'

'Let's ask brother Geoffrey to play drums and Wally Wilkinson to play guitar and do the Mayall tour.'

'... Yeah, why not?'

Geoffrey jumped at the chance. He had watched the burgeoning

Split Ends scenario and relished the opportunity to join in, even if it did mean abandoning the guitar for the drum kit. Wally Wilkinson was now playing bass in Orb and accepted readily; it gave him the chance to get off the bass and go back to his first love, guitar.

With 12 days to go before the first Mayall show in Auckland, we gathered in my bedroom at 469 Parnell Rd. By now, Brian, Phil and I were decided on the exit of Mike Howard, particularly in the face of a new, electric line-up. So, as none of us had the guts to fire the man, we turned up our amplifiers and drowned him out. He gave up and stormed off.

The songs that fit the electric lineup fell into shape quickly while others such as *Wise Men, Buffs* and *Hermine* disappeared forever. Brian took to the new sound quickly. He now owned a Fender Rhodes piano and played a larger musical role, although the trusty tambourine was still there for *Split Ends*.

On Friday April 13, the big night came and we walked onto the stage at the YMCA stadium, Auckland, to a full house of Mayall fans and hit them between the eyes. The songs flowed and we held tight, kicking off with *True Colours* which was new to the repertoire. We finished with *Spellbound*. Back in the dressing room we beamed and Coburn beamed and we felt it. It was joy.

The next day the reviews came through and Phil Gifford in the *New Zealand Herald* confirmed our suspicions: 'Opening was an excellent local group Split Ends. They write all their own material which had a touch of (Jethro) Tull but a lot more of themselves. If you have a chance to see them, do so, your time won't be wasted.'

The other Mayall shows sustained the impact of the Auckland performance and we returned home in high spirits. Waiting for us were copies of our single, hot off the press. As far as we were concerned, the success of *For You* was going to be a natural progression from the success of the Mayall dates but we soon learned otherwise. This was 1973 and private radio stations had arrived, bringing with them strict Top 40 formats and particularly conservative playlists. The single made no impression at all, sinking without trace.

Coupled with this, Coburn promoted a concert at the Peter Pan Ballroom, Auckland, with Split Ends headlining and the place was packed. This proved to be regrettable when we noticed most of them leaving halfway through the set. The sound system was way below par, no one could hear anything and Brian lost the plot as the performance slipped through his fingers. For the first and not the last time, he dragged us all down with him. (To be fair – we all played like crap as well).

Coburn was running short on options. We had made it perfectly clear to him that we refused to play the pub circuit. Brian knew full well that Phil would not take kindly to flying jugs and bubbling chatter. And he himself was committed to a level of excellence that surpassed the tawdry confines of a sticky beer barn; he knew, in his heart, that the music he and Phil had created didn't belong there. We had set a standard that we wanted to expand on, not fall back from. Consequently Coburn did what he had to do – enter us in a 'talent quest'. The only one worth bothering with was called *New Faces*.

In May, we went back to Stebbing Studios to record a track for the heats. We chose a song called *129* which brought mandolins to the Split Ends soundstage. With Wally on guitar and Geoffrey on drums, the track kicked along in sharp contrast to the acoustic arrangement of the first single. This time Brian and Phil were ready for some experimentation, and we enlisted a string quartet (some friends of Miles') and Rob Gillies on saxophone. Phil and Brian arranged the string and brass parts, and the end result was varied and intensely melodic with theatrical references and a confident Finn vocal. We also recorded a recently written number entitled *Home Sweet Home*, an eccentric fable about Martin the deaf, dumb and blind kid who danced the highland fling. Phil took the lead vocal.

These sessions confirmed the Split Ends ethos. We were never to stand still: we reached for ways to break down the predictable and used the studio, primitive as it was, for new sounds and new effects. With the Beatles still fresh in our minds, Phil and Brian arranged string quartets and wrote brass parts; we threw in percussion, bagpipes, banjos, gongs, and sound FX. (The opening babble on *129* is a recording of punters drinking in the Gluepot Hotel). Life in the studio was magic and in contrast to the fragile live shows, Phil, particularly, was in his element. By now, his acoustic guitar playing was masterful and *Home Sweet Home* was proof of that. Wally was shaking his 'metal' roots and conceiving some hooky parts that weaved in and out, and Geoffrey and I enjoyed the rejuvenation of the Sibling connection.

In the end we walked out weary and delighted. We had taken another step forward.

6

TALKING TO MYSELF (I DRANK THE BEAUTY)

The New Faces talent quest had national attention. In those days, this, the *only* television channel, was a government department and was able to spend exorbitant amounts of money flying contestants from all around New Zealand to mime out heats in their Wellington studios.

The year before, two of the finalists, John Hanlon and Shona Laing, had gone on to fairly substantial careers with Top 10 records as a result of the exposure they had received from the series.

That was our plan. Having toured New Zealand twice with little real penetration outside the university campuses, we now had the chance to grab the country by the throat with 129 and clamber up a few rungs. All without having to gamble off live performances. In midyear we had played Hamilton, Wellington and Palmerston North concerts to small crowds and while the feedback was good, the effect was minimal despite the new line-up finding its feet. The material that had transferred from the Miles Golding era was now sitting comfortably and the acoustic flourish of the summer of 1972—73 had become a historical perspective.

We did have a huge article in the Wellington press that bolstered our pride: 'Split Ends – probably the most innovative and original group in New Zealand. The minute you begin to write about this group, you begin to take away their magic because they really defy classification.'

This was what we wanted – exclusivity – and *New Faces* was going to allow us the chance to go up against the fire-eaters, folkies and comedy acts and blow them all away. With 129, we felt we had the song that would do it.

We flew down to Wellington in August, recorded the video segment for our heat and returned to await the judges' decision as to whether or not we would be in the final.

Barry Coburn, disappointed with Polygram's failure to achieve much with *For You*, was in a state of glee: on going to the Polygram office to secure a photocopy of our contract, he had been handed the original by the receptionist. Goodbye, Polygram.

By this time, Brian and Phil had reached the end of their tenure at Malmsbury Villa, with people coming and going and privacy at a premium. They rented a basement flat at 18 St Georges Bay Road, Parnell, when it was still a derelict suburb, and three of them moved in: Brian, Phil and his partner, Julie. Tucked away down a rocky side path, number 18 was as private as you could get. Draped in permanent shadows and with a view of nothing but tall trees, the house, not unlike Malmsbury Villa, had an unstable quality to its aspect and appeared to be sliding down the slopes to the valley below.

It was here that Brian dedicated himself completely to Split Ends, to such an extent that his compulsion was virtually a deterministic obsession. For many months, he had little contact with outsiders, particularly women. He had little else to talk about in his day-to-day life other than his vision for Split Ends.

Phil painted the walls of the flat, set up an easel in his room for more oil painting and, late at night, would drive off to the Viko photo processing factory and raid rejected prints from its rubbish bags. He would come back with photos of gang members flopping their cocks out at a party, smudged copies of middle-aged men speaking at weddings and the odd out-of-focus baby shot. And so on. These flawed slices of New Zealand were auditioned for his artwork. And new songs flourished as a parallel. Songs like *Hermine* and *Blankets*.

When Phil wasn't at his easel, the two of them concentrated on writing new material and drinking wine. The composing process was now more evenly shared, with Brian at his piano directly contributing and conceiving. Behind the flat and buried in the forest was an A-frame hut, which we set our gear in. We rehearsed the new songs that Phil and Brian had concocted in their new home. Songs like *Walking Down A Road*.

On the odd weekend, Phil, Julie, Brian and I would all go out to my parents' bach at Bethells Beach. We would walk through the thick native forest to the volcano crater that had become a deep, mysterious lake called Kawaupaku. On all sides the ferns and twisted trees rolled steeply into the water and the sense of space and timelessness was extraordinary. At night we would fire up the old reel-to-reel tape recorder and play the final mix of *129* at half speed with our heads between the speakers. Large, pumping ad hoc headphones. The half-speed phased violins were like a royal ether in our skulls. And we would talk about the future.

Most of us, including Brian, knew we had only just scratched the surface of the effort required to gain commercial success. Phil had achieved the establishment of an amazing musical entity and, more surreptitiously than Brian, now looked to spread his vision. While less able to handle the logistical upsets and twists and turns that flew in our faces, he was nevertheless determined to see Split Ends' music spread far and wide. He had little choice however than to leave this to the rest of us and the likes of Barry Coburn.

In October, we heard that we had won our *New Faces* heat and needed to come up with another song for the final. Brian and Phil had written something in anticipation of this, and we took off to Stebbing Studios to record it – *The Sweet Talking Spoon Song*. This light-hearted ditty shook off our usual serious, adventurous spirit and tackled the story of a man obsessed with a pin-up poster. Once again the arrangement was intricate. Rob Gillies came in with his trumpet and a tuba player was hired. We had mandolins, and some accidental weird harmonies crept in.

Near the end of the track, Phil played a spoons solo that captured the attention of everybody who heard the song. The end result swung in a neat fashion and we flew down to Wellington. *New Faces* was going to be the start of it all.

We didn't look at each other when the judges' points placed us second to last.

The next day Brian was interviewed by the *Sunday News* and put it on the line: 'Our sound is very complex and it takes a lot of work even in a studio, to make it work. And we want the right situation ... We definitely won't be doing concerts at the moment'

Back in Auckland, Coburn gathered us together and presented us with two-year management contracts with options at Coburn's discretion. We agreed to sign on the condition that a clause was added: 'If, in the last six months of the period we had individually earned less than $50 a week, options could not be taken up.'

Shortly after, Brian rang to say that Phil didn't want to perform live any more so we shouldn't look for any work. Brian adopted Phil's plans of existing as a recording act only and 1973 ended in a limbo. While at the time this development seemed sudden, it now appears almost logical. The 'rejection' of our performance in the *New Faces* final was an enormous let-down for Phil and Tim, who had imagined the show would send the band soaring into the stratosphere. When the reality struck, their natural reaction was to retreat – and that meant avoiding live work.

But it wasn't just the talent quest. Miles had gone, and the live shows were fraught with technical problems and small crowds. The only real achievements in Phil's view had been the records we'd made, in that they had reached his expectations and he found the recording studio to be the ideal canvas. And Brian followed suit. They virtually disappeared into the shadows of St Georges Bay

Road; Wally, Geoffrey and I ended the year not knowing if we would ever meet as Split Ends on a stage again.

This state of affairs was mirrored in the release of *The Sweet Talking Spoon Song* backed with *129*. It followed the path of *For You* to nowhere in particular. In the NZ Top 10, The Carpenters were toppermost of poppermost.

Brian returned to Te Awamutu for Christmas, where Dick was again wondering what Brian was doing with his life and questioned him on the subject. Neil was in on the conversation and Brian told them both that Split Ends was his mission, his quest, and that he was convinced that if only someone would finance an album then Split Ends could be the next Beatles. Dick respected Brian's intensity of belief and Neil ... well, it just soaked in.

In late January, we were all back in Auckland from our various holiday distractions, assuming nothing was happening which it was. Then Barry Coburn rang me to say that we had a 30 minute television special, courtesy of Television New Zealand, as a result of being one of the *New Faces* finalists. The show would be entitled *Six Of The Best*. We needed to record four more songs to add to *129* and *The Sweet Talking Spoon Song*. And there was the possibility of concerts ahead as Radio Hauraki were planning a series of Buck-A-Head shows at His Majesty's Theatre.

'Buck-A-Head, Barry?'

'Yes, Mike. A dollar to get in.'

I rang Brian and explained this to him. He immediately saw the worth of the TV show so we got Coburn to book time at Stebbing Studios to record the tracks. And the concerts sounded ideal. Radio advertising support and the magnificent His Majesty's Theatre to play in. We talked more and decided that even though Phil wasn't interested in playing live, we would expand the group and Phil could be involved from the sideline – contributing ideas, concepts and songs.

In early February 1974, we asked old buddy old friend Rob Gillies to come in on sax and trumpet. We had a few rehearsals and, after the hiatus, were breathing new life into the songs. Brian was uncomfortable with Phil not performing but kept it to himself; as far as we were concerned, his enthusiasm was on a par. He had just purchased a mellotron keyboard, courtesy of a loan from Dick and Mary, which used strips of magnetic tape that reproduced the authentic sounds of violins, cellos and flutes. This was going to help recreate the string sections that had featured so prominently on the records. Consequently, we needed a second keyboard player to play it and he had to be brilliant.

There was only one choice: Tony Rayner. Rayner's reputation as a master keys man had grown considerably during 1973 as Orb became more and more notorious. And with Wally as an ex-Orb member we had an in. Wally asked him along to a rehearsal so we could audition him. We now had a new rehearsal place. My parents had bought the three townhouses in Parnell Road (one of which they had been renting as the family home) for a steal and as the family spread out into two of them, Split Enz nabbed the third. Hidden away behind double brick walls at 473 Parnell Road, we set up our gear in the ground floor front room in readiness. The Chunn piano had come from Otahuhu and it stood quietly against the wall. (I still own that piano).

Tony turned up with his innocent face and long blond hair, and took a seat next to Brian at the piano. He had a knowing eye, swirling hair and an odd pair of trousers like a Russian politician. When he played a couple of chords on the piano his hands played them like he'd played that piano a thousand times before. Hands that weren't skinny or delicate. Quite fulsome fingers they were. Like his legs.

Very little was said because very little was always said to people outside our enclave. We just plugged in our guitars and hit young Tony right between the eyes with a thumping, desperate version of *Lovey Dovey*. I looked at this young musician as he sat watching carefully. We finished. Again nothing was said. Until:

Tony – 'Can you play it again?'

'Sure,' we said.

As we started the song Tony spun on the piano stool and played the entire song with us. How did he do that! Indeed, we weren't auditioning him. He was auditioning us. We passed and Tony Rayner joined Split Ends.

At the same time, Phil and Brian decided to re-title the band 'Split Enz'. The graphic symbolism inherent in 'Enz', with the New Zealand reference, was clever and we were happy with the new moniker.

Rehearsals with this six-piece continued at a furious rate. We had less than a month before we were in Stebbing Studios. In the end, over two days in February, we recorded *No Bother To Me*, *Malmsbury Villa*, *Lovey Dovey* and *Spellbound*.

The sessions found us excited at the fuller sound. Thrilled at the broader perspective, the general consensus on hearing the final mixes was that this line-up had surpassed any before it, and that the contributions from Rob and Tony to the arrangements were cool.

Rayner in particular showed a talent of extraordinary proportions. He had a definite, lyrical style, and his flourishes and whirls were founded on those masses of Yes and Bowie songs he had performed with Orb. (If you think Bowie and Yes had no link, take into account the fact that Rick Wakeman had played all the piano parts on Bowie's *Hunky Dory* before joining Yes.) There was no doubt the Rayner chap was technically majestic, with the piano his true forte. Coupled with this discovery of Tony's musical talents, I found Geoffrey and I to be knitting as a rhythm section. His simple, direct drumming style layered with rolling tom-tom fills suited the lavish arrangements.

Brian's vocals on the tracks, particularly his harmonies, were on a par with Tony's dexterity. In spite of this, Brian was still uncertain, believing that the results would have been better had Phil been a full member of the band. While half of him was happy that the momentum of the band was back on track, half of him lamented Phil's absence from the line-up. This was mildly allayed by Phil playing acoustic on most of the tracks (rather magnificently, I might add). But he was no longer a member and Split Enz without Phil was not really Split Enz as far as Brian was concerned. With this in mind, there were no plans made to release any of these recordings as singles.

Brian's vexations were not shared by the rest of us, who felt that Phil's fragility in the live situation made it easier for us to charge on confidently without him. The recent sessions had proved he was nothing less than a boon in the studio; the rigours of the stage were a different story. Our feelings were compounded further when Barry Coburn rang to say we had a headline slot at the first of the Radio Hauraki Buck-A-Head shows in May. This was going to be the relaunch of Split Enz and nothing could go wrong.

In the March issue of the new rock mag, *Hot Licks*, a half-page story on Split Enz quoted Phil on the subject of live concerts: 'I hate it. It disturbs me.' It was now in black and white.

We continued rehearsing madly, with Phil occasionally sitting in, reworking the old songs around the new line-up. As a warm-up to the Buck-A-Head we flew to Christchurch for a concert supporting Quincy Conserve in the Christchurch Town Hall. No one came. As well we recorded a video clip of *Spellbound* for the TVNZ rock show *PopCo*. It was shown once in April and then wiped. TV magnetic tape was expensive. And recycling was a new buzz word.

We cast the Christchurch trip from our minds and concentrated on the Buck-A-Head ahead. Phil had taken to scouring more junk shops and bric-a-brac outlets for old 78s (Bing Crosby, Flotsam and Jetsam, Louis Armstrong and so on) and ancient sheet music. I would borrow the old records and wonder at the eccentric, polished music of the thirties and forties, and decided to incorporate a selection before and after the His Majesty's Show. This started a general hubbub of planning of theatrical concepts for the show and very soon we had a phantasmagorical series of sound effects planned for the occasion.

Singing monks, breaking glass, peeling laughter, birds singing, children playing, passing trains, rivers running; they were all recorded in readiness for playing at pertinent moments. Geoffrey Crombie was back on the scene as he and Rob were flatting together at Bankside Cottage with Rob's partner Geraldene, and a sketch was devised featuring Geoffrey as a psychiatrist pursuing Phil Judd in bandaged head and straitjacket. They would do this during the middle section of *Stranger Than Fiction*. The stage would be decked out with coloured light bulbs, large pot plants and stuffed animals.

Brian had a large mask with a microphone in its mouth, which he would use when he sang *No Bother To Me* and *Malmsbury Villa*.

Finally the night arrived – May 12, 1974 – and by 8.00 pm the theatre was full, with 1,200 people drawn in by curiosity and Radio Hauraki's powerful promotion campaign. We shuffled, sat, shifted, and stood backstage in a complete state of anticipation and nerves. This was our chance.

The support band was Crow (sponsored by Black Crow bourbon) and they performed Boz Scaggs and Isley Brothers covers in flared jeans and tight t-shirts. We watched them from the wings. Like coiled springs. For now we were dedicated even more to isolating ourselves from anything remotely resembling what the rest of the musicians in the country were up to. We had all cut our hair, shaved our faces and had the most eccentric clothing we could find to wear. Brian was a harlequin; Wally in a burgundy crushed-velvet suit; brother Geoffrey in a suit that looked like pyjamas. Tonight, we were going to muster every possible deviation we could think off to position ourselves as 'unique'.

When the curtain rose, our knees were knocking (literally) and Brian's eyes were jammed shut. And we started with *True Colours*. The songs rolled out. The sound effects were all on cue and Brian found springs in his feet and leapt, swayed, pranced, and lunged as he buried his fright, held out his hand and scooped that entire crowd into his palm.

At the start of *Stranger Than Fiction*, he spoke to the audience: 'I'd just like to mention a certain somebody who's with us tonight – he's not on stage but still very much a part of the show. His name is Phil Judd and it's his music which is our privilege and our joy to be playing.'

In an extraordinary public moment, Brian confirmed our suspicions; he was only too ready to undercut his own real contribution to the writing and, in fact, the philosophy of Split Enz. His lack of self-belief was battling against his stage persona, which was extrovert to the extreme. His almost manic stage presentation was his way of putting himself into the Enz songs, which he didn't seem to want to admit were partly his in the first place.

With that unexpected speech, Tony Rayner kicked into the opening riff that had been written by Miles Golding seemingly centuries before and, for the first time, Split Enz performed *Stranger Than Fiction*. It was during this song that it all fell into place. We had a unique musical piece. It seemed the quintessential Split Enz musical statement and as Tony finished it, Miles' riff trailing over and over into His Majesty's Theatre, around the pillars and down the aisles, I felt totally and unashamedly proud. I looked across at my brother, his brow sweating and glistening. Otahuhu dreams, brother!

The theatrical side of the night also ran like clockwork. On cue, Phil came out in his straitjacket completely disguised by the bandages. And Mr Crombie came running after him. The crowd roared. After the final song, we walked off stage completely liberated. And the applause rang on, so we returned to do a newly arranged, instrumental version of *Split Ends*. During this rousing, loose jam, Phil walked across the stage, his bandages gone and his identity revealed. The crowd cheered in recognition and the wall of resistance inside his head dissolved as he, once again, sensed victory and relished the sense of euphoria.

As Phil danced across the stage, his eyes alight, I thought to myself that something was afoot ... that the achievement of the night's performance might not be the start of a long harmonious road for the six of us.

The success of that first Buck-A-Head was set in concrete when the May *Hot Licks* edition came out. The editor, Roger Jarrett, wrote in his editorial: 'The Split Enz concert may well go down in history as one of local rock music's major events. Certainly it will be a great stimulus for other groups to get off their arses and perform for the people as a creative unit and not merely as music makers.' Elsewhere in the same issue there were two separate reviews that heaped on the praise. We had crossed the Rubicon and, better still, given the rest of the bands in the country a sock on the jaw.

The New Zealand music scene was then one of two things, if you excluded us. There was the long-haired, r 'n' b based, flared jeans and Indian shirt brigade. They reeked sleaze and dope and slouch and arrogance; they played lead solos and wrote original music that was a strange mix of Lou Reed and English progressive, with echoes of Hendrix flying around for the extra-inquisitive. The other side of the coin was the glam infiltration from England, which was championed by the likes of Ragnarok who were purportedly a mix of Pink Floyd and Viking folklore! Their stance was a minority one, and they took on the pub circuit and lost. As did others who followed in their wake. The musical base was too intricate to endure the pubs and the material often fell short in a concert environment.

In the end, the underground likes of Dragon flourished because good r 'n' b is timeless and no matter what context you dress it in – pop, dance, whatever – there's someone waiting for it. Back in the early seventies, the r 'n' b legacy threw up more and more bands but the presentation failed to match the musical expertise. This allowed us the opportunity to grab attention.

A few days after this watershed concert, still revelling in the sense of achievement, Brian came to rehearsal and told us that Phil wanted back in the group. Brian was adamant that it should happen and talked of the opportunities it gave with songs like *Under The Wheel*, previously discarded, being brought back to life.

The reaction from the rest of us was, on the surface, 'We'll give it a try' – but it was couched in pessimism. At the next rehearsal Phil came along with his electric guitar and the period of re-adjustment commenced. Brian was relieved to have Phil back ... it was Split Enz as it should be, although the reunification between Brian and Phil was soon to shift in Brian's eyes.

Julie Judd was pregnant and Phil's attention was, naturally, on his forthcoming fatherhood. Brian sensed this and on the night Julie went into labour, Brian, although sharing in the excitement, realised it was the end of the incredible bond that the three of them had fostered at 18 St Georges Bay Road. The night Julie went to hospital, Brian went out alone and got drunk. Happy for Phil and his fatherhood, he was nevertheless having to come to terms with the new sum of things.

From the moment Amy Judd arrived, the dynamic between Phil and Brian would never be the same. And they would never discuss it because nothing was ever discussed. The two of them, and, for that matter, all of us, moved in silence to the point of least confrontation.

There were problems, as well, at rehearsals. Phil's electric guitar capabilities fell short of his talents on an acoustic guitar and his vocals were in contrast to Brian's efforts. Phil was uncomfortable with his prodigal son status and felt he had lost some of the presence he had in the previous year's line-up, which in his eyes had been a smaller, more manageable unit.

This new line-up had a more complex political base and, once Rayner and Gillies had come on board, a musical direction without Phil had been forged. Now that balance was wavering.

Uncomfortably.

It was only a short time before Rob Gillies and brother Geoffrey decided for themselves that the new line-up was not on a par with the previous one, and both left the group in July. In keeping with our internal lack of communication, their departure was accepted without discussion and a replacement drummer was sought. It wasn't felt necessary to replace Rob.

Once again, an ex-member of Orb was recruited and a week after Geoffrey's departure from the skins, Paul Crowther was loading his drum kit into the front room of 473 Parnell Road. I say this as a matter of fact. And it was. But my brother and I had set our sights on a grand musical adventure together in our Otahuhu home and it was happening.... And now he was walking away. I was very saddened.

But I was in Split Ends. You don't say anything. And his leaving haunts me to this day.

Paul Crowther had an innate enthusiasm and a wide vision of what was 'going on out there.' He was older than any of us so a gentle authority emanated from him. In time he would be the one to drive the vans and stretchy Holden cars. He brought with him an enormous talent with electronics, and soon Tony was zooming, bubbling, sustaining, and buzzing away on a synthesiser. *Under The Wheel* took on another dimension with this extra-terrestrial keyboard.

And so what went around came around and following Crowther's crash course in the repertoire of Split Enz, another Buck-A-Head was booked, this time at the Mercury Theatre on August 18, 1974. And once again the Theatre was full. I had recently started working at a Fisher and Paykel factory machine press shop and wore my safety glasses for a laugh. Little did I realise at the time that they were to become an integral part of my Enz 'face'. We kicked off with *Under The Wheel*; Tony's new synthesiser swooped upon the crowd.

Halfway through the concert, it dawned on us that three weeks' rehearsal had not been enough and we floundered. We had extrapolated the theatrical concepts of the first Buck-A-Head to an absurd degree: we employed schoolboys who were caned by the Crombie, whose role this time was that of a headmaster. There was a tap-dancer (Tony Rayner's aunt actually) who clacked out a routine in the piano solo of *The Woman Who Loves You*, which we were performing for the first time, and we had a choir of 20 schoolgirls singing the final, grand choruses of the first (and last) performance of *There's A Way*.

Confounded by the logistics of these extra dimensions, we knew we had failed. After the show I came across brother Geoffrey. 'An abortion,' he said.

The review in *Hot Licks* went: 'I saw their concert at His Majesty's and that was a much better show. This time the theatrics were better conceived but overshadowed the music.'

Once again we slid down a few rungs on our ladder of quest and thought to ourselves:

'These rungs have a familiar ring.'

With these concerts so few and far between, we were all obliged to seek day jobs as a buffer against starvation. This was done with gay abandon as it was 1974 and jobs were plentiful. One would open the 'Situations Vacant' page and ask oneself, 'What shall I be today?'

Brian had the wildest array of occupations. A previous summer he had been an orderly at the Tokanui Psychiatric Hospital where unspeakable things happened. He then tackled life as a drone on a sausage line at the Southdown Freezing Works. As the sausage meat shot out into the long miles of pig intestine, he would tie a knot to cordon off each individual banger. Of course, his mind was only on one thing – Split Enz – and the variety of size, length and girth of the sausages was so extreme that he was quickly turfed out onto the street.

Another time, he, Tony and Phil all worked at the Heards confectionery factory in Parnell.

It was a surreal environment and they fantasised. The liquorice allsorts were made on the second floor, a vast room of ancient conveyor belts with everything permanently ghost white from the decades of fine icing sugar that hung in the air. Like warped servants in a strange, Gothic passion play, they wheeled their trolley-loads of lollies around the building. (Think Ghormenghast again). The foreman was round and fat as if stuffed with chocolate fish; on the first floor (hard and soft jubes) was a kid who would offer a comment every time anybody said anything. It was always the same comment: 'Hard to believe!' The three of them worked in the packing and despatch section, and they would hide boxes of jelly fish, chocolate rats and rainbow bars in the cool room and stuff their faces every now and then. Acne was prevalent.

By mid-1974, Judd, Finn and Crombie were at the Post Office mail-sorting centre in the city, where they would deftly abuse the work ethic and go on deliveries for hours at a time to nowhere in particular. In the end, they were all chucked out when the Crombie was caught flogging a motorcycle helmet.

While the rest of them were playing havoc with employers, I was playing havoc with myself. My partner Paula was in Australia with her family for the university August holidays, so I took the opportunity to spend a night in her family's empty house with Brian and a friend.

We tried some blotting paper LSD, a Thai stick and some whisky. Brian was a tough nut and he laughed his way through the Isaac Hayes special on television. I proceeded to kiss my sanity goodbye and wallowed in a morass of fear, hiding in an upstairs room. I pulled through the night in one piece but found myself, a few weeks later when out of town, crippled with a panic attack that came out of the blue as night fell. It was the same frightening experience but there wasn't a cause.

Three weeks later it happened again. And again I was away from home. I hid in an empty room, my mind speeding with fear, thoughts unable to be retained for more than a fraction of a second. In a word? Terror. It would be eight more years before I would realise that I was suffering a phobic disorder called agoraphobia. But at that moment in time – I was just simply mad.

During all this mayhem we found time to travel to Wellington for some shows that Coburn had put together. All were poorly attended but there was a milestone reached. For the first time, in the smokey, dingy confines of Ziggy's nightclub, Geoffrey Crombie walked out from backstage halfway through *The Woman Who Loves You*, peeled off his white gloves, removed two spoons from his coat pocket (with real style), and proceeded to dance across the stage: clicking and clacking, with his long legs shooting out, his body buckling down and spinning round, his face cast like a statue's. This was magic for our weary heads; we grinned and laughed at this wonderful display.

Geoffrey Crombie became a full-time member of Split Enz after that trip. And with the announcement of his arrival to our ranks, Coburn confirmed another concert; this time at the Founders

Theatre in Hamilton, supporting Spacewaltz led by Alistair Riddell. Riddell had folded Orb when he lost Tony, Paul Crowther and Wally, and had put together Spacewaltz from the members of his covers band, Stewart and the Belmonts. He had Greg Clark on guitar and Brent Eccles on drums. Spacewaltz had ventured onto the *New Faces* merry-go-round and also won their heat, with a song that went on to spend 10 weeks on the national chart peaking at number one! That was the toppermost of the poppermost. It was called *Out On The Street* and featured Tony on piano as a guest. On watching this national onslaught, we blossomed an envious vert colour at Riddell's success. Still, he would drag in a huge crowd at the Founders and we were ready to go. Tony's bonds to Riddell were still fairly strong and he was enlisted to play keyboards with Spacewaltz for the show. Riddell was short of a bass player so I was asked to fill in on bass. This sort of thing only happens in New Zealand!

Backstage, in readiness for the show, Mr Crombie walked in with a bulky suit-carrier and pulled from it a selection of brightly coloured suits. For the first time we looked upon a set of Crombie original costumes designed and sewn by the man himself. In wild, pastel colours, distorted shapes and angles, the suits stood before us as a symbol of the new era. They were quickly entitled (at times) 'the Zoots' or (at times) 'the Twits'.

This night we had everything right and we shook off the Mercury concert in a wild, tight show that featured the beautiful, uplifting 'Instrumental' for the first time. Geoffrey was on stage for the entire performance, banging his tambourine while standing stiffly beside Phil. It was his first chance to contribute in full, all the while waiting for the big moment – the spoons solo. And when it came, he played as if he was born with spoons in his hands. As the crowd roared, we knew that his entry into our ranks had been an auspicious decision. In the new costumes we moved our stage presentation a few more steps outside the boundaries.

Three weeks later the momentum rolled on, with another Buck-

A-Head at His Majesty's booked for December 1. Flushed with the renaissance in Hamilton, we were powering.

We abandoned the idea of a support act and split the show into two halves. We employed no extras and we fine-tuned the old songs as well as learning a newie, *Amy (Darling)*, Phil's ditty to his daughter.

When the curtain rose, it didn't matter to us that the theatre was half full. The plan was tight and prepared. We played hard; Brian rang out loud and clear; Crombie killed with his spoons, whistles and bass drums, cavorting across the stage in duet with Brian, his droll expressionless face speaking louder than words. That night our mix of theatrics was in just the right balance.

As usual, we went mad on sound effects: feet stamping, gnomes, chaos, monks, death noises, Bing Crosby, boings, DC10 jets, carousels, etc. etc. In the second half we came out in the new costumes, feeling like we looked – a million dollars. We kicked off with yet another new song, *Prophecy*, with Phil on lead vocal.

The review in *Hot Licks* by Roger Jarrett said it all: 'How can one describe their concert? The Oxford University debating team on acid? Peter Rabbit as seen/played by Syd Barrett? Monty Python visits the Queen Mother under the direction of Pasolini, Marcel Marceau and Ray Davies? Split Enz are the cream of the crop. The finest band New Zealand has ever seen.'

On reading this, along with the huge story on the front page, we had to go outdoors such was the expansion of our egos. But it was just this response that we had strived, rehearsed, sweated, and longed for, and we had it.

Seven days later, sitting in his room at St Georges Bay Road, Phil picked out a few chord sequences on his guitar. He wrote them out on a piece of paper and dated the page December 8, 1974. Above that he wrote *Weekend of Nightmare Stampede*. I don't know why.

Radio Hauraki were also deeply moved by the success of the recent concert and quickly booked three more shows for the 19th, 20th and 21st December. We gave them a Christmas flavour by entitling the series *The Christmas Pantamonium*, and utilising Geoffrey as a mental Santa Claus, miming Hendrix-like versions of *Jingle Bells*. We went to town on the theatrics, coming onto the stage in a huge gift-wrapped bag. This allowed the mischievous ones the opportunity to break wind, etc., with the others having no means of escape. We were starting to relax at long last.

We drew in a few friends: Rob Gillies' partner, Geraldene, was a Christmas fairy with blood dripping out her mouth and an axe in her head. There was a beach scene – with sand and seaweed all over the stage and people sunbathing – and a layered tier of four drummers playing along with Crowther in *The Instrumental*. Brother Geoffrey and Brent Eccles were two of them. Magic, nuthouse stuff. By now, we had developed the stage performances to a more unified musical/theatrical cohesion.

The skits and vignettes merged with the music. During *Stranger Than Fiction*, as Tony broke into *Red Roses For A Blue Lady*, Brian and I danced jerkily to the front of the stage and toppled off the edge into the orchestra pit. As we clambered out, we threw buckets of confetti over the incredulous faces in the front rows. It was all in a night's work.

Mind you, hardly anyone came. Radio Hauraki advertised the series as a Christmas show for the family and the name Split Enz was hardly mentioned. So be it.

The New Year found us back in rehearsal. We had vacated 473 Parnell Road for a house in Heather Street, Parnell, which Coburn was renting. It changed shape quickly when, in order to get our piano into the house, we pulled down the entire back porch and threw it into the yard. Thick as thieves.

At one of the practices, Brian presented us with a new song, one that he had written alone with the title *Lawdy*. It was to be the last new song for many months.

By now Brian and Phil had evolved their own separate writing methods and rarely worked together. And the old songs from the Malmsbury Villa days were just that – old. We never considered recalling the likes of *Hermine, Wise Men* or *Blankets* to the repertoire. Why?

The fact of the matter was we had around 15 songs without them, which was enough, and we were intent on getting these sounding nothing short of brilliant. Some were reworked and others fine-tuned; after three weeks of intensive rehearsal, we were really rocking.

Barry Coburn then turned up to tell us we were doing a tour of the universities for Orientation, which would be followed by a trip to Australia for three weeks – an exchange with an Australian group called Hush. This would be followed by another full New Zealand tour.

Australia? Hush?

Australia? The effect was one of excitable curiosity.

While the whole momentum of Split Enz was pointed north to England, the distraction of a left-turn to Australia (a land we knew NOTHING about) appealed – although it wouldn't stretch the truth much if I were to say there were those in the band who held their noses slightly aloft at the thought. Still, in a three-week flurry of live dates at presumably huge concert halls in Sydney, Melbourne and Wagga Wagga we could perform our spectacular theatrical shows and return the conquering heroes, ready to set New Zealand alight and record our first album for Coburn's new label White Cloud.

This news threw us into a state of deep concentration. Suspecting that our standard of performance would have to be nothing short of excellent if we were to annihilate whatever bands existed in Australia (we couldn't have told you the name of one of them), we rehearsed solidly through February until the university tour and relished in the results of the *Hot Licks* Readers Poll in which we took Group Of The Year and Concert Of The Year. Tony Rayner was announced Musician Of The Year and we weren't surprised.

At the same time, Coburn secured a licence deal with Pye Records for White Cloud; a remixed version of *No Bother To Me* backed with *Home Sweet Home* was scheduled for release as a single.

The idea of singles still loomed over us as an echo of our youth. A hit single. That must be cool. What was the chance? In early 1975 the toppermost of the poppermost was *Mandy* by Barry Manilow. Our single didn't sound like that.

The university tour covered the seven campuses. We took brother Geoffrey on the road as support; he was now a fully-fledged singer/songwriter type and had a batch of originals to perform. The beauty of this tour were the venues – virtually all concert halls – and we were honed down and ready to go. Geoffrey had designed a new set of costumes of extreme eccentricity, which we called 'the Clowns'. We took to the stages throughout the country, more often than not to full houses. The copious positive press we had received via *Hot Licks* was paying off. The flood of reviews was positive and uplifting.

When the tour was over, we had three days before leaving for Australia. But there was nothing to prepare because we would only be gone three weeks – two in Sydney, one in Melbourne – and Barry Coburn had a tour manager waiting for us. We had just completed a very successful tour of New Zealand and were confident of making an impression across the Tasman.

The only persistent disappointment was the continuing lack of success of our singles. We all felt that we had to record an album and that this must be done after the next New Zealand tour in May. We had put down demos for the album at the new four-track facility in Auckland, Mandrill Studios, with Glyn Tucker Jnr and Dave Hurley engineering, and all seemed in place. We were ready for the next step.

Gone were the carefree days of Malmsbury Villa and the acoustic ramblings of Levys Saloon. Gone was the trip. The search was on for a new batch of dimensions. Whitianga was a moment in time that was slowly sliding away, as were the rehearsals where song after song would be offered up and devoured by the hungry imaginations of excitable young men nurturing dreams in their heads.

Now there was work to be done. New songs would have to wait in the search for full houses, press reviews and record deals. There was a nation to be conquered and we only had three weeks to do it in. But we felt greater than the sum of our parts; we believed in the concept of Split Enz. With smiles on our faces, we boarded a plane to Sydney. It was March 13, 1975 ... and even though we didn't know it, we were going for good.

7

HOME IS WHERE YOU FIND IT

In a flurry of suitcases, bags and guitar cases, jackets, ties and floppy hair, we drove from Sydney Airport to Bondi where we checked into a boarding house called The Bondi Lodge. The next morning we checked out again. The pungent smell of urine and the threadbare furniture made it a simple task.

As we drove off to find better accommodation, we took in our tour manager. His name was Dave Russell and he had once been a guitarist with Ray Columbus and The Invaders. This was mildly interesting. Fairly cool, really. With our conversational talents still decidedly skimpy, it would be a while before we warmed to him. We were champing at the bit, you see. Distracted boys.

After a scout around we checked into two rooms at the Squire Inn which was adjacent to the Bondi Lifesaver nightclub; a fortuitous position because this was to be the venue we would be playing at that night. Finn, Crombie, Rayner, Crowther and myself all crammed into Room 416. Two beds, three stretchers. The others – Russell, Murray Ward (soundman), Wilkinson and Judd – were a floor above. I can't recall ever going to that room. Maybe they all slept in a double bed. We then drove off with Dave in a hire truck to pick up our sound system. On our arrival at a distant garage, a bleary, bedraggled roadie from the Hush camp informed us that he knew nothing about the Hush gear being used by us while his employers were playing in NZ. It was in a state of disrepair.

I looked at Brian who looked at Phil who looked at Dave. We blew out the Lifesaver show. On the way back to the hotel, weaving through the miles and miles of Sydney suburbs, we read a small press mention in a music rag. It heralded our arrival as 'New Zealand's raunchiest rock 'n' roll band.' Brian looked at Phil and Phil looked at me and I looked at Dave. On our return to the Squire Inn, Dave Russell went mad trying to find a sound system.

While he was distracted, we took in Sydney and found it to be loose, fast, bent, and full of semi-derelict and submerged life-forms; an extraordinary contrast to the staid, plain and protected social structure back in Auckland. Pornography had flooded in and newspapers bulging with hardcore sex lined up at corner shops beside the *Sydney Morning Herald*. Prostitutes lined the Cross; it was at its sleazy height. Teenagers in hot pants and fishnets lolled around, their eyelids filled with lead; a few feet away, the squinting eyes of a pimp with slicked-back hair and a wide collar. Light brown loafers. Cars were advertised on television, phones were push-button and the hi-fi shops stocked exotic, slick machinery. It would be some years before New Zealand joined the party.

Back at the Squire Inn, we lived on cereal and Vegemite sandwiches washed down by continuous cups of instant coffee and non-dairy whitener stolen from the maids' trolleys. In time the 'boy's own' ethic came to the surface and we pranked and played on each other. One night we walked across the Sydney Harbour Bridge to Luna Park, where I refused to go on the roller coaster because of my fear of heights. The Crombie insisted the ride was a breeze, that the car never got very high and there was nothing to worry about – so I agreed to join him.

As the car started to climb the first ramp, Geoffrey, seated beside me, turned to me, looked me in the eye and spoke slowly and precisely: 'It's going to go really high. So fucking high you're not going to believe it. This ride is absolutely T-E-R-R-I-F-Y-I-N-G!! AAARRRGGH!'

While the rest of us were playing the fool, Dave had found some gear and in a last minute panic we were ready for the rescheduled show. The Lifesaver changing room was so small we changed into our costumes at the hotel and ran across the road, halting traffic en masse.

We performed to a small crowd; they stood and stared. We went back to the hotel and watched television. I'd never seen a Humphrey Bogart movie before. *'We don't need no stinkin' badges!'* It made me think of my folks.

Three days later there would be another show, this time at the Oceanic Ballroom, Coogee Beach. Another press clipping had surfaced. This time we were described as New Zealand's answer to Skyhooks.

'Dave, who are Skyhooks?'

'They're a glam band that's just spent six weeks at number one.'

'Glam band?'

That night on television we saw Skyhooks. They wore makeup ... end of comparison. Their music was hooky pop and they were a teen sensation. We drove off to the Oceanic Hotel ready to set the record straight. We played well on the miniature stage; Brian lurching and leaping, throwing out his soliloquies to an enthralled crowd.

He had evolved a real style of patter over the past few months and it was captivating ... strands of the court jester. *'And from him full of vim to the brim and nimble at that, goodbye, bye, come again, be good, keep in touch and until we meet again, good luck to you all, see ya and so long for now.'*

While Brian was the immediate focus, it became obvious very quickly that the Crombie was on his heels. Using his minimalist philosophies, Geoffrey captivated the unsuspecting Australians with his mere presence and dazzled them with his spoons solo. He was heading for celebrity status and provided a neat foil to Brian's wildman persona. As far as the players went, by now we knew the songs backwards and were in complete harmony. We took them up, we took them down. That night we felt we had achieved what we wanted with the limited facilities available to us; we had managed to set ourselves apart and show that we weren't like any others, that we had a niche of our own. So what next? Nothing.

Red Symonds (Skyhooks)

My first recollection of Split Enz was at one of their first gigs in Sydney shortly after they had arrived in Australia. What motivated us to see them was probably the early warning that they, like the Skyhooks, wore costume and make-up which meant that they were presumably working in the same territory as we were.

In fact they were working quite different than us in that at that time they were working much more in the British melodic angst area than we ever did. I suppose what we did have in common was that we both felt that there was much more to the rock business than just playing the tunes; that presentation was an imperative not an embellishment.

My strongest memory of the individuals, on that first night, was of Phil Judd, or 'old paranoid in the corner' as we preferred to call him. I always find fascinating the breed of performers who relentlessly radiate a sense that they do not want to be on stage in front of an audience. In my experience these performers often have a paradoxically long career. Poor loves.

I can remember an early piece in Rolling Stone in which Eddy (sic) Rayner was invited to comment on the Skyhooks who were enjoying their 15 minutes of massive and unprecedented fame at about the time the Enz arrived. With a cheek that many would find offensive he brushed us off. 'Yes. I used to play in a band like that two or three years ago.' My kinda guy.

I remember a post-gig mortem when we were playing on the same bill and Tim Finn saying 'We've got to perform more confidently.' The band nervously agreed.

My only measure of success nowadays, and I believe things are judged best in retrospect particularly in the pop(ular) field, is that the band individually and collectively invented themselves. They were no one but themselves.

What else is there?

T he next day, we learned that the week's work in Melbourne had never materialised. The tour had been set up far too late for any work to be available. We watched television instead (*'You know how to whistle, don't you, Steve?'*) and Brian wrote home: 'It would not be an exaggeration to describe the trip as a disaster. But who knows? Something may come of it. Next week we are playing a pub – something we swore we'd never do! If only the right person was to see us play. It is painfully obvious that if we could just do one concert of a standard even approximating the standards set by our Buck-A-Heads then the whole city would be talking ... At the moment, it seems we will sail from Sydney on the Northern Star on Tuesday April 1 (an extremely fitting day for this pack of fools to leave these foolish shores).'

Shortly after, Barry Coburn turned up and we said nothing. So he said. 'I think you guys should stay in Australia, It's going to take a while to get things happening.' Then he left, and we watched some more television. *'... of all the gin joints in all the towns in all the world she walks into mine.'* Where were we? Oh. 'Australia'? Yes, Australia ... We knew he was right.

So, in an emotionless, almost resigned fashion, we decided to send some of the band back after the final week's work to close shop in New Zealand and return for the continued campaign. I didn't go back because I didn't care either way. My panic attacks (still randomly hanging over from the year before and still a night-time phenomenon) were keeping me preoccupied and I came to the odd conclusion that the cause must be physiological, somehow related to food. Consequently, when the sun set each day, I stopped eating. I very quickly achieved considerable frailty, which luckily no one seemed to notice. I still had no answers. And I kept it all very secret.

In our third glorious week of conquering Australia we played another club, Chequers, and then returned to the Oceanic Ballroom on the Wednesday night. Word quickly reached us that some members of Skyhooks had come with their manager/ record company boss, Michael Gudinski, to see what this lookalike band was made of. Brian did his sums very quickly: Michael Gudinski was a manager, owned a record company with the current number one album and co-owned an agency booking live work. This was our man!

That night, with a blessed charge, we blew them all away.

Bob Starkie from Skyhooks, who was there with Gudinski and Red Symonds, recalled the occasion in RAM magazine: 'We thought they were great. Gudinski used to listen to us in terms of what we liked and what we thought would be a goer ... The Enz were just so fresh and so theatrical, which was sort of over our side of the fence: we were theatrical as individuals, had our own personal identities, whereas they were theatrical as a band – they were all the same kind of thing – absolute fruitcake characters! And the music was really together – I mean, Phil Judd-phenomenal! It really suited that post-hippy, crazy, drugged period – I thought they really suited the period.'

Well, err yes. What can I say? The unified effect was the end result of our actual unity as a bunch of disenfranchised New Zealanders tossed into the fray with gloriously good songs coupled with the immaculate conception of Geoffrey's costumes. There can be no denying that the full brunt of our performances in those days was intensely musical – Phil and Brian's material, Brian's rich vocals and Tony's dexterity saw to that. But the initial impact, the reason why people would later tell us they couldn't take their eyes off us, was the fact that Split Enz as a visual whole was greater than the sum of its parts.

The next day Gudinski rang Dave Russell and asked, 'Are the band signed to recording and publishing agreements?' Dave looked at

Brian who looked at me and I looked back at Dave. We all shook our heads.

Gudinski said he would get back to us.

The following weekend, there were two shows booked at the Hordern Pavilion, a huge 12,000-seat barn, where we would be opening for Australian bands Buffalo and Finch. Once again the advertising ran: 'New Zealand's raunchiest rock 'n' roll band.' We were starting to sense doom. We checked into the Hordern to find an assortment of young males with long hair, tight t-shirts under sparkly glitter waistcoats and flared jeans on top of platform shoes. They were Buffalo and Finch.

Buffalo who were headlining (methinks) had been around for years and were on their dying legs. They were of the Free/Bad Company school without the material. The show's promoter asked each band what kind of music they played. Each answered, 'Rock 'n' Roll!' When we were questioned on the matter there was total silence. How do you speak? We set up our gear while two roadies, one from Buffalo and one from Finch, decided to punch the daylights out of each other. This was a zoo.

Back in the changing room we dressed into our 'Zoots' in silence, knowing full well what was ahead. As usual nothing was discussed. We looked at the wall. The 'Roadie's Creed' was scrawled on it.

If it's dry, smoke it
If it's wet, drink it
If it moves, fuck it
If it doesn't, throw it in the back of the truck

Then we took the stage to face 1,500 13-year-old Sydney glam-rock freaks intent on banging their heads on the front of the stage and getting smoke bombs up their noses.

Brian kicked off with his usual soliloquy, an opener to *Walking Down A Road*: *'How to get from A to B which is ab which is drab and you've been had which is sad ...'*

Fifteen hundred hard-nosed belligerent Sydney children stared at him and, after a short period of collective adjustment, broke forth:

'Fuck off!'

'Go back to where you came from!'

'Get off!'

This was the moment of truth; the realisation of our fate. The whole trip had been a farce.

No one wanted to know about Barry Coburn's twerpy bunch of twits from New Zealand. New Zealand sucked. Australia was revelling in a teenage music extravaganza with Skyhooks at the helm. Bombs, smoke machines, Gibson Flying Vees, Skyhooks, speed, huge cleavages, cum shots, Marshall stacks and AC/DC ruled. The anger welled inside us. Brian stormed around in an increasing frenzy. Phil retreated to the back of the stage, his head down. Wally cranked up the volume of his Gibson Black Beauty to drown them out, and I walked to the front of the stage and brought my guitar down on the head of some particularly obnoxious, fat upstart. It felt good and after the show we retreated to the Squire Inn in haste to watch some television. *I'll be blowing pretty soon. Heading back East I guess.*

Two days later all of the Enz except Brian, Geoffrey and I returned to New Zealand to kiss it goodbye and shut up shop on the past. While they were away, the three of us remaining were called to a meeting at the Festival Records boardroom (Festival distributed Mushroom), where Michael Gudinski and his partner in Mushroom Records, Ray Evans, offered us a recording deal with studio time guaranteed for an album. Gudinski was always on the move. He never seemed to sit down. But you sensed his attention to detail was, while short and swift, built on a keen understanding of how the game worked. He came across like he knew what turned the right buttons on and who and what was needed to advance from stage 1 to stage 2. We certainly didn't. And he would fix his gaze on you for a second or two. It wasn't a glance. It was a fix. And Mushroom were in the process of signing the band Ayers Rock to A&M Records in the States and Gudinski was on the phone to the Los Angeles office.

We were all impressed. And he kept pacing up and down, tugging his beard and drawing fingers through his hair. We liked his energy, his overseas connections – even if he might have been talking to the Festival rep in the next room!

Brian wrote home to Teasdale Street: 'Well, at last it seems the tide may perhaps be turning. Our spirits are a lot higher and a general feeling of optimism prevails.'

We'd been in Australia three weeks. Brian and I got to talking about the album and we agreed that we didn't have an obvious single. So Geoffrey, he and I spent some time on the Squire Inn house band equipment up in the restaurant, piecing together an old song Brian had been writing. The opening verse was culled from the nameless piece we had played as Mellodrone in 1972 at the Student's Arts Festival in the Peter Pan Ballroom. At the same time, in this limbo, we decided to change our identities. During a particularly contemplative moment, Brian and Geoffrey reached the momentous decision that we should all adopt our middle names. On the return of the others, Brian became Tim, Geoffrey became Noel, Tony became Eddie, Paul became Emlyn, I became Jonathan, Wally stayed as Wally seeing as his real name was Paul anyway and Phil stayed as Phil.

This change was more significant than we realised. It was the subconscious adjustment to our new home because we knew, in our hearts, that the beautiful isolated world we had created for ourselves in New Zealand would never be experienced again. There would be no turning back. We decided then and there that we had to give Australia a go. Our belief in the short-term conquest had vanished and, as each day dawned, the task of achieving commercial success appeared more daunting. At least we had a record company.

Phil, his refusal to change his name a hint of his reluctance to face the slog ahead, retreated into himself creatively. He and Tim no longer had the opportunity to write – the quiet room in St Georges Bay Road and the sun-drenched back yard of Malmsbury Villa had been translated to a single hotel room where the whole focus was on existence and survival in the face of apathy. And while Phil yearned to retreat to the days of creativity and excitement, Tim pinned his sights on the Australian market. His dream became a series of pragmatic stepping stones leading ultimately to that magic city where he firmly believed Split Enz was destined to make waves: London. His awareness, however, of Phil's sliding attitude was hard to gauge and he seemed set in his belief that Split Enz was a sphere that revolved around Phil. His focus was so obsessive that he spent many hours in his hotel room brooding on the struggle ahead. The rest of us dreamed of the day we could afford a prawn sandwich.

In mid-April, we signed a recording contract with Mushroom Records, and Phil and Tim signed writer agreements with Gudinski's publishing company, Mushroom Music. At the same time, Gudinski kicked his agency into gear and a stash of live work was scheduled in Sydney and Melbourne. First up was a support at the Sydney Town Hall before Captain Matchbox. And then the cruncher ... support at the Hordern Pavilion before Roxy Music.

Tim wrote home: 'Tonight we are doing the support for a Roxy Music concert at the Hordern Pavilion. It will be interesting to see if it goes better than our last Hordern performance.'

Four days later, from Melbourne, Tim wrote again: 'The big news is that our Roxy Music support last Wednesday was a big success. We went over well with the audience but, more importantly, most of Roxy Music were watching and we really surprised and impressed them ... The guitarist, Phil Manzanera, wants to produce our album, no less. However it seems it will be impossible to fit it into his schedule ... I believe they are trying to work something out ... Michael Gudinski is now very enthused ... and it seems we are a band destined for a little fame and fortune at last. But still we are living on $2 a day ... It seems I have been over here years and years ...'

It had been 41 days.

In Melbourne, against our better judgement, we tackled another teenage hysteria session. This time we were not up against the paltry likes of Buffalo and Finch, but the cream of scream, Skyhooks and AC/DC, together in the vast Festival Hall. It was an afternoon concert which no one had told us (or perhaps we weren't listening) and we were pulled from our motel beds 50 minutes from the 1pm show time. Without time to fret and ponder we scrambled into our 'clowns' and tumbled on stage, to be confronted by 8,000 restless, spotty kids. We had a familiar feeling as Tim slammed his eyes shut and Phil slid away. I scoured the front row for a skull to crack.

It wasn't long before the familiar chorus prevailed upon us:

'Go back to where you came from!'

'Fuck ooorrrffffffff!!'

I looked side stage to Gudinski. He was watching the crowd. He was learning something ... and as we sloped off to chants of 'good riddance', we knew that we wouldn't be doing any more teenage shows in the foreseeable future.

Gudinski then coerced the promoter of the monthly bohemian concert series, The Reefer Cabaret, to squash us on to the bill of his next show in three days' time. To his credit, the young man, Michael Roberts, had an inkling that he was doing the right thing and we performed, in a theatre setting, to a full house of students, beatniks, hippies and adults. We felt at home and were able to muster the old Buck-A-Head sense of presentation. Noel's spoons solo found them so quiet you could hear a pin drop. They were captivated! *The Instrumental* pinned them to their chairs, and Juddsy's rendition of *Under The Wheel* was powerhouse as he exorcised the dud shows of the past few weeks. Able to relax and not feel the pressure from thousands of youngsters wondering why he wasn't turning out raunchy riffs, the Wal (Wally) stood to attention and sent his lyrical guitar notes into the hall. As usual, he was standing right beside me. We'd been on stages together for what seemed a long time now. How long is three years?

The press reviews spoke volumes. The following are from *Juke* magazine:

'Kerrist, they're madder 'n us. Leaping about the stage, pink suits, blue shirts, red suits, long legs, short legs. Doll faces, human faces, new faces. Cackling, screaming, leering, bounding, jerking, lurking, always prepared to pounce on my poor nut. Pictures of the giggle palace thrashed through my scone.

'In Split Enz you will find classical and neo-classical; music hall honky tonk and sleazy vaudeville; acoustic and electronic, good ole rock 'n' roll, a piano full of cool jazz and some Gregorian chants or Calypso shouts for good measure.

'We had a resurrected James Dean, (Judd) white-faced and hollow eyed in a teddy boy suit of bright red ... the lead singer (Finn) moves like a sped-up movie of Charlie Chaplin doing an imitation of Harpo Marx – or is it vice versa? He comes on with a patter that sounds like *Waiting For Godot* done by a music hall M.C.'

This show was to Australia what the first Buck-A-Head was to New Zealand. A peak moment in which we transcended the former 'curiosity' status bestowed upon us. But it was more than that because it was a turning point. We were still adamant on holding an inimitable position in this very active, commercially-driven market but we realised that it would be impossible to spend weeks planning one-off extravagant and theatrical concerts. We were going to have to play hotels, cafes and clubs because we had to eat. So we developed, very quickly, an extreme presentation in which each of us hid behind a fanciful disguise, cloaked in one of Noel's extraordinary costumes.

Tim and Noel had started their transformations in New Zealand but the Australian situation, with its sense of isolation, of alienation, schtick stock station cemented us together and we closed ranks on the outside world. It came down to the fact that we didn't relate to the Australian rock 'n' roll lifestyle, in which we were now inextricably immersed. In New Zealand, we worked outside any system if only because, when it came down to it, there wasn't one. But in Australia we were confronted by managers with quick tongues, record company people (we had never met any in New Zealand), agents, flared jeans, roadies, mandrax, coke, trucks, overnight drives, schedules, Polaroids, mogadan, t-shirts, Quaaludes, blotting paper and abuse.

The only aspect we rarely came up against were groupies. We

were ugly and asexual and we rebounded into ourselves seeking out a collective sense of purpose, to avoid being part of this menagerie. New Zealand slipped into the past. LSD was gone, the Buck-A-Head concerts had gone and the vast expanses of time that we had in New Zealand to develop our music and writing were now hours, not weeks. We wanted to create a musical unit that presented itself to such an extreme that it had to be noticed. It had to be unique. We had to continue our natural policy of reaction and if we had to do it by the Aussie rules then so be it. We weren't prepared to buckle. In fact, we were going to take it further.

Tim and Noel cut their hair in oblique shapes and sizes, teasing cones and pyramids out of their heads. Make-up was now being applied in large quantities, each of us in control of our own persona; some more extreme than others. On the musical front, committed to performing the same songs every night, we started to toy with them, adding sections, rhythms, breaks, and bridges to keep them interesting. We never had time to rehearse and there were no new songs to learn.

Meanwhile, Mushroom Records and Roxy Music management had failed to find a time for Manzanera to produce the first album so it was decided to charge ahead with Dave Russell in the control-room chair, ostensibly co-producing the album with ourselves at Festival Studios in Sydney. We didn't have much of a fix on what a producer was supposed to do anyway so, if someone had to be producer, it may as well be Dave. We liked the guy. On May 8 we walked in with our gear, ready to quench the craving we had been hauling around for years. We were brimming with expectation and, unbeknownst to us, a fair quotient of paranoia, which had leaked into the band's psyche over that time. The rhythm tracks kicked off reasonably well; within three days, my Gibson Les Paul Recording bass, Croth's drums and Eddie's basic keyboards were down. Then started the overdubs. By now it was clear that the engineer was uninterested in the whole exercise and it would not be unusual to find he had literally gone fishing. Otherwise, he would sit with a blank face staring through the glass at nothing in particular. Dave Russell, while being a loyal friend, was perhaps too respectful of the band; he was failing to channel the sessions and give some firm instruction when it was needed.

Phil, in a stroke of opportunism, rushed in after the rhythm tracks, recorded his vocals and was done. He then followed that with a colourful array of guitar parts that he had concocted, and was able to clock out of the studio and into the control room. Smart move. The follow-up sessions were fraught with problems. The guitar overdubs found Wally sweating in a tiny room with a huge Marshall amp screaming out, while in the control room it resembled a twanging rubber band. Over and over he would play, and the sense of jinx set in.

It got no better when Tim came to do his vocals. After one session he wrote home: 'Well, it's been a tortuous week. The tension and nervous strain have been unbelievable. Because we have waited so long for this album we've been striving for perfection and any imperfections that have arisen due to musical fumbles or emotional traumas have appeared worse than they actually are ... I feel very drained of energy.'

I wrote home at the same time: 'I'm writing this on the control desk at Festival Studios. We have put down the rhythm tracks for *Lovey Dovey, Amy (Darling)* and *Spellbound*.

After tea we are doing *The Woman Who Loves You*. This morning I had to redo my climactic bass lines on *Walking Down A Road* because one of my strings was out of tune. Such a silly lad. Such a twerp. If only I could afford a prawn sandwich. ... None of our songs are really singles. Gudinski will probably want to choose one so that's not our worry. He will stress and strain. Yesterday I walked the eight miles from the studio to Bondi Beach'

Why did I do that? Panic in Festival Studios. Like that Panic In Needle Park. But no needles. Nothing to blame. No reason. Just panic.... So you run. I ran to Bondi and dived into the water. It's odd when you wait years to get into a studio and record an album and when you do – one day – terror wraps its fingers round your throat and you run.

Certain tracks for Tim ultimately failed, particularly *Time For A Change*. Phil was in the studio coaxing him: 'Tim, remember what it was like when we wrote those songs. Put yourself back there ... you can do it.' But it wasn't helping because Tim was possessed by the importance of this album, his own need to make it supreme – which blocked any chance of relaxation. He tightened up, and his deliveries became mannered and contrived. Coupled with this was the mish-mash of overdubs, all thrown in without a real plan for the final arrangement.

The end results were a far cry from the streamlined arrangements that Miles, Tim and Phil had put together for their early stuff. Even that first Buck-A-Head in 1974 found the band still able to create space in the sound. But here, at the moment of truth, there was a general rush for parts without a blueprint. Another possible contributing factor could have been hunger. For the past few weeks we had been on $3 every two days. I recall standing at a deli window, gazing at a prawn sandwich. (Sorry to harp on about prawn sandwiches). Make that a pastrami.

The title of the album, *Mental Notes*, was conceived by Tim; the cover was a brilliant painting by Phil, based on a photo of the band taken at the Auckland Domain in December 1974. He had rejected the original transparency of the painting and asked for it to be done again. During the recording sessions, he received word that the photographer re-shooting the painting had dropped a large studio light on it and it was cracked. Phil retrieved the canvas and painted a series of cracks on it, all neatly matching the real ones. One of them passed through his face. I kept the original photo just in case. It's now with Phil. It's also on the cover of this e-book.

On June 11, we returned to New Zealand with the album unmixed, leaving Phil behind with Dave Russell to oversee proceedings. We left the Squire Inn behind with one last burst of excitement as we leaned out our windows and observed a young couple fornicating in the adjacent wing. Voyeurs. In this Australian sojourn, the time-honoured legendary culture of sex and rock 'n' roll was just a dangling image for this band. And there they were. Acting it out for us.

While still in Sydney, Phil was interviewed for *RAM* magazine: 'Coming over here, facing a new kind of audience, has started to bring it home to me, for the first time, why people can't assimilate our music the first time they hear it.' He didn't say why.

When we arrived the New Zealand tour was in place, with Barry Coburn promoting in conjunction with Bruce Kirkland and the New Zealand Students Arts Council; it looked certain that we would have finished travelling the country by the time the album was released. This continued the, by now, stumbling nature of our enterprise.

Phil returned and we kicked off in Whangarei on June 22. Once again we had brother Geoffrey on the road as support act, except for Tauranga and Hamilton where Neil and his musical cohort, Rod Murdoch, were booked. Noel had produced a vivid set of black and white costumes and the tour was quickly dubbed the 'Black and White' tour. It received huge media attention and a rash of full houses, with the Auckland Town Hall sold out for two nights.

Raewyn Turner was reunited with Noel and he suggested she operate the lighting panel. We still had old friend Murray Ward mixing the sound.

Reviews ran hot, particularly as so many had never seen us before. But there were those who felt we had shaken off too much of a good thing during our time in Australia. Roger Jarrett was one and said so in his July *Hot Licks*: 'For many, Split Enz' complex music is made palatable by their credibility as a band of creative and intelligent rock 'n' rollers not above sending themselves up – a humorous parody if you like of rock 'n' roll in general. At Whangarei, I felt that parody had been replaced by misguided cynicism – if so, their credibility rests on a very fine line and any loss could cost Enz success before it rears its gilded head.'

The extreme costumes and make-up that we had developed in

Australia looked pretentious, and Tim's new jittery persona and vocal style was too much of a contrast for many. The overall effect was one of appearing up ourselves, particularly when we performed live on Max Cryer's *Town Cryer* television show.

Tim had prepared with a guest interviewer, Bryan Staff, for his first question to be, 'Tell me Tim, why do you look so foolish' for which Tim had a rat-a-tat, stagy reply based around the word 'fool'.

Bryan Staff asked Tim; 'Tell me, Tim, why do you look so stupid?'

Off guard, Tim lost the plot and in front of the nation with his pancaked face sweating profusely, he came across as a bit of a tool instead. As we mimed the single from *Mental Notes, Maybe*, the rest of us also looked particularly toolish. The next week, Dick Finn was fined at his Rotary club for having produced such a wayward son.

The other Finn son found his chance to perform before Split Enz, a moment of intense excitement. Neil and Rod Murdoch took to the stage in Hamilton and Tauranga as if they had been doing it all their lives. Tim watched from the wings, pleased at having provided this opportunity for Neil ... and intrigued at how Neil could perform with such confidence and bravery with so little experience. In essence, the opposite of himself.

After the Hamilton concert, Neil relished his first press mention in the Waikato Times:

'Finn's younger brother Neill (sic), from Te Awamutu and Hamilton musician Rod Murdoch, contributed three interesting pieces, with Neill Finn sounding reminiscent of his brother.' We all read it and thought 'mmmm that journo isn't Gay Talese!'

Near the end of the tour, Barry Coburn's sideman, Ian Tilbury, had a meeting with us in Palmerston North where we were presented with new management contracts. We avoided the issue, the memory of $3 every two days fresh in our minds.

Three days later, back in Auckland, we all received a letter from the Tilbury lad: 'This is to confirm that under the terms of your management agreement Coburn Artists Limited will be exercising the right to an option of one year under the same terms, commencing on the third day of December 1975 ... This further confirms that ... you will be guaranteed an average nett weekly earning of fifty dollars between 3 June 75 and 3 Dec 1975.' We decided to wait until December 3 and see what had transpired by then.

Besides we had a wedding to go to – Emlyn was tying the knot with his partner, Jo, and it was a night in which we could afford to forget Split Enz for a few brief hours. I was particularly at ease, having made a move to alleviate the panic attack problem that still jumped up and slapped me around. It was a short step into my father Jerry's surgery office.

'Hey, Dad, old Doc. Out touring and all ... I get really scared ...'

'Stage fright?'

'Well ... I guess it is like that. Only much worse.'

'These should help.'

Jerry Chunn gave me Serepax (Google that) and saved my life. He was that kind of guy. I could live each day without the possibility of terror. Back to Croth's wedding. There I bathed in an almost forgotten sense of normality. Little did I know at the time that my virulent sense of adventure was about to be buried under a metaphysical wad of cotton wool as the Serepax slowly (very slowly) but surely (very surely)started to bury me. Three days later, we returned to Australia.

At the end of July, *Mental Notes* was released on the Mushroom label in Australia and Coburn's White Cloud label in New Zealand. The reviews ran hot to cold. The Australians had yet to decide what to expect from Split Enz and were tentative; the album reached number 35 nationally. In New Zealand it was generally received favourably, with writers relieved just to finally have the thing. It charted well, albeit briefly, and reached number 8 on the national album chart in mid-August.

Tim wrote home to *Hot Licks* magazine: 'The good feelings shown to us by *Hot Licks* is indicative of a strain of life and heart ... not yet given over to cynicism and jaded armchair melancholies.

Thankfully New Zealand is still a little green.' Back in Australia we ran blindly into a vast workload, with a Lou Reed tour for starters.

Raewyn Turner had crossed the Tasman to join Noel and be our lighting operator. She quickly came to grips with the vast underbelly of the Australian rock 'n' roll industry roadies. She showered us with coloured lights and was soon dubbed a whizz. The travelling was relentless and young Eddie became crippled with quinsy, if only because he was a whacker, so we had to herd him on stage and place him gently on his piano stool. By the time we reached Adelaide he was in hospital, so we left him there. The press started hounding us and we received masses of copy.

Tim was even asked to review singles for *Juke* magazine, one of which was Quincy Jones' *Is It Love That We're Missing*. He said: 'This song finished before I was aware it had started. Either I missed it or it wasn't there.'

Noel was asked to describe himself in *Juke*: 'Haz tha beegist nooz an smorlist chin. Absalootlee unmuzikill.'

Phil was asked to describe his favourite composers: 'Dvorak, Lennon/McCartney, Ray Davies, Jimmy Page & Robert Plant.'

In late August, we moved into flats in St Kilda and Elwood, Melbourne. We had decided to move to Melbourne because Mushroom was based there, as was our new tour manager.

After the New Zealand tour, Dave Russell became disillusioned with the management situation. He returned to New Zealand and while he was there, Tim wrote him a letter suggesting he not return. (Tim has always been good at this *letter* thing). We had decided we needed a local chap with contacts who could speed up the processes. Dave took it like a man (he was probably relieved) and we were alone.

We were directed by Mushroom to a fellow who was tour manager for Skyhooks and who carried out their front-of-house sound mixing duties. We approached him to join us; he agreed, and one John Hopkins came into our fold. He dealt with all admin. duties and mixed the live shows. Made good sense ... at the time. By now we were on $30 a week and putting butter on our bread. I even partook of the odd prawn sandwich.

Hopkins set about putting work schedules together at Gudinski's Premier Artists and September, October, November, and December were all a jim-jam of pubs, universities, clubs, halls, and theatres in Melbourne, Sydney and Adelaide; playing three to five nights a week and driving over 25,000 km in the process. Each time we careered down the Hume highway or drove through heatwaves across to Adelaide, we slowly but surely grew to know intimately every gum tree, cockatoo, dead kangaroo, car restaurant, petrol pump, fly-blown carcass and pistol-toting cop on the road. Our car was once stopped for speeding and Emlyn at the wheel was asked to produce identification. He had none so he produced a copy of *Mental Notes* and, pointing to his photograph with name printed underneath, explained: 'Look, Officer, that's me.'

'Yeah, but how do I know it's you?'

We laughed the laugh of the innocent and he gunned us in our seats, his bullets ricocheting around our skulls. Perhaps he didn't.

It was always with sighs of relief that Melbourne came into view after hours on the road.I liked Melbourne. If I were there right now I would like it. I'll always want to be there. It's one of those places.

I was flatting in Elwood with Eddie and Emlyn; for the first time, since our arrival six months before, we had a base. There were six of us at Elwood. I had married Paula and parenthood was imminent; Ed had flown his old flame, Janice, over from New Zealand. Wally was also in Elwood, in Wave Street down the road in St Kilda, Tim, Phil, Julie and Amy, Noel and Raewyn had also settled in for the haul.

The stable location gave Tim and Phil the chance to write again, although they wrote separately. Phil was still grappling with the whole scenario of pressure cooker live work but found it in his head to produce new material. He was always writing. Filling sheets of paper with phrases, words, possible titles, chord sequences and so on, Phil spent hours of his spare time poring over musical possibilities much as he had done at St Georges Bay Road. The only difference here was he did it alone and, with the touring so consistent, he rarely had the chance to bring his stuff to fruition. Those that he did pointed to a new approach. The self-analytical lyrics of New Zealand were now replaced by storylines and oblique love songs. *Nightmare Stampede* and *Late Last Night* are two examples.

The single *Maybe* had completely failed on the charts while Glen Campbell's *Rhinestone Cowboy* was up near the toppermost of the poppermost. But the relentless touring paid off and by the end of the year we were headlining all shows to full houses. We capped off the year at the Dallas Brookes Hall, with two sold-out concerts to an excellent response. We started each show with our new 16-minute epic *Nightmare Stampede*, and the first one of us to play a note was Rob Gillies.

Rob Gillies?

In late November, we fired Wally Wilkinson. The seeds were sown during the *Mental Notes* sessions when the results from his guitar were unsatisfactory and we, in our ignorance, blamed him. The situation worsened during the four months of touring, as Phil found his feet on his Gibson SG electric guitar and started to play more and more. At somewhere like the Sundowner Hotel in Geelong or the Wagga Wagga Workingmen's Club, Tim and I would glance at each other as all around us a caterwauling of duelling guitars and Eddie's by now multi-stacked keyboards fought a running battle. It was clear there had to be some compromise and so, instead of sitting down and talking about it, (how do people talk?) we fired the Wal. None of us had the guts to do it. John Hopkins was sent over to his flat and, with the thud of Hoppy's linguistic guillotine, Wally was told. That still haunts me too. And he flew home.

Rob Gillies was rung the next day and two days later he was on stage, standing beside me again and blowing that trumpet as beautifully as ever.

At the same time, we witnessed the arrival of the 3rd of December. So I plugged in the trusty calculator and worked out that in the past six months, the following weekly income had been earned:

Tim Finn $34.70
Phil Judd $38.25
Mike Chunn $5.51

We duly wrote to Barry Coburn to excuse ourselves from his future and carried on.

Meanwhile, Phil had plans. I wrote home on the 3/1/76: '... Phil has handed his notice in. It seems he's had enough of the whole business etc. and will probably go back to New Zealand. At the moment we're considering possible replacements. I'll continue the letter after we've nutted it out ... Monday 5th Jan. I'm back and so is Phil. He's decided not to leave. False start.'

Phil had been ground down to the point where he was ready to go. There had been warning signs as he gradually sang less and less; he would shy away from various songs, leaving Tim to fill in his (Phil's) vocal duties. This outraged the Finn chap but he preferred not to confront it; he would walk the stage in a depressive state of contagious proportions, picking us up in his downward spiral. On stage, Phil had developed a motionless remote persona, watching the rest of us in our double-speed manoeuvres through haunting, sad eyes. While it may have appeared to the punter that this was a clever disguise and a neat balance to the circus around him, the illusion was basically reality. Phil's decision to leave prompted the rest of us to try to convince Tim that Phil's exit would be for the better. We did this by not talking to him. We hoped he would pick up our telepathic vibrations. While we enjoyed Phil's company and found him off-stage to be no less one of the team than any of us, it was too fragile a situation live and we were still remembering the first Buck-A-Head where the sense of unity was magnificent. Tim wasn't convinced and Phil's decision to leave was nullified with the promise of a less hectic schedule. This first week of the New Year heralded our first recording session since *Mental Notes*.

At Armstrong Studios in Melbourne, we put down Phil's *Late Last Night* for release as a one-off single. How we seriously thought such a warped piece might assail the pop charts I cannot begin to guess. Mushroom accepted the track, as always. They should have come in and belted us around the ears. Built on the early seventies ethic of artistic freedom, Mushroom let us pick and choose what material was recorded; with no producers in the real sense of the term, we made the decisions in toto. This was exactly how we wanted it, even if we didn't really know what we were doing. Gudinski, in fact, was of the assumption that Split Enz didn't really care whether its records scaled the Top 40. He had decided we were more intent on achieving musical satisfaction. And, for the majority of members, he was basically right although we all yearned for fame in whatever manifestation it might arrive. Global fame. We were buffoons in essence when it came to strategy.

After mixing the track, we buried ourselves in Perth for three weeks while Michael Gudinski sorted out our future activities in the UK. The Phil Manzanera connection had sustained through the months and his interest in working with us had rubbed off on Island Records in London. The plan had been to go to England in December to start recording.

Unfortunately, on viewing some of our videos, a director of Island had cringed sufficiently for them to pull the plug on the whole deal. This put Mushroom on the spot. With no UK record company in place, Gudinski would be risking large sums of money in flying us there to record the album. The trip was delayed to allow him time to work on it. Phil Manzanera found another project and set aside April for us. So we flew to Perth for three weeks where we played before Frank Zappa and Santana, and killed them in pubs such as the White Sands and the Sandgroper. I sat across the aisle from Mr Zappa on the flight from Melbourne to Perth. His whole persona was elegance and restraint. Until I stood side stage at the WACA oval and watched him from about 20 feet away as he played his show. Then he was elegance and violent sophistication and I thought 'Perhaps he could give us some tips.' I had forsaken the Sydney prawn sandwiches so every lunchtime in the White Sands hotel where it was 41 degrees outside I ate alone a lunch of deep fried Tiger prawns while the bar

TV showed porn videos. There's no reason to all this. I just did it. And I fattened my calves.

With the projected lack of Barry Coburn in our lives, Michael Gudinski presented us with management contracts whereby a tripartite entity under the moniker Mental Management would represent us globally. Mental Management would comprise Michael Gudinski, Ray Evans and John Hopkins. Gudinski wasn't keen on basing himself outside of Australia so Hopkins, by virtue of his commitment to and experience with the band, was elected a corner of the triad. He would be the man on the spot. Manager/tour manager/accountant/meaningful conversationalist etc. etc. While we were okay with Hopkins, if only because we knew he wouldn't try to direct or mould us, the others were an unknown quantity in a management sense.

Discussions on this contract took place in Gudinski's Toorak home. He had Skyhooks in one room and they were getting right up his nose, so he had little time for our queries and points of detail. We had about as much negotiating skill as a Carmelite nun and it was over quickly. We knew that if we didn't sign we didn't go, so we signed.

With our recording, publishing and management secure, Gudinski agreed to take the gamble and fly us to London to record with Manzanera without a UK record deal in place. There were 11 in the party and it was shaping up to be an expensive exercise.

Manzanera was contacted and April was still free. There was resolution in the air. It was now late January so New Zealand and Australian tours were hastily booked, Tim sojourned briefly into Adelaide to collect Radio 5KA's 'Live Group Of The Year' award, and we all flew into Auckland on February 19 after stopping in Melbourne the day before to film the video clip of *Late Last Night*. It was Noel's first effort in video concepts and he succeeded admirably. In it I smoked cigarettes and was a drunk which was quite clever considering I didn't smoke and had stopped drinking over a year before once agoraphobia became my sidekick.

The tour was entitled *The Enz Of The Earth* and it was a joy. By now, there was a strong awareness through New Zealand of our material from the *Mental Notes* album and the five months endless touring in Australia had honed our performances to a polish.

Noel was now playing a major role: one minute spooning, the next whacking huge bass drums and clashing cymbals, to be followed by a distorted guitar solo where he would play with his teeth and then buckle over spitting broken teeth out into the crowd. Tim was the supreme master of ceremonies, his soliloquies rolling out between the songs:

... Tis the glad season of life
The time of singing birds
A time for celebration for the new fledged, the unripe, the callow,
the not quite dry-behind-the ears, beardless, flapperish, vernal,
unlicked, new born and for darling daughters everywhere especially
Amy (Darling).

He was now completely and utterly immersed in his stage persona.

As well, the many months of continuous playing in Australia had tightened our performance; we were in total sympathy with each other, always on the button, meticulous and aware.

In our hearts, we knew this was another peak time. Our musical stratagem had taken another direction with the likes of *Nightmare Stampede*, the three minute pop songs of our youth clearly out of mind. With twisted arrangements and oblique structures we presented an intricate musical showcase in yet another set of multi-coloured costumes; these were dubbed 'the Harlequins'. Songs such as *Malmsbury Villa* and *For You* were distant memories, ill at ease with the atonal and multi-layered extravaganzas we were devising.

In sharp contrast to this festival of light and sound was the support act on the tour. His name was Neil Finn. Performing alone, Neil, now a mature 17-year-old, strode on to the country's stages with his now customary confidence and aired his original material; songs like *Late In Rome*. His voice was now rich and strong, and those hours of piano and guitar practice at Teasdale Street had paid off. The reviews said it all:

'I would like to get it on record now that Neil Finn is a singer of great potential. Timothy's 17-year-old brother sang and performed (on mandolin, guitar and piano) his own material along with two or three Lennon/McCartney numbers ... The standard of both lyrics and tunes was astounding. Neil's writing and use of voice is already quite sophisticated and sensitive ... We await more from (him).' — *Christchurch Press*.

Mention should also be made of the excellent opening act of Nick Flynn (sic), a sensitive and versatile performer who was the ideal entree for the inspired lunacy that followed. — *Christchurch Star*.

Nick Flynn?

Once again the tour was shrouded in a media surge with advance publicity splashed everywhere. One small piece in the *NZ Herald* was especially interesting:

'Coburn Artists Ltd (In liquidation). Notice is hereby given that ... dated the 23rd February 1976, the above named company ... is unable to continue in business ... and that the company be wound up.'

Another item as interesting: 'Phil Judd ... has been awarded one of the Australasian music industry's top titles – the award for "Cover Of The Year" for their album *Mental Notes*.'

We all thought: 'YEAH, Juddsy. Go, go, go!'

The Auckland shows at His Majesty's Theatre were the pinnacle of our run through the country. From the opening bars of *129* to the clacking spoons finale with all seven of us playing the cutlery, we shook off the inconsistencies of our last visit – and that old adrenalin came rushing back again. Playing in His Majesty's was always a buzz. During the intermission, a court bailiff handed my father Jerry a writ from the Coburn Artists liquidator suing Tim, Phil and I for $13,000. Jerry handed it over to an old friend of his – one of the country's best QCs, Lloyd Brown, who sat on it throughout the concert, presumably breaking wind irreverently over the threatening legalese.

We left Auckland for the Australian leg of the tour but it was a mere shadow of the victorious New Zealand series. The agency had too many tours running. There were major inefficiencies and on arrival from Auckland, there was no one to meet us. We cancelled shows in Newcastle and Canberra that were looking shonky, but we forgave all when our old home, Melbourne, turned on a full house at the Dallas Brookes Hall and the tour finished on a high note. This concert epitomised the standing we had in Melbourne and it focused again on how supportive that city had been to our development. From our first visit there – when punters took the time to absorb our music and tolerate our bolshy stance right through to the full houses, there had been a tangible endorsement. Without that initial support, we may well have perished.

We returned to Auckland for some gazing blankly into space, although I was heavily preoccupied with the birth of my offspring. On March 31, a son arrived to Paula. We called him Nicholas. He is now called Nikko. I had a brief five days to witness his growing 0.05 inches before saying an uneasy goodbye; on April 5, 1976, we all boarded a plane for London – without John Hopkins. He had flown ahead to set up our accommodation, rehearsal rooms etc. etc.

On the plane, Emlyn produced the April issue of *Hot Licks* hot off the press. The review for the Auckland His Majesty's concert by Roger Jarrett was on page five:

'I can only comment that my dimmed hopes of July 1975 turned to absolute jubilation when Split Enz gave the finest rock concert I have witnessed in Auckland since Roxy Music last year ... Split Enz are certainly the most conceptually evolved and sophisticated group to come (sic) this portion of green world ... I'm sure the world is their private oyster and I wish, hope and know they'll do it all the way. Thanks for the vision, thanks for the trouble and thanks for the time!'

. . .

Peter Garrett (Midnight Oil)

When I saw Split Enz play Mental Notes *from start to finish whilst at university in Canberra in 1975 I was instantly won over.*

Split Enz at first sight. I will never forget it. Compared to the blue singlet hard rockers, tie-dyed jazz soloists and the pretty-boy pop popsters of the time, the Enz were so different. The crazy costumes, this kaleidoscope of obtuse movement and all the songs that seemed to go on voyages to places further than could be imagined.

Every time that I saw them after that, including the Hammersmith Odeon show in London in 1980, sitting next to Nigel's parents with two standing ovations, in a small pub in Cremorne in 1983, cold, wet, Noel on drums, or completely spinning out the American audiences on the West Coast – wherever – they were always great.

There are lots of things I liked about the Enz. They were creative, intelligent, strikingly original and, at the end of the day, turned out to be decent people as well.

There was a raft of great songs. Time For a Change. I Got You ... *well, don't get me started. But let's face it – I'm a fan and I always was. From the first note to the last.*

8

ONE ROAD LEADS TO LONDON

S plit Enz flew into Heathrow and stood around waiting for some divine guidance as to where we were. John Hopkins wasn't there to meet us and he couldn't be found. After three hours of waiting, we decided to just get going. We piled into two black cabs and as we cruised down the M4 into the city, quickly lost our irritations and basked in the sights, sounds, smell and feel of our Mecca, London town.

London was the City of Dreams, literally. For more than a decade we had relished the music that emanated from that place; we had looked at photographs of The Beatles, The Kinks, Abbey Road, Carnaby Street, and the peacock revolution of youth, and imagined ourselves there, being part of it. As we weaved through Kensington, the two-dimensional artifice transformed into a three-dimensional landscape of possibilities and opportunities. We were in London about to record an album.

We found Hopkins at the Australian Club; he had no excuses for his absence. He informed us we were staying on the Kings Road so we tumbled off to Chelsea into two, expensive serviced apartments.

Because of the high cost we planned to rent flats immediately, but it was a slow process. We left that up to Hopkins and settled.

I was a long way from home. I had pills but in the morning I acted out a small routine as a supplementary vibration. Instant coffee with a dash of whisky and a Romeo Y Julieta cigar puffing. In bed. Bob who was prostrate beside me with his toes sticking out from under the crispy English sheets looked over. He didn't know but I suspect he understood. It was a difficult time when the pause button was on. But really – I just woke up far too early and nerves frayed. The whisky helped. The cigars made me feel like Winston Churchill. On rising we hopped on a tube to meet up with Phil Manzanera at Basing Street Studios.

Three days later from the Kings Road, Tim wrote home: 'Here I am writing again from the other side of the world. We met up with Phil Manzanera at Basing Street Studios where he showed us round ... He really is a charming guy, incredibly respectful of us and our music, which makes us feel pretty good. He is convinced we are going to be big over here and is genuinely determined to do all he can to help ... He has been coming to all the rehearsals and is interested and involved ...... We are mainly running over and polishing up the old songs. We are certainly being given the chance to make a great album.'

Manzanera quickly focused on the tracks he wanted on the album. We would re-record a substantial number from *Mental Notes* as well as *Sweet Dreams, Lovey Dovey, Late Last Night,* 129 (retitled *Matinee Idyll*) and *The Woman Who Loves You.* By mid-April we were ready and we walked into Basing Street Studios on April 19.

Tim wasn't there; he was considered a liability because of his paranoid tendencies when it came to recording sessions. It was an amicable, practical decision if a little harsh. He stayed back in Chelsea reading, sleeping and pondering. Over the road from the Kings Rd apartments, at number 430, was a shop with a huge purple sign above the door that read: SEX. Although only three letters long it was indeed the writing on the wall. Tim and Noel walked in one day and eyed up a couple of oddly attired gents behind the counter, and the gents scrutinised them. Tim Finn and Noel Crombie didn't speak to Malcolm McLaren and Johnny Rotten, but presumably all parties appreciated the others' outrageous appearances irrespective of the difference.

A difference that, in a few months, would cause Split Enz a whole head of problems.

The recording sessions ran smoothly. *So Long For Now* and *Spellbound* were deemed unsatisfactory and rejected, partly through weak performance but also to allow newer tracks on the album so that it would have a market in Australasia. Manzanera and engineer, Rhett Davis, were unflappable and consistent, keeping a steady flow and ensuring proceedings never became bogged in impossible pursuits. Old friend Miles Golding was rediscovered playing for the Royal Philharmonic Orchestra and he dropped in to play violin on *Matinee Idyll*.

After a week, Hopkins and roadie Peter Woodward had secured three houses in Forest Hills and Streatham, and we moved in. Tim, Phil, Hopkins, and Eddie in Canonbie Road; Rob and Noel in Colt Cottage: myself, Emlyn and Woodward in Covington Way.

By now, Tim was allowed in the studio: 'It's coming along really well and the good atmosphere and lack of tension is still there, thank God. Last Friday I went in and did *Time For A Change*, which I am really pleased with. I had observed the relaxed atmosphere with the others but didn't really appreciate it until I actually did something myself – a very good working atmosphere. Michael Gudinski came over and seemed impressed with our progress so far.'

Gudinski set about interesting UK record companies in the album and had a bite from Chrysalis Records. They were interested in the music but wanted to be convinced about the live presentation, so halfway through the recording sessions they arranged for us to travel to Southampton to support one of their acts, Gentle Giant. We drove down ready and poised for the big audition. The Southampton Gaumont was an old picture theatre and the perfect venue for us. We walked around backstage in the afternoon, sifting the imagined images of past British giants who had readied themselves in those cold back rooms for their shows: The Beatles, The Stones, The Who, Hendrix, Kinks and so on. All had stood on that stage before us. Now it was our turn in front of a crowd of 1,000 UK punters and five Chrysalis employees.

The next day another letter flew south: 'We are now a band that has played on English shores. Our debut gig at Southampton was a success ... We got a genuine encore and the feeling throughout the performance was one of receptivity and complete attention ... the Chrysalis boss, Chris Wright, seemed particularly interested in everything about us ... I think it could be in the bag but they played it very cool ... Gudinski comes back in a couple of weeks so it should be sorted out pretty quickly.'

While waiting for the record deal to be resolved, Manzanera completed mixing the album, we started doing some rehearsals, and Phil shaved all his hair off.

By now we felt a brimming confidence. The UK was a market that had reached stagnation point with the major artists such as Genesis, Yes, Jethro Tull and so on all sliding off their blazing trails. There seemed to be a vacuum that we could fill and we felt that, with this airy nature permeating the industry, we could capitalise on the chance to break in.

The beat boom, the psychedelic era and the progressive rock of Led Zeppelin and Yes had all slid into the history books. This sense of right time/right place was further compounded when Gudinski and Chrysalis struck a deal on June 8, my 24th birthday. With the contract signed sealed and delivered, our resolution was no longer in the air – it was on the ground.

June 8 also saw Paula and Nikko arrive from New Zealand. They settled in as well as could be expected in the Streatham mansion, where the nearest laundry was a mile away and the nearest tube station a good hour's walk.

We celebrated the signing to Chrysalis with a lunch date, and

found them all to be enthusiastic chaps with public school airs and
gentlemanly graces. The tone of the soiree was lessened rather when
I ordered steak tartare. (Any of you done that?) In my extreme ignorance, I was expecting an agreeable rare slab of hot roast beef with
dollops of tartare sauce in the vicinity. On being presented with what
looked remarkably like a high quality uncooked hamburger pattie, I
wrapped it in a napkin, put it in my coat pocket, and fried it up when
I got home. Back at lunch, the Chrysalis lads outlined the path ahead
and projected a release date for the album as the second week of
August. The first step they said was for us to secure the services of an
agent as, without one, we would be stationary. No agent; no live
work.

Later we talked to John Hopkins, now known as Hoppy, and
sent him scurrying off to look for an agent. He came back an hour
later and said there weren't any around. We pushed him out the
door again and he ferreted away, his eyes peeled for this mysterious
entity. He eventually found himself in the offices of the Cowbell
agency who weren't interested in us. Chrysalis told him to
persevere.

We had to have them because they were the best. In the meantime, while waiting for this small task to be completed, we returned to
the E-Zee Hire rehearsal rooms.

E-Zee Hire was one of London's premier rehearsal complexes.
Outside the front gates we would find Aston Martins and Porsches
waiting patiently for the rich bottoms of Jethro Tull or Procul Harum
to drop onto the soft leather bucket seats. Our particular room was
large and adorned with large cut-outs of giraffes and elephants,
gazing down upon us as we wondered what to do next. E-Zee Hire
became a routine; a half-way house between the past and the future.
We travelled by bus to South Kensington and then by tube up the
Piccadilly Line to the dank Caledonian Road underground station.
This was followed by a 400-yard walk past greasy spoon cafes and
bric-a-brac shops, stepping gingerly over the dog dung, dried spit and
discarded Wimpy burger bags that seemed to litter every street in

London. Streets lined with grey walls and grey doors ... all leading to the E-Zee Hire entrance.

As the days rolled along, Split Enz began a slow but sure decline to boredom, inefficiency and frustration. With an album waiting in the can and everyone poised for the release, the agency problem gradually grew to become a suffocation that prevented any forward motion.

There was little we could do; it was all in Hoppy's hands as it dragged on through June and into July. Nothing. And the toppermost of the poppermost was Demis Roussos and his *Forever And Ever*. We sat around in the heat, we played tennis, we walked down the road and back again. For the first time in our career we were faced with a daily routine, a routine of nothingness but waiting. Eventually it all rolled into a haze.

Weekends found Hoppy and I cruising out into the English countryside in his ancient Morris Oxford, affectionately known as the slutmobile. We were both members of Chris Wright's Chrysalis cricket team (try and say that quickly) and under the steaming hot Sunday sun I would send down seamers and outswingers to the likes of Tim Rice and Adrian Hopkins. Wright had a private cricket pitch in the back yard of his expansive country property, with a huge oak tree in the middle. Truly eccentric.

I wrote home: 'By gosh, it's bally hot at the moment. 30 degrees and dashed uncomfortable. Last Sunday the Chrysalis team played a Tim Rice XI in some respectful English village and we thrashed them. After I bowled one swerving swinger past Rice's off stump he called out: "Every time you bowl at me I don't understand, why I let your outswingers get so out of hand." Silly man, what!'

Come the week, we would spend days and days in the rehearsal rooms swimming in opposing circles, trying to finish two new songs that had arisen. One was called *Another Great Divide*. That one did reach a stable conclusion. Occasionally the suggested paraphrases of this locked-in stifle would make us laugh. Tim cried out.

One plus one equals two; now that's addition

Two into two goes one; now baby that's division
And one into three? That's after the show.

Long periods of time were taken up trying to find complementary notes, bridges, intros and the like. One conversation was recorded on tape. We find Juddsy trying to find a note for his fourth finger to play in one chord in the *Fascination* bridge.

Judd: 'What chord is that in?'

Rayner: 'C major.'

Judd: 'What's the next chord then ... let me see. C Sargeant?'

Finn: 'Try B-minor.'

Judd: 'I'd end up with a major seventh.'

Gillies: 'Try B Flat.'

Judd: 'No, that's a sus 4th p'raps. What makes it the sus 4th?'

Chunn: 'It's an F sharp with a F.'

Gillies: 'Try an N.'

Rayner: 'Naa. Tell him to get fucked. It's F sharp with a B.'

Finn: 'Play the G.'

Judd: [plays note] 'Hey ... very nice. But B always has an F sharp.'

Finn: 'B minor with a C sharp?'

Gillies: 'It's F sharp with a B flat.'

Rayner: 'Troublemaker.'

[Judd plays note]

Finn: 'You can't have the E Flat. Take the E flat out of it.'

Judd: 'Out of what?'

Rayner: 'You want the C sharp.'

Judd: 'C sharp! That's way up there, man! What a long way!'

Finn: 'You can do it, Juddsy. You can do it!'

Gillies: 'Listen, you guys. I'll give you 10 for an A sharp!'

Finn: 'Okay, you guys. Bring us back from the cosmos.'

Chrysalis had decided that none of the tracks on the album were suitable as singles, which was akin to telling us that we had shot ourselves in the foot. Stumps afoot. Tim decided to concentrate on writing a single and would bus around to Colt Cottage to work with Rob. He would walk up Canonbie Road, guitar case in hand; Phil would watch him go, dragging their past up over the hill and out of sight.

Phil wasn't the only one watching him. A young woman who lived on the other side of Canonbie Road took note of this unusual-looking man as he came and went. Her name was Liz Malam and soon she struck up odd conversations with the occupants of number 17 as they passed in the street. She was in the world of entertainment, too; dancing underneath the lights at clubs in the city.

The composition Tim and Rob pieced together – titled *Are You Sad* – was never presented, as Phil's *Another Great Divide* became the choice for the single. Our choice. Tim was unable to bring himself to offer his new song in opposition to Phil's.

The Judd/Finn writing partnership was now history. Phil continued to find the drive for commercial success to be virtually anathema whereas Tim was now sharply focused, particularly as this was London and there was nowhere else to turn. Phil would still spend hours working away on his compositions. He had a screed of lyrical ideas strewn across loose pages that littered his room. Phrases that might be useful for whatever song he was working on. One of them had a working title of *Address Four Walls* and he had an array of possibilities with which to finish the song: 'beggars can't be choosers; living on borrowed time; fat between the ears; once metaphysical man', and so on. He had lists of working titles such as *Jamboree, Frenzy, Three Irish Twins, The Perfect Stranger* and *Sugar And Spice.*

Unfortunately, without the moral support Tim had given to Phil in the past and without Tim's natural inclination to push material at the band, very little of Phil's new stuff came our way. Tim, on the other hand, had so little confidence in his own work relative to Phil's that he offered us nothing in 1976.

Back in New Zealand, Neil had decided, during his time at Te Awamutu College, that he wouldn't study for a university degree. With the start of the 1976 year, he approached the headmaster and asked if he could write his own curriculum, concentrating on music studies. This was frowned on, so he quit the academic life for a job behind the counter of the local record bar. He was summoned for the *Enz Of The Earth* tour and followed that with the decision to live in Auckland, spurred by a letter Tim wrote from London on May 5: 'Fang. I hear Geoffrey Chunn is doing well at a few concerts in Auckland, so get into it, man, and show those Aucklanders what a Finn is capable of.'

Neil journeyed up a few weeks later and moved into a flat with one Mark Hough, who hailed from Napier. Hough was a Phil Judd acolyte with a strong artistic bent and Neil first met him at Malmsbury Villa where both were staying overnight. He found him at dawn taking time-lapse photos of the sun rising over Kohimarama.

During the *Enz Of The Earth* tour, they met up again and Hough suggested to Neil that he avail himself of the opportunity to stay with him at the Remuera home of his old girl's parents. Her name was Miranda, she was sitting on the veranda and the house had been vacated by a peripatetic mother and father. Neil moved in with the two of them and looked for work. He found a job at Pye Records, which had gone into liquidation (taking Coburn's White Label and *Mental Notes* with it), where he worked in the warehouse sending out boxes of records to stores who were lapping them up at a dollar a copy.

At nights he would play out songs and compose with Hough; Neil at the piano moulding the thing while Hough would sit at the kitchen table scribbling out lyrics. These would be pored over by the both of them and dissected. With the recent Judd material fresh in their heads, they were unable to avoid plagiarisms. Phil was now writing outside his heart as he slipped further from the passionate times of old. He concocted twisted scenarios epitomised in his recent works *Late Last Night* and *Nightmare Stampede*. Vignettes of struggle, loss and whackiness. And with Hough's focus on all things Juddish coupled with Neil's starry view of Split Enz, the young lads were destined to, subconsciously perhaps, emulate the Enz style.

This creative life in Auckland appealed to Neil although he was perturbed at the domestic predicament he found himself in. Hough and Miranda lived a tempestuous existence; Neil would wake at nights to the sound of running feet, distant thuds and crashes of altercation coupled with the odd blow. But it wasn't to last, and Hough and Neil ended up in a Remuera flat where they continued their musical doodlings.

Pye Records passed into the history books so Neil found work as a hospital orderly. Around the same time he met a young keyboard player so he and Hough decided to form a band.

Neil got in touch with brother Geoffrey, who was ready for a play, and the four of them set about rehearsals with Hough on drums. There was a thread of seriousness and they tried to think of a name for their combo. Easy Keys was the likely contender but it was discarded after Neil wrote to Tim asking his opinion.

Tim replied: 'Not sure … sounds a bit like Easybeats. Anyway, Fang, my advice is to keep looking for a good solid simple drummer. A vital ingredient. But it does sound as if you are making considerable progress. Keep it up, even for its own sake, the struggle is worth it. How about some tapes? I would love to hear them.'

Neil immediately borrowed a tape recorder and four originals were put down by the nameless foursome. They were dutifully sent to London.

Tim replied: ' … received the tape this morning. Many thanks, and congratulations, Fang, from all on a fine effort. Phil, Jonathan, Eddie, and I sat down and had a listen this morning and thoroughly enjoyed it, particularly the singing. Your voice records very well and it was nice to hear the extra arrangements, particularly on *Late In Rome*. Glad to hear of the writing with Mark Hough. Songs or bits? Phil thinks that you could make it on your own so if the band thing doesn't work (hoping it does of course) take solace in the fact that Split Enz believes in you.'

While happy to believe in Neil and his adventures, Split Enz was having problems believing in their bad luck. By early August, with still no agency in sight, we were mere shadows of the stout-hearted

New Zealanders who had charged into E-Zee Hire for a short burst of practice.

We'd been in there for 95 hours and had almost completed one new song. But, with the whole focus now on agents, record companies, live work, and an album (of mostly old songs), we were blind to the decay. Weeks had passed with nothing to show for it and we didn't seem to care.

In sharp contrast to the hordes of wandering New Zealanders clambering over the Tower of London and drinking in corner pubs, we stayed entrenched in south London. The routine of waiting had numbed us to an extraordinary extent and, as if paralysed, we found ourselves playing tennis in the Forest Hill gardens and not much else.

Chrysalis decided to act and booked the Marquee club for a showcase concert on August 19. They decked the place out with huge posters, displays and marketing devices, and invited a large contingent of music media. We were happy just to be doing something and relished the history that the Marquee is steeped in.

I wrote home: 'Chrysalis have hired the Marquee for a reception-type thing for invited press, record bods and friends. Phil Manzy has invited Eno and his 10CC buddies. Muchos nervosa. The club will be decorated with blow-ups, adorned with press kits, and littered with free booze. There might even be an onion dip! Jimi Hendrix played there in 1967 – nine years ago. I will stand on his footprints!'

Decked out in the Black and Whites, we shook off the E-Zee Hire syndrome for a night and played to a crowd that had never seen us before. Afterwards, the Chrysalis contingent seemed happy and the following day we spent the whole day being interviewed by UK, US, European, and Japanese press. A startling volume of chatty people.

'Split Enz su potpuno čudno i tako čudno da mi je skočio gore i dolje i pio previše.' List iz nutty Europe.

We finished the day exhausted but happy to be seemingly on the move again. Tim wrote it down: 'There were lots of important people there. Some loved it, a few hated it and a fewer still were not sure ... Hard to say what the results were. (It was) quite a subtle encounter.'

The album, entitled *Mental Notes*, had been released on August 9 with the same Judd painting as on the 1975 *Mental Notes*, except Wally's head had been replaced by Rob's. The painting was bordered by pink candy stripes which perturbed us. *Second Thoughts* was chosen by Phil as the title for Australasia. He had been working on various options for the album's name such as *Second Leg, Second Fiddle, Second Person, Second-helping, Second-class, Second late*; he had even worked on a title song that was accompanied by a mandolin in a strange tuning. He had scribbled a few lines and phrases down for the thing: 'Change yeh, Change my song; Wait and see how the wind blows; Ransack my brains; I gotta do some heavy thinking.'

It was never recorded and the album winged its way south as *Second Thoughts*. We waited expectantly for some positive reactions. Unfortunately, with our being so immersed in the project and many months (years?) away from an objective assessment, we hadn't realised that the album fell short of our expectations. We had re-recorded the original *Mental Notes* songs to satisfy the demand in the UK but we were unable to bring them back to life. Most had been performed more than 300 times since we learned them and the original spark was virtually extinguished.

Phil Manzanera did not know our capabilities so he wasn't able to sense the almost automaton nature of our performance, our virtual weariness and blunt edges. The music press were also unknowing and tended to take us on at a conceptual level rather than as a purely musical entity. Of course we gave them little option with the rash of extreme press photos in which paraded in gross make-up and poses. The reviews were plentiful and encouraging, if a little guarded.

'We've heard this sort of thing before ... music with the quality of a nightmare. But these seven musicians ... are particularly good at it.' — *Daily Express*.

' ... they are one of the few bands of any originality to have emerged over the last twelve months ... They are I suspect likely to be viewed with suspicion by those who originally dismissed Roxy

(Music] as facile and pretentious. For, like the early Roxy Music, they have evolved a group personality which accommodates both their visual and musical idiosyncrasies.' — *Melody Maker*.

'Split Enz are preserved from aesthetic obscurity by their compulsively droll humour and exacting musicianship. The band's two writers, Tim Finn and Philip Judd, have chosen as theatre of operations a curious environment: the baroque and the berserk, alternately reminiscent of early King Crimson, Genesis with Gabriel and Roxy Music.' — *NME*.

'It's hard to believe that such a bizarre looking bunch of characters could have produced the very charming music to be heard on this album.' — *Shepherds Bush Gazette and Post*.

While the music press were receptive to Chrysalis' badgering, the general media were a problem. To this end, Phil Manzanera introduced us to Lyn Franks, who was a fashion publicist and friend. She found Split Enz to her liking and offered to dredge up some action as best she could. Next thing you know, we're on BBC television, beaming out to over 10 million people. The programme was essentially a chat show entitled *Today* and we were guests of the host, Bill Grundy. It was a theatre set-up and we sat fully costumed and made up in the front row. Noel was asked how to describe our music and a ping-pong ball popped out of his mouth. A short excerpt was shown from the video clip we had just shot of *Lovey Dovey* and Grundy asked a young woman in the crowd if she liked it.

'No,' she said.

A few days after that fiasco, we tried to get our clips played on the BBC but all were dismissed as unsuitable for teenagers. *Late Last Night* had cigarettes (I was convincing), *Lovey Dovey* was too epileptic and *Sweet Dreams* had the line '*only got as far as the back seat of my car ...*' which was immoral.

Around then Eddie and I dressed in drag (that's not the right word – we were profoundly effeminate) and went to see Sherbert who had a top ten hit in the UK with *Howzat*. The show was at the Victoria Palace theatre. We had a banner that said 'Fuck me, Darryl.'

(The truth is we were jealous). The only part of this tawdry story worth acknowledging as colourful was – we lost our car keys dancing in the aisle and had to stand outside Victoria Station looking like two bedraggled transvestites. Never again.

This was getting us nowhere and the compounded setbacks of the past four months began to bulge. No agency, no airplay for the album, no new material and a sliding confidence in the management situation. John Hopkins was out of his depth in London and it was becoming clear to Chrysalis that his efforts were yielding few results. I overheard Chris Wright saying as much to promoter Adrian Hopkins at one of our cricket matches. Wright was bemoaning the lack of an agency and stated quite simply to Hopkins (he of the Adrian variety): 'The band has a management problem.'

Instead of moving to redress this problem, the absurd thing was that we acknowledged Hoppy was not achieving, by virtue of his lack of experience in the UK market, and decided, only, that it was a pity. We did nothing about it. We couldn't TALK about it. But something had to give. So we fired Emlyn.

Emlyn was an easy option. He had always been on the periphery, finding the make-up and mannered presentation uncomfortable. As well, Tim, being a closet drummer, wasn't able to prevent himself giving undue attention to the drum arrangements and he found Emlyn's style high on technical expertise but low on solid simplicity. Years later, however, he missed Crowther's wayward, brilliant drumming. It's all about the wood and the trees.

I was given the black hood and sharpened axe. At 5.30 pm one evening, as the heatwave submerged London into soporific nonchalance, I said to Emlyn as he sat in the Covington Way dining room surrounded by oscilloscopes, circuit boards and rheostats: 'Croth, we're getting a new drummer.'

'Is that right?'

His increasing frustration at the lack of work and his minimal confidence in John Hopkins had buffed his fighting spirit and he flew home to Auckland.

The search for a drummer was now on and, of course, we wanted a New Zealander. The only one in the United Kingdom was Dean Ruscoe and he was playing with the Maori Volcanics at the Lakeside Country Club in Surrey. Ruscoe was a past member of Quincy Conserve and Rob Gillies knew him, so the two of us drove south to watch him play. This simple task was more difficult than we had imagined as the club management would not let groups of just the one sex into the club. Presumably this was to stop roving packs of English hooligans from upsetting the gentle, harmonious atmosphere of the Benny Hill establishment. We enlisted Ruscoe's help to lobby the management and were duly allowed in to witness the show, although it was impossible to concentrate on Dean.

For one-and-a-half hours we drank in the hilarity, satire and musical mastery of the newest Volcanic member who, only in his mid-twenties, was setting the room on fire. His name was Billy T. James and it was patently obvious he was destined for greatness, a greatness duly and honourably bestowed in the passage of time.

After the show we offered Dean the job and he said no.

An ad was then placed in *Melody Maker*: 'DRUMMER wanted for touring band with record contract playing original material.'

The use of the word 'touring' in the advertisement was not a misnomer. Cowbell finally came to terms with our refusal to go away and, still reluctant to sign us to an agency agreement, fobbed us off with the support slot on an upcoming tour by a Geordie band Jack The Lad with a total of 26 concerts throughout England and Wales. We took it and found ourselves, yet again, a few weeks away from a tour and one member short.

Drummers were whittled down on the phone.

'Hey, I believe you guys are looking for a drummer.'

'Yeah, what kind of music do you like?'

'Medicine Head.'

Click.

The balance were interviewed at Canonbie Road and a final tally of 11 invited to audition at our new rehearsal room: a dark, dank basement room in Lots Road, Battersea. Dylan Taite came and filmed us there. It's on YouTube. The standard was generally abysmal, with Rayner hiding behind his vast tower of keyboards buckled with laughter. The rest of us had nowhere to hide. Two lads impressed: Dinky Diamond, who had played with Sparks, and Malcolm Green, who was a mystery. The votes ran Diamond 2, Green 5. Mal was in and the heat was on. There were 10 days before the first Jack The Lad show in Aylesbury.

Eleven days later, Tim was in the letterbox: 'Had to write and tell you of our stunningly successful first night of the tour ... a very sincere encore and generally a total success. The English kids seem very eager to be entertained and they picked up on quite a few subtleties – it bodes well. Malcolm, the new drumming "end" did extremely well ... there are quite a few personality differences but his drumming is good enough to dispel any fears in that direction. Given time I think we can mentalise him.'

The *Jack The Lad* tour was relentless and just what the dreary, resigned mob that Split Enz had become needed. We quickly found Jack The Lad boys to be ready to party; our first encounter with them was four pink, Pommie sphincters staring at us as they drove past on the way to Pinewood Studios for the dress rehearsal. In sharp contrast to the drug-infested vagaries of the rock 'n' roll circus in Australia, Jack The Lad stuck to Guinness and filled whatever room they were in with deep Newcastle laughter. We wore the 'Black and Whites', which by now were deemed to be lucky charms, and in this new atmosphere we re-found ourselves.

Cooped up in the van for hundreds of miles a day we had the chance to take up the slack on the loosening rapport we once had ... and for me – the Serepax had me nodding off all the time in the van and time passed in rapid fashion.

It was a joy to shake off the unnatural months we had endured. We were back on stage at last and playing to people who had never seen us before. A challenge we thrived on.

By mid-October the tour was receiving reviews in the press.

Media space was at a premium as Malcolm McLaren had just held his 'Punk Festival' at the 100 Club in Oxford Street, with new bands the Sex Pistols, Clash, Siouxsie & the Banshees, Buzzcocks, and Damned playing over two days. The previous month in *NME*, Tony Parsons had cracked open the movement with a full page rave which espoused a new attitude: 'When a band like the Sex Pistols gets in a punch-up with members of their audience halfway through a performance it probably gets a big larf with all those coke-snorting superstars up there on Olympus, as secure as the Tzars of Russia. Just maybe, if things work out as they should, this time next year they'll be laughing on the other side of their faces.'

A month later, *Melody Maker* and *Sounds* were running huge expanded 'punk' sections, heralding the new movement in which musical expertise didn't matter and the three minute song was the bedrock. The philosophy was one where music was outside any code and anyone with a notion could walk on a stage. It dovetailed neatly into the deepening late 1970s social depression and attracted massive negative attention from the non-music media which is exactly what was necessary to ensure its success. The biggest selling newspaper in Britain, the *Sun*, gave the punk movement a two-page spread, warning of 'nightmare, chaos, safety pins, swastikas and slagging off hippies.'

Against this wide media surge Split Enz managed to get mentions with varying degrees of positivity:

'To me the visual grotesquery, though undeniably more interesting than a bunch of geezers stood around in worn-out denims, was a barrier. I had nothing to relate to ... But not for the students of Durham who gave them one of the most insistent ovations I've ever seen for a support band.' — *Sounds*.

'Tim Finn, the band's vocalist, told me the band don't actually listen to much music. This I can believe as they don't sound much like anything I've heard. The numbers are well structured and generally long, but the manifold rhythm changes act as a grade A boredom deterrent.' — *NME*.

Coupled with live reviews, we had major feature spreads in *Melody Maker*, *NME* and *Sounds*, generally focusing strongly on image.

Tim was quoted in *NME*: 'The theatrics just developed. They mushroomed out when Noel came into the group and started designing all the costumes ... They're not a gimmick, although I sense a backlash against our sort of image at present. Still, for those who want an alternative to the punks, here we are and intend to stay. Split Enz is a very close, cohesive family and we've worked very hard to get this far.'

The tour covered a huge territory and took us to thousands of people, with the majority of the shows being successful. As in Australia, Noel was quickly hoisted to celebrity status by virtue of his spoons display and unique persona. We shook off the hangover from the arduous summer months.

The final show of the tour on November 2, 1976, was at Manchester Free Trade Hall to a full house; as usual we were finishing our set with us all playing the spoons. This night, Jack The Lad wandered on in their Black 'n' White Newcastle soccer jerseys, all clacking spoons, and they joined in for the final bow. Hearty stuff. During their set we devised a complex routine whereby various Enz members walked across the stage during the final Jack The Lad number in increasing levels of undress. The climax featured Phil, Mal, Eddie, and myself running naked through the lot of them, clutching underwear in case we were tackled by the lithe Geordies. They didn't get us. After the show we drank Guinness and sparked in the glow of a successful tour. It was with a hint of sadness that we farewelled our hosts.

In a way, this tour, loaded with pranks, humour and full houses, was a panacea, a relaxant that distracted us from the horrors of minimal album sales and nil radio exposure. We had crowds in front of us, a defined unique presentation and we were sticking with it.

As the tour finished, we found Cowbell more interested in a long-term arrangement and dates were put together through November and December. This included a trip to Amsterdam for a show at the prestigious 'Paradiso' club and we arrived there on November 4. Amsterdam was wild, and the porn shops and hash houses were quickly absorbed. With a spare night to kill we dribbled out of the hotel and wormed our way around the streets, occasionally passing each other. I would catch Noel and Raewyn leafing through an S&M book, or Eddie perusing a wild array of motorised dildos to-ing and fro-ing in a shop window.

I passed Hoppy staring at a bunch of photos in a window. 'Wow, that's some cum shot!' he exclaimed. Over black coffees we would notice the odd poster advertising our show. The anticipation built. Rob, Noel and I took in the Rembrandt museum. After a few hundred of the huge oils we found ourselves running through the vast labyrinth of walls decked in gilt frames, as if in a maze searching for a way out.

The next night we found ourselves backstage at the Paradiso in high spirits. The sheer volume of UK music press that we had had over the past two months ensured a full house.

The show was stunning, and the reception long and sincere. The ensuing reverberations took our album into the Dutch and Belgian charts, and a day of interviews exhausted Tim yet again.

Coverage was enormous although the emphasis was still on the presentation:

'Split Enz – kaputter geht's nicht.'— *Music Express*.

'Een stel serieuze gekken.' — *Nationale Hitparade*.

On returning to London we recorded *Another Great Divide* at Air Studios, with Manzanera producing and Rhett Davis engineering. The song had been receiving a brilliant response live and it made sense at the time to try it. There were no other options in fact. The results were exciting and Mal's drumming sat perfectly in this, his debut session. This would be the intermediary single that would garner massive airplay, etc., etc.

On hearing its myriad pieces, the A&R chap at Chrysalis suggested it would make a good album. And he was right, of course.

Once again we proved that we had no real idea of what singles were about or were meant to be. Meanwhile at the toppermost of the poppermost was the band Pussycat with *Mississippi*. Simply – while we were proud of *Another Great Divide* as a piece of music, it had negligible commercial potential.

The real development of this single was Tim's vocal. Gone were the twittery mannerisms and inflections that he had originated in the paranoid environs of the *Mental Notes* sessions and felt obliged to perpetuate on Second Thoughts. He realised, under pressure from the queries and questions that had been thrown at him relentlessly in the UK asking 'Why? Why? Why?', that his rococo vocals were in need of a natural death. So they went, never to surface on record again.

On November 24, we kicked off a 13-date headline tour of universities. Because of the high cost of hotel accommodation, we would more often than not return to London after each show. Consequently we were in a van, wrapped in coats and scarves against the cold, driving up to 12 hours a day. We wiled away the time by dividing ourselves into teams and flicking small wads of paper at each other from rubber-band slings. Mind you, I was often falling asleep as bullets flew. It became an artform, a jovial, if at times painful, war.

Occasionally, we would lift our heads and look through the windscreen at some approaching city. The first sign would be a grey, almost insipid haze on the horizon and then the sharp defined edges of the factories, smoke stacks, wire fences, brick walls, funnels, pipes and gushing steam of some county metropolis would materialise. It might be Sheffield or it might be Hull. Preston, perhaps. We came upon Bury St Edmonds. Was the next town going to be Destroy St Albans ... followed by Smash St Farthings!

Did anyone know where we were? Who was driving? Was this the M1, the M4, the M3, or the M64? Was there an M666? Were the doughnuts in the next service centre going to be stale? Was the coffee real? The toilets locked? Football Hooligans loaded with darts ready and waiting? There was an inherent humour in the proceedings but

Phil and I had a subdued growing concern. As parents, we weren't overly enamoured of the time we were spending away from families. We were learning quickly the massive and complex emotions that can fill a father's head ...

There was one city that met us with a sweep of sheer beauty. On the Welsh coast, we savoured the history and timelessness of Aberystwyth and, as if to emphasise our sense of satisfaction, the local university students gave us a resounding reception in a setting that was pure Dylan Thomas. I can't remember now if they clapped for 10 minutes and we played three encores, or if they clapped for three minutes and we played 10 encores. Whatever; it was a winter moonless night in the small town, starless and bible-black.

The tour was well attended and the receptions excellent. And, as usual, this gangly group of New Zealand males failed to attract any female attention. Still ill at ease with women, it was only the occasional odd disenfranchised fan who would follow us around. The face would flash up out of nowhere but nothing was said. We would clamber into the van ready for another dart fight and drive away.

The concert at London's Imperial College in Kensington was a full house with a large punk contingent. The press coverage in the music media had aroused the curiosity of the still small but virulent punk fraternity, particularly with the strong focus on our image. We had Siouxsie, some Clash and some Pistols in the crowd. Liz Malam, from Canonbie Road, was also there ... watching closely. Siouxsie was later to record a track entitled *Spellbound* with a strumming acoustic guitar intro. Perhaps? Outside the dressing room after the show we could hear punks discussing the whys and wherefores.

'But, you gotta admit they're fookin' brilliant.'

'Yeah, okay ... but they're not punk. Know what I mean, like?'

Three days later, we drove to Liverpool, ready to fill the town with our music and eager to immerse ourselves in Beatles' memorabilia. We had to cancel the show as the club heating system didn't work and the room was frozen. The venue was called the Cavern and above the entrance was a statue of four men in collarless suits. An inscription was written underneath: 'To the four lads who shook the world.' I looked up. A perfect moment really. And we drove back to London without playing a note.

The tour ended on December 11 with plenty of ovations echoing in our heads but no money in our back pocket. There was only one way to stop having to suck money out of Chrysalis – return to Australasia for a tour. We closed up flats, packed suitcases and boarded a plane to Melbourne on December 14, leaving behind a frozen, wet London town. A grey contrast to our first sighting that bright, clear April morning eight months before.

With 28 hours of staring at the seat in front of us, we had time to reflect on the UK trip.

We had made an impact, indeed; but it was confined to the music industry and had been overshadowed in the end by the punk movement. Chrysalis had been delivered a flawed album; it was up to us to solidify our writing and come up with something that was going to surpass the pretensions of *Second Thoughts*. Chrysalis needed an album that was more accessible and more likely to sell outside the minority of *Melody Maker* and *NME* readers that had handed out cash for *Second Thoughts*.

The ball was in our court. We had to ensure that Phil was encouraged to bring his writing out into the open and try to get Tim to get back in there with him. They may have developed differing views on the long-term objectives of the band but on a musical level there was work to be done and it couldn't wait. Tim may have been writing alone but he was still convinced that Phil was the mainstay of the writing arena and he would always back off in deference to Phil's works. But Phil wasn't handing them over.

For the second year in a row Split Enz had stalled creatively as our attentions became focused on material success in a new market. It was draining us and we had to consolidate. I say all this in hindsight. What is now the past was once the future and, at the time, we knew nothing. We just flew home for the Australian and New Zealand tours, and then the United States.

9

THE FALL OF THE HOUSE OF CARDS

I n November, Chrysalis Records in Los Angeles had declared its intention to get behind the release of *Mental Notes* in the USA and wanted the band to travel there in the New Year for a showcase tour.

This would entail small club dates through most of the country, which would allow Chrysalis to have us play before important press, radio and other VIPs in suitable, intimate venues. Hopkins and Chrysalis UK agreed to the trip and we were to fly us from Auckland to Los Angeles on Jan 30th. In the meantime, we had the Australasian tour to do.

Back in Australia, the surprising volume of English music press had rubbed off and we were deemed to have virtually conquered the Motherland. The tour, entitled *Courting The Act*, kicked off in Canberra and, in direct contrast to the *Enz Of The Earth* fiasco twelve months before, ran like clockwork to 90 per cent full houses. The attention lavished on us was massive and we were flown hither and thither for interviews with every conceivable paper, station and channel. I was flown alone to Adelaide where I did radio and television interviews. Dreamy languorous interviews in my benzodiazepam stream.

In much the same way as New Zealand had embraced us on the *Enz Of The Earth* tour the previous March in the afterglow of the time we had spent in Australia garnering record deals, press, television and continuous live work, the parallel was now happening in Australia.

We had been around long enough to be considered an integral part of the Australian music infrastructure and we were championed. And the beauty of it all was that it was national.

From Brisbane down to Adelaide, we received the red carpet. The only sore point was the wholesale lack of success of *Second Thoughts* but then we hadn't done a very good job on it, had we?

Once again Melbourne was the highlight, with two sold-out nights at the Dallas Brookes Hall. As a single, *Another Great Divide* was looking like the proverbial Split Enz stiff; on stage, however, with Malcolm's rumbling drums and Eddie's powerful keyboard arrangement, we threw it out to sustained applause.

On December 23, we flew into Auckland where we quickly disappeared into the undergrowth, savouring the delights of peace, tranquility, clean air and – for Phil and I – family. Tim and I took the opportunity to check up on the Coburn case. The writ was still in force with our man, Lloyd Brown, demanding a breakdown of Coburn's $13,000 claim. A search for discovery they called it; a search that ultimately took them nowhere – the receiver gave up on us four years later.

The whole thing was dragging on so we departed for the University Chapel, where Rob Gillies and Geraldene were getting married. Geraldene was going to travel through the States with us on some kind of bent honeymoon. Having rejoiced in the vows and drunk our fill, we went off to rehearsals at Epsom Normal School. There Phil presented a new song which he had conceived at Canonbie Road but finished off in Auckland. It's called *Sugar And Spice*.

Littered with sexual innuendo, *Sugar and Spice* was essentially a superficial, flippant work with nothing of the Judd psychological process on offer. His lyrics were now colourful, at times humorous, slices of escapism, as if concocted from dreams. Other Judd bits were moulded together in rehearsal and another song evolved as a group effort, although you will recall the title from Phil's Canonbie Road list. It's called *Jamboree*.

Tim contributed the song's coda and Eddie made various musical contributions. Another was rehearsed but never performed. It was one of Phil's Canonbie Road creations, called *It Would Be Nice To Know*. He only had one line and Tim wound a melody around it: 'Oh, wouldn't it be nice to know.'

Phil had one of his sheets of 'physical ideas' as suggestions for the verses. They read:

'Licking my wounds; biding my time; I been crossing fingers; I been picking pockets; climbing mountains; stealing kisses; been on a wild goose chase.' In the end it failed to come together and was laid to rest.

The situation regarding public perception was the same in New Zealand as in Australia and the tour kicked off with gigantic coverage, including front-page spreads in virtually every city to herald our arrival. The costumes this time were the 'Medievals' and were particularly outrageous. As well, we had further enhanced the make-up and hair styles to the maximum. The concert reviews were laudatory although the *Star* in Christchurch had some comments to make:

'If England had any effect on New Zealand's Split Enz, there was little visible of it in their performance in the town hall last night. They left the country our best rock product and they are still our best, but their progress seems minimal.'— *Christchurch Star* (some would say that was more to do with losing a rugby match to Auckland than anything else).

'Personally, I have a suspicion that they will never give me more than they did that Friday night in early '76 which was plenty.' — Terence Hogan, *City News*.

As in Australia, the tour was mostly full houses with repeat shows in the main centres. *Another Great Divide* was released at the same time and failed to dent the radio stations; there was no television exposure as we hadn't made a video clip of the song. And the tour finished with two nights at the Auckland Town Hall where, once again, *Another Great Divide* was given an ecstatic response.

Sam Neill, actor

1975. I think we're talking about the old Town Hall in Wellington and on stage run Split Enz. Already much talked about. From Auckland and therefore a little suspect, but here they are and they are ... well, different. They wear make-up for one thing.

Dubious. The lead singer seems kind of spastic. The odd looking fellow on the left doesn't even play anything. And one of the guitarists, a decidedly androgynous number, seems actively hostile.

A year or two later, I've seen them again and have become a devotee. I'm on an NAC flight to Dunedin and on run Split Enz. But disconcertedly they seem to be dressed as All Blacks on tour. Normal haircuts, normal black track suits, normal silver ferns. Of course it's a joke and of course it takes me a minute to get it.

They always were one step ahead.

We had little time for reflection on the road as less than 24 hours after the second Auckland show we were 35,000 feet in the air on our way to Los Angeles.

In sharp contrast to our original flights into Australia and England, we had no expectations as to what might befall us in America. We went to Australia thinking we would conquer it in three weeks; the UK was the golden land where our final concerted efforts would be made.

But the USA found us couched in uncertainty. America was gripped in Fleetwood Mac and Al Stewart fever; long hair and flared denims were still the uniform. New bands like The Ramones and

Blondie were kicking up dust in the alternative press but, as opposed to the UK, this meant little on the grand scale of things.

To further collectivise ourselves as an impenetrable unit, we took to wearing black track suits en masse, emblazoned on the chest with silver ferns. In many ways, this was clever stuff as it held up the genuine pride we had managed to sustain over the years for the homeland – although it further enhanced the prospect of Split Enz being regarded by flash Americans as a pack of wandering minstrels each short of a few brain cells.

The reception on arrival was also a sharp contrast. In Australia we had a bemused, uncertain Dave Russell waiting with a clapped-out Holden car. In the UK, there was nobody.

Here in LA we had a Chrysalis reception party and a fleet of stretch limousines. We drove off down the freeway with FM stations blaring, televisions clicking off and on, cocktail cabinets opening and shutting, electric seats swishing to and fro, electric windows zooming up and down, electric sunroofs sliding back and forth, heads popping out scanning the wide vista of palm trees, and rows upon rows of enormous, clunky American cars driving beside us as if in a silent pilgrimage to nowhere.

Karl Malden from *The Streets of San Fransisco* was in the next lane, his gaze blank and fixated, his spongy nose a dead giveaway. (True!). I squizzed the bucket seat beside him for the outline of Michael Douglas but it was empty. A small whirlwind of cigar smoke was spinning out the top of the electric window. I watched it spiral into the sky where it was lost in the brown muck hovering over our heads.

Our Chrysalis rep, Russ Shaw, signed us into the Hyatt Hotel on Sunset Boulevard and we threw our by-now battered suitcases onto the wide beds and threw open the ranch-sliders to gaze out across the dark haze that was settled on top of the huge metropolis of LA, each of us clutching our fresh, unmarked tour itineraries in our hands. Upon reading, we knew this was going to be one organised six-week trip.

Wednesday Feb 9th

9.30 The following persons will meet the group at their hotel:

Maury King: MS Dist.

Barry Freedman: MS Dist.

Kenny Hamlin: MS Dist.

Billy Taylor: Chrys Rep.

10.00 Billy Taylor will take the group to Peaches Record Store for an appearance, located at 6666 Hollywood Blvd.

11.00 Billy Taylor will take group to Music Plus at 1440 Vine Street.

12.00 Billy Taylor will take the group to Licorice Pizza at 8878 Sunset Blvd.

1.00 Lunch in parking lot of Tower Records. Lunch, champagne and a photographer will be on hand.

2.30 Rick Ambrose will take two members up to be interviewed by Teen Magazine.

3.30 Two members will be interviewed by Kathy Kaiser of K-ROQ-FM news.

4.00 Rick Ambrose will take two members to interview with Record World.

They will be required to talk.

We spent the first five days in Los Angeles doing just that. Talk. And talk. And talk. A myriad of interviews weaved their way through our waking hours, coupled with record store appearances during which we summoned all our minimal conversational skills to endear ourselves to the staff. Tim and I visited a radio syndicated show called *The Magic Mountain* (a long way from Thomas Mann) and we were introduced to two black kids who were being interviewed after us. The little one had a handshake like warm plasticine. His name was Michael. His older brother was Jermaine. The Jacksons.

At nights, we'd be herded off to restaurants to meet radio people. We would dress as absurdly as we could, taking on their leisure suits, tight body shirts and splayed collars with stove-pipe trousers, jerkins and thin black ties. This was the era of heightened seventies kitsch, with loud mouths and relentless hyperactivity.

LA was a society languishing in sex and coke, not yet ready to heed the warnings of fried brain cells and the hollow victory of me me me. Aids was what you did when you helped somebody cross the road. The West Coast ethos was overdrive and the likes of Russ Shaw would spend all their spare time driving us in a convertible Mercedes high above Los Angeles, to view the city lights, or cruise along Holly-wood Blvd and the like. One gentle night we slid past 10050 Cielo Drive, Benedict Canyon. The sign at the front said 'Entry will be met with armed resistance.' (Google that one)

And we dropped in on enchilada joints and Maple Syrup diners and one-stop-doo-drops and a Dickey's Barbecue Pit. The Twisted Root was unusual. There was a definite feeling that these Los Angeles people thought of us as simpletons. We thought they were lunatics.

This was exemplified by a pot-bellied cop who, on stopping me for weaving all over the road at two in the morning, asked me what I was doing. I was very intrigued by my proximity to a hand gun. I'd never seen one before.

'Why you driving funny, son?'

'I get confused with these traffic lights, Mr pot-bellied, gun-toting officer, suh!'

'Well, son, where you from with that funny accent?'

'New Zealand, suh.'

'Where? Well, let me explain something, son. When the red light's on, you stop; same with the orange. The green means you can go. So get your cotton-picking weasel face outa here before you make my day!'

Sitting in the ground floor coffee bar of the Hyatt one smoggy afternoon I was gazing out the window, my brain gently to-ing and fro-ing in a state of pax while Tim coped with a journalist from *Teen Date* who wanted to know why we were so zany, spoony, daffy, flipped-out, doltish and corybantian. Malcolm McLaren walked past in zippers and pins and winked his eye. One short fragmented piece of body language that said many things. Presumably one of them was: 'Get ye out of this place, kiwi ignorami. Regroup, refocus, shake off that wrinkled facade and return to conquer!'

I couldn't be certain. But it was him alright.

We had our first taste of the Chrysalis promotional thrust when we were presented with a gimmick that they were sending to all media. It was a clay model of Noel's head with holes on the moulded hair sweeps for planting grass seeds. You were then supposed to water it and watch Noel's freaky hairdo materialise. This gauche marketing ploy was presented to us at a Chrysalis restaurant dinner to which they had invited some major radio honchos. The blond, large-breasted thing escorted in by one particular ham picked up Noel's clay head and exclaimed: 'Am I supposed to suck it?'

We squirmed in our seats and in our pants. We were lost in the inept setting but said nothing except to Hopkins, who did nothing. There was the rub. Hopkins was the supposed buffer between us and the record company but his role had reduced itself to one of tour manager (which, in hindsight, was all it had ever been). Gudinski and Evans were light years away, embroiled in the Australian struggle that had seen Skyhooks slip from the popularity stakes with nothing to replace them. The two of them were unable to focus on the evolving tawdriness creeping over the horizon. We were at the mercy of the Chrysalis vulgarity and were powerless to prevent it.

The first show was in San Francisco so we high-tailed it out of LA, cruising in long V8s up the Ventura Highway with Chip helicopters hovering overhead. We arrived in San Francisco, which appealed instantly. Stylish, colourful, varied, almost European, San Fran had a feel and we readied ourselves for the first show at The Boarding House. The tickets were subsidised by Chrysalis at only $4; we wore the Black and Whites and we walked on to a full house.

What is it, when a moment predicted as mundane turns into euphoria? Confronted by 300 San Francisco residents who, over the years, must have seen and heard it all and more, I anticipated a struggle. It was not to be. From the first note they beamed with delight, whooping, laughing, intense and wide-eyed; at the final, crashing chord of *Another Great Divide*, they rose to their feet shouting and cheering.

We had scooped them up and taken them to another place. The real spirit of the performance came from our desperation at the whole Los Angeles media focus on haircuts and zaniness, wackiness and silly clothes. Here, tonight, we were going to prove that we could overpower the whole theatrical monster we had created and drive home a bunch of songs that would prove our musical worth. Songs – words and music – that we loved. And we did.

Backstage after the show, a long-haired chap walked into the changing room with a stetson hat on and exclaimed: 'You guys are good. I want you out of town by sunset!'

'Mumble mumble ... ha ha ... mumble mumble.'

'You guys know who I am?'

Noel replies: 'You're not anybody if you don't have our record.'

Presumably the bass player for the Tubes grooved on the flippancy. He hung around. We liked him.

The next day in the breakfast room of the hotel, surrounded by fake palms, blueberry short stacks and bottomless coffees, we read the *San Francisco Examiner*:

'... Last night at the Boarding House as they played I wondered why this septet, calling itself "Split Enz" monkeyed around the stage like a collection of idiot robots. But popular music has always had more than its share of pseudo-freaks, the down-groups, the anything-for-a-buck (and maybe success) ensembles ... Tom (sic] Finn, vocalist (with the most ridiculous of hair arrangements) prattles on endlessly between tunes, spouting silly poems and making like a Shakespearean jester ... Better the embarrassingly contrived dance steps and amateurishly handled lighting effects had been lost.'

We chewed our short stacks in silence. After another three Boarding House nights of enthusiastic receptions, we drove back to Los Angeles for the big show at the Roxy on the Strip. It was an

invite-only Chrysalis affair and during soundcheck Tim was inter-
viewed by a television anchorman for an evening news broadcast.
This, we were told by Chrysalis, was a coup. It screened at 7pm and
Juddsy and I watched it in our hotel room:

'About your hair?'

'Yes, it is *about* isn't it ... an approximation of a hairstyle that I'm
working towards.'

'How would you describe your music?'

'Neoclassicosmoidalcosmeticmental rock.'

'You oughta try a little calamine lotion.'

'I don't know what that is. We don't have that in New Zealand.'

'Classy group ...'

Cringe.

After soundcheck, Tim returned to the Hyatt and walked into
the lift, where a gent with a London accent put out his hand and
introduced himself.

'Hi, I'm Ray Davies and I'm a fan.' Ray Davies. The Kinks.

Davies spoke to Tim about how he liked the album and that he
had friends, serious music lovers, who liked it too. He suggested to
Tim that when he was next in London he look him up. Tim walked
off to his room a few inches off the orange, purple and mauve carpet.

That night the cognoscenti, codgers and aloof gathered at the
Roxy to decide for themselves whether or not Chrysalis were backing
a dark horse. We charged out in the 'Zoots' and ran around to a
muted response. This one was hard work, particularly for Tim who
had to try to wring some life out of the silhouetted masses. It never
came to be and we ran back to the dressing room, with its light-
bulbed mirrors and chrome, and looked vacantly at each other.
Buffalo Springfield had sat in this room. I wondered if Neil Young
was in the audience.

Questions flew around the room unspoken and there were no
answers to be had. Most of us sloped back to our hotel rooms where
we retreated behind locked doors. Phil and I were rooming together
... he gazed at the television, wrote home to Julie and Amy, and

slugged from a small bottle of brandy. I gazed at the television, wrote home and looked out the window.

The next day we visited more record stores and were interviewed by more magazines. We were asked how to describe our music and how important the image was and what were our influences and where was New Zealand? From there to more record stores and so on. And more interviews.

The following weekend, February 10–13, we played three nights at the Golden Bear, Huntington Beach. We were performing as support to the Sons Of Champlin who attracted a staid, unadventurous crowd of medium size (34 waist) in this medium club on a medium midweek night. There were two shows a night, which entailed sitting around waiting for two hours between sets. So we sat patiently, spoke a little nonsense, smoked a little weed and Phil would slug from his small bottle of brandy. I would have had my pill round 4pm so I drank water.

The first set was received with negligible response from the small crowd. We sat backstage like patients in a queue waiting for the next injection. The second set kicked off about 11.00 pm, again to a small crowd, but was cut short when Phil walked off. He was having tuning problems ...

Four days later we were in Houston where the roads were twice as wide as the freeways of LA, we eat grits for breakfast, the sidewalk was awash with ten-gallon hats, the pavement ground by Cuban heels. Odd to think that Beatle boots and cowboy boots both had Cuban heels. We visited a record store and played one show to a confused response. We found out later that Cheap Trick had screamed on down from some mid-west town to catch our show but we'd finished by the time they arrived.

And the next day found ourselves in Dallas.

By now some of the national press fostered in LA had reached the news-stands and there was a bustle of curiosity. Boz Scaggs and a few cohorts checked us out. We relished in the sudden burst of attention, although the reaction to the show was far short of that which was showered on us in San Francisco and Phil's stage presence was in retreat mode. He would stop playing at seemingly random moments and his guitar parts took on an increasingly abstract tack, trembling and reeling as if out of control. He was by now failing to sing with Tim at all. Tim was unable to confront Phil with this and drove himself on stage like a fanatic, damping his eyes shut and pounding the stage.

Once again, Tim's despair was contagious. That was the thing about him. His emotions ran wide like a net and it was impossible to avoid being scooped up in it. When he was cooking we all cooked. And when he was down we would find ourselves struggling to stay afloat. The power of the man. He was painting it all from a wide palette onto a wide canvas and it drew us in ... At times I thought, 'Timmy boy, you're being hard on yourself.'

By day, we stuck to hotel rooms, except for visits to record stores and radio and press interviews, which allowed the odd free lunch. I grabbed a hire car and drove off into the suburbs alone, amazed at the luxury and extravagance that littered the Bible belt. By now, it was obvious that Chrysalis had only a slim chance of getting this album away and that there was no single for the record company to focus on (in this, the country that invented the Top 40). The toppermost of the poppermost was David Soul's *Don't Give Up On Us Baby*. We put the charts aside and watched more TV. Our day-to-day routine was steady and unvaried, although some of us did notice Raewyn coming out of Eddie's room instead of Noel's.

There was one show where we got an attentive crowd. At Dallas airport waiting for a plane Tim and I tried out a new entertainment concept. A video game. It was called Table Ping Pong. We had one gloriously elongated rally – ping ping ping pong ping ping pong. You get the picture. I forget who won but one of us did. We threw ourselves back into our seats as it finished and took immediate notice of the large crowd that had gathered to watch our fierce video battle.

The next stop was Atlanta, Georgia. By now the tour was tedious. We could see from the gun shops, peach-tree plazas, Ford pick-ups, gridiron helmets, checked golf trousers, baseball caps and platform shoes that 'contemporary' was a word outside the Atlanta dictionary. There were very big bellies all over the place. That's an aside.

We checked into the Holiday Inn and charged off to record stores and interviews, then charged back again to our hotel rooms where we flicked endlessly through TV channels and radio stations, watching beauty pageants or listening to religious zealots calling for hard cash: 'People, on this week although I will not be sending you a physical piece of bread I will be sending you bread from the word of God. As you already know it is the Lenten season and we are asking the Lord for something very special – a message of hope and help.

During the next 40 days, I am expecting an outpouring of God's choice and divine blessings upon the city of Atlanta, Georgia. Now, I want you to hear me well. Give me your money!' After overdosing on that we would wander the streets drinking bottomless cups of coffee and eating Danish.

Chrysalis were desperate and they conceived the ultimate in gauche, cheap promotion: a lookalike competition sponsored by themselves, a record store, a radio station, and a hair salon. We were playing four nights, two shows a night from February 23–26 at the Great Southeast Music Hall.

The first night's performances set the tone when we drew four people for the first show; the second, ten of them. Once again we found ourselves waiting backstage between sets, the sweat drying on our white, orange, pink and blue striped faces. We talked about toasted sandwiches and boredom, and how we were going to solve it. During the second set, Phil walked off early so we played on without him. We didn't care for our own various reasons.

The next night we resolved to ignore the serious, conscientious attitude demanded of us. We walked onstage and as we faced the audience of two people, Tim called out: 'Are you having a good time???!!!!!!'

At the deep silence that followed, he continued: 'Well, we are ... and majority rule!!'

We sniggered and cackled and lurched off into *Late Last Night*, forgetting where we were. Forgetting the album and Chrysalis and fame and fortune, we found some semblance of sanity coming back. Between sets we pranked and laughed and kept to ourselves. Phil threw back his brandy and laughed along. We opened the second set with *So Long For Now*, said goodbye at the end of it and left the stage. Stuff 'em all!

By Saturday night we were anarchic, playing hokey to the minuscule crowds. The whole situation reached truly imbecilic proportions when it was discovered that there had been only one entry in the lookalike contest. Chrysalis honchos quickly rounded up some of the club staff and employees of the hair salon sponsor, and threw them into our changing room where they slapped on make-up in a valiant attempt to look like one of us. They were then paraded out in front of the crowd of around 30 people and the only chap stupid enough to enter was given his first prize of air tickets to California to watch a Jethro Tull concert. He looked like me. In fact, he looked more like me than I did. Second prize was 50 Chrysalis albums, third prize was free admission to the club for a year and fourth prize was a year's free haircuts but there was no one to claim them.

This insane siege was too much. Tim took refuge in a trip that elucidated the whole scenario into a vapid fantasy. We moved onto the stage like soldiers climbing out of the trenches and methodically struck up our respective notes. We wormed our way through about three-quarters of the set before we noticed we were one member short – Phil was gone.

We played on regardless and finished the set. Backstage, Phil, in defence mode, pleaded tuning problems. Eddie and I had had enough so we went back on stage and checked the guitar – it seemed fine. This was passed on to Tim. Instead of letting it go as he would have done in the past, his altered state swept aside his usual reluctance. He confronted Phil and accused him of lying about being out of tune. For the first time in his life, Tim stood up and threatened the safe haven that Phil existed in.

Phil was taken aback ... in a corner ... and he punched Tim in the face, at the same time exclaiming: 'I'm leaving ... I'm leaving.'

As Eddie and I held Phil back, Tim stared long and hard at him – letting everything that had bonded them together, every support structure remaining, no matter how slender, slip away. But for how long?

The next day we were in Boston and Phil announced his departure to us all. In hindsight, he had to go. He was missing his family and found the continuous opening and shutting of suitcases, pressure-cooker tours and the alien drive for fame too much to bear. Throwing back brandy was just the short-term answer.

There were many reasons, however, as to why Phil was walking away. He desperately needed someone outside the band that he could confide in and relate to. And that person could only be in the management role. An objective confidant could have instilled a direction and a sense of worth in Phil; but he was now so low, so backed into a corner, that he wanted to disappear.

In the suppressed environment that we somehow managed to sustain for so long and with the external forces now so in control of our movements, he was unable to confront the situation and we were unable to help him. There was no one he could turn to and I believe he felt victimised. A scapegoat for the drudgery we were steeped in.

He would continue to play through to the end of the tour but then that was it ... out, gone, finito. We met afterwards and decided to follow Eddie's suggestion of asking his old Orb cohort, Alistair Riddell, to join us as Phil's replacement.

In earlier times, Tim would have been shattered. But now, weary with the struggle that this US trip had become and more confident in himself, in his ability to focus the direction of the band, he accepted without comment. There was no contemplation of an end to Split Enz by virtue of Phil's departure. There was a definite will amongst the rest of the band to carry on; Tim would have to carry the writing role on his shoulders. We knew he had the confidence to do it.

The rest of the tour slipped by. There were nights when crowds in small numbers shifted aimlessly. And others, like the Bottomline in New York, where as support to Polish comedian(!) Henny Youngman we played our hearts out, seemingly free as birds and without a care in the world, to an enthusiastic reception. And in Boston's Pauls Mall we nailed it. Maybe that was right. We were all facing, with certainty for the first time, a new frontier within ourselves. Instead of asking 'Why, why, why?', we were asking 'Who, what and where?' The uncertain future we faced on arriving in America had been replaced by a different uncertain future; one in which the band had to change within, as opposed to just another reshuffle of the external circumstances it found itself bashing its head against.

At Washington's Cellar Door club we peaked and the crowd gave us long, zealous receptions. Phil never left the stage early, and we played wildly and exuberantly, shaking off the stigma of Chrysalis' zany emphasis. We focused back on the material and fired. There was change in the air and this American tour was now just a ride.

The natural development of Split Enz, from its beginnings at Levys Saloon in Auckland to the Bottomline in New York, had taken so long in so many different markets that we were now defeated. We had pushed the one particular concept to such an extreme level that it had to explode. And Phil lit the fuse.

On March 11, 40 days after our bubbly arrival at Los Angeles airport, I flew to Auckland; Eddie and Tim flew to Baltimore to write songs at Tim's uncle's house; the rest sloped back to London. Nothing was said. There was nothing to celebrate. It was the quiet, timely end to the first phase in what was to be the long life of Split Enz.

10

WE WHO START FROM SCRATCH

In contrast to the murder, mayhem and genocide about to be foisted on Split Enz in the United States, Neil Finn had been having a fairly easy time of it as he sojourned in the lazy New Zealand summer of 1976—77.

The Finn/Chunn/Hough combo that might have been called Easy Keys gradually crumbled away, and Neil found himself back to kitchen writing sessions with Mark Hough. As 1977 rolled around, he left his job as a hospital orderly, although he failed to report his departure to the authorities and they continued to pay him for about a month. Divine sustenance.

Brother Geoffrey was cavorting on guitar at nights and silk-screening by day, when the offer of a support slot for a Waves concert at the University Maidment Theatre came his way via Graeme Gash. Geoffrey rang Neil and said: 'Let's put the band back together.' And they did.

One of the rejected names from 1976 was hauled back and deemed to be satisfactory and Geoffrey Chunn, Neil Finn, Mark Hough, and a bass player by the name of Alan Brown became After

Hours. They kicked off rehearsals and immediately there was a strong musical rapport.

Hough played percussion and accordion, Geoffrey guitar, Neil piano and guitar, and Brown bass.

The songs came together well: *Late In Rome, Fall Out With The Lads* and *Ice-Shakers*, which had been complemented with verses by Geoffrey, and a fourth number by Geoffrey entitled *Benu Benu.*

The first thing that Geoffrey noticed was Neil's vast improvement on the acoustic guitar. This unit was far more accomplished than the nameless group they had grappled with the previous year, and Geoffrey found the conscientious approach and determination Neil displayed to be very similar to that found at Split Enz rehearsals. Neil's optimism was paramount; anything seemed possible to him, and Geoffrey could see clear as day that Neil's dream of a life as a musical performer was vivid. Geoffrey himself was writing more and more, and his new songs blended well with Neil's.

They polished the material in time for the concert and on the evening of Sunday, March 13, After Hours took the stage at the Maidment Theatre to a sizeable crowd, which included me. I had arrived from Chicago four hours beforehand and, on learning of the show, decided to get along and surprise the siblings. As they walked on I noticed Neil was wearing fake glasses and the stage was decked out with standard lamps and furniture. Flashes of His Majesty's Theatre circa 1974 skimmed by.

The audience, there to see Waves, was quickly swept up in the intricate arrangements and melodic mastery that After Hours possessed. Neil's voice sounded far more mature than his seventeen years, and he and Geoffrey had arranged their songs carefully, particularly *Late In Rome*, which had expanded instrumental sections with detailed guitar/piano interplay. Geoffrey's guitar playing had mushroomed. I was impressed, and after they left the stage I walked into their dressing room to announce my arrival home. They were glowing with the post-gig adrenalin rush and it was great to see. It had been a while since I'd seen the wide eyes and rapid conversations that accompany the rush of joy when a new group delivers a solid debut and nothing goes wrong.

The next day, I rang Alistair Riddell with an offer to join Enz. He said he would think it over so I sat back in the peace and serenity of the cool Auckland weather. I rang Alistair two days later and he said he needed more time. Back to that vacant gaze into space ... it felt wonderful.

I caught up again with Geoffrey and Neil; on the strength of the Maidment show, they had been booked as headliners for a lunchtime concert at the same venue on Wednesday April 6. While waiting for Alistair to call, I soaked up New Zealand. Although it had been only two years since my departure, the country had changed considerably.

Oil shocks had shuddered the economy; inflation, having spent decades as a simple, dull statistic for the Treasury, now burgeoned into the headlines. Each week price tags were scribbled out and another dollar or two added on. Muldoon was in power and the austerity from protectionism, prohibited export of money out of the country and increasing unemployment all added up to a new buzz-word – recession.

This of course meant that New Zealanders wanted some enter-tainment to soothe their stressful lives. The pub touring circuit exploded and zigzagged across the country, allowing a whirlwind of new bands the opportunity to play regularly. This beery environment encouraged guitar bands to flourish and very soon Hello Sailor were the country's top draw. As well, the punk movement was filtering through via the UK music press and there were rumblings in inner-city Auckland. Who would be first to dress up and be a punk?

In essence, though, I found myself not wanting to leave New Zealand. Back home in the security of family and friends, I found myself emerging from the cocoon of Split Enz. It quickly dawned on me how repetitive, frustrating and mind-numbing the seemingly endless pursuit had become to me. All weighed down by the tranquil-lisers which worked their numbing magic so that panic attacks were very rare. But it was a hollow victory. And now, being in Auckland I realised that the susceptibility to panic attacks was much less. Why? What was this? I still didn't have a name for it. That name. At the time I didn't think there was one.

This endless haze slowly shut me down as the tangible rewards of our hard work continued to evaporate like a desert mirage. I had to come to grips with the reality of life with a phobic disorder and the homelessness of touring, coupled with the myriad of changes that the group was undergoing, was too much. I had had enough of my own private hell, and the glorious moments on stage were now too few and far between.

I fully understood Tim's commitment. Having conceived Split Enz, led the group for so long and now developing a song-writing talent without Phil, he had to forge ahead and prove himself. His dedication was now as much for his own personal thirst for success as for the band's. And he wasn't torn by personal family commitments as were Phil and I. My decision on the shores of Lake Michigan only days before stood in front of me. When to say 'I'm leaving'? I found I couldn't give it a date. But I knew it had to be.

A week after my arrival, Eddie called from Boston in a state of glee. He and Tim had clicked in a big way and songs were pouring out. He wanted to know what Alistair was doing. I said I didn't know. Three days later, I rang Riddell and he said he wouldn't be joining. I rang Eddie back and informed him. He and Tim were about to leave for London and it was decided that another advertisement in Melody Maker was called for:

'Guitarist wanted for band with an increasingly complex history, shaky record deal and a new batch of songs.'

A week later I flew out to join them, shacked up with Hopkins and the crew in Crystal Palace, and heard about Baltimore.

Baltimore doesn't jump out and hit one as one of the USA's prime cultural or historic highlights. But in the history of Split Enz, it was a watershed, at a critical time. Tim and Ed arrived there bruised and confused from the American trip. Tim was charged with his own determination to push ahead and, much as Phil had needed Tim as his moral support in the early days, Eddie, with his enormous musical knowledge and willingness to be involved, urged Tim on. Songs flew out and new titles arrived. *My Mistake*, *Crosswords* and *Parrot Fashion Love*.

Here Tim was able to draw completely on his own influences: the short, hooky pop songs of his youth that meant so much to him, such as the Kinks' *Waterloo Sunset*. Deeply immersed in his subconscious, they surged forward and in a completely natural flow of melody and imagery he brought back to Split Enz the concise, memorable song.

Back in London, early April, the writing continued. In fact, instantly. On arrival in the familiar, grey terraced house environs of London, Tim and Eddie booked into a sleazy hotel near Forest Hill. They found the old men peeping though the toilet keyholes at them a charming addition to the warped atmosphere. Tim was in explosion mode. Charged with the release from Phil's shadow and bristling from his new writing spree, he decided the time had come for female company. He taxied round to Canonbie Road and dropped in on the only woman in London he knew ... Liz Malam. His reception was welcoming and he woke up in her room the next morning. Back in the confines of the crumbling hotel, he picked up his guitar and wrote a song; a song that poured out in a pure moment of release – the first time it had ever happened. He wrote a paean with imagery once again spread thinly over the real subject: the exorcism of Phil. The song became *Charlie*.

Rima Te Waita, actress

The song I love the most is Charlie. *It's the only song I've ever heard where my sympathy lies with the violent offender. And what a story-line. Even Bert Brecht would have been hard pushed to come up with one like that!*

All Split Enz lyrics take an unusual point of view and often use odd words and phrases. Set to equally unusual rhythms and soaring vocals, the band shines. They were completely original. I still think they deserved a lot more success internationally.

A few days later, Tim, Ed, and Mal found a house in Ravensbourne Road, Catford. From there Tim would drive around to Colt Cottage, sit down with Rob and together they would fasten lyrics to pieces of music that Tim had composed in Baltimore – one was a song called *Bold As Brass.*

What exactly was going to be happening to this new material was in the process of being sorted out with Chrysalis? The US company had kissed the band goodbye with nothing less than confusion to show for it. They had never really got a handle on where we were coming from and they weren't sure exactly where we were going to. Presumably, they had nary a clue as to whether or not they would ever see us again. In fact they didn't so we will never know.

But, in London, Chris Wright and the boys were keen to keep the ball rolling; Phil's departure was not of real concern to them once they learned that new material was chugging through.

Gudinski had secured a commitment to a second album and Geoffrey Emerick was approached as a possible producer. Emerick had a glorious history as far as we were concerned from his time as engineer for The Beatles, working on albums like *Revolver* and *Sgt Peppers*. His recent activities were a little hazy but it mattered not. The guy had pedigree.

He dropped down to E-Zee Hire rehearsal studios on the first day back and showed an affable nature.

The real concern now was the guitarist problem. The ad in Melody Maker had elicited a huge response and once again phone calls eliminated vast numbers. This left around 20 to be interviewed – although it was felt that it would be difficult to find someone who could absorb the Split Enz consciousness quickly enough, particularly when there was a tour looming. This sense of the impossible loomed large in my head especially.

The thought of dragging scores of Eric Clapton or Steve Howe clones through hours of auditions suddenly appeared anathema. I racked my brains for a way out; for some answer to eliminate this seemingly impossible task. Before the first young hopeful had a chance to knock on the door of the flat, I made a suggestion to Tim and Eddie.

'Guys ... what we need is someone who knows what Split Enz is all about. They may not be the greatest guitar player in the world but then that's not really what we want. We want someone who is going to be a natural member – someone who can fit in instantly and commit fully. That person, you fools, is Neil Finn.'

'But what's he like on guitar ...?'

'Not wonderful ... but there's potential.'

Tim, Eddie and I immediately climbed the stairs to the telephone and Tim rang Mary Finn in Te Awamutu. Could she find Neil and ask him to ring Tim in London? Neil rang shortly after and Tim spoke: 'Neil, how'd you like to join Split Enz and play electric guitar?'

'I'll have to think about it. I'll call you back.'

' ... Oh ... Call us back?'

This seemingly impertinent response from Neil ran contrary to our expectations of the lad falling to the floor in paroxysms of delight screaming at the top of his lungs, 'Take me ... Take me!' We were unaware of Neil's true perspective. In his mind he had always thirsted for a slot in the Enz line-up but hadn't imagined it would be so soon. He certainly hadn't envisaged being asked to replace Phil, as he didn't even own an electric guitar let alone know how to handle one. On top of this was the After Hours scenario and the flush of success they had achieved just a few weeks earlier at the Maidment Theatre. But he couldn't turn it down. And he rang back to say 'yes'.

The decision to bring Neil into the band seemed perfect once it was in place. Here was somebody who would assimilate instantly; he was young and keen, not likely to display ego or personal problems as he didn't have a responsibility in the world. And, from the songs I had heard, his writing talent belied his young age. For me this solution was a catalyst ... a clear moment in my head that enabled my subconscious to force aside any feelings of guilt and confusion.

Less than 24 hours after suggesting Neil join, I found myself having to leave. I had to get back. I had to find a home where I could throw away the suitcases and tackle the demons. I qualified my timing knowing that Enz were about to put Neil through the learning process; they may as well do it with two members than have to repeat the process sometime in the future. Tim, Eddie and I were in the Catford flat waiting for the first guitarist to turn up so that we could tell him to go away.

'Tim, Ed ... I'm going to have to leave the band.'

'You may as well leave now,' Tim replied.

They knew nothing about my phobic straitjacket and I couldn't tell them. My departure was put down to family ties and lack of stamina.

As Tim would say a few years later: 'Split Enz is like a tree and sometimes the branches fall off.'

Perhaps in the grand scheme of things, it was that simple. I booked a flight home. Shortly after, there was a knock on the door and the first hopeful guitarist introduced himself. This one was a Neanderthal with red hair down to his waist and a miserable look on his face, reminiscent of whichever sensitive guitar hero he was emulating. He was promptly informed of his journey being totally unnecessary and he sloped off down the path, a vanishing symbol of all Split Enz could have had.

Back home, Neil was making plans. Brother Geoffrey was shattered at Neil's announcement.

The After Hours potential fell away to nothing as Neil readied himself for his departure to London. He planned to leave after the next Maidment concert and, in the interim, committed himself fully to rehearsals. At the same time, Geoffrey booked demo time at Harlequin Studios so that their material could be recorded for posterity. On Thursday April 7, After Hours played their second and final concert at the Maidment Theatre, recorded five tracks at Harlequin

Studios, and Geoffrey went home to Newmarket while Neil flew out to London. The After Hours demos remain, today, a glimpse into a combo that showed real promise.

An hour after announcing my intention to fly home, Mal, on hearing of my departure, suggested a replacement for me. He had a bassist friend currently playing in a covers band in France, which gave us the image of someone who had complete mastery of the Charles Aznavour repertoire and who spent his post-gig hours slipping halter-tops off the backs of gorgeous French women with a head full of Gevrey Chambertin. Mal quickly assured the others that he would be ideal and complementary. His name was Nigel Griggs. He was rung straight away and on April 4 he reported for duty at E-Zee Hire. I went along to check him out.

As I stood against the wall, watching the starts and stops, I can't say I didn't sense the dispossession, the sad forfeiture of my special corner of the rehearsal room. It seemed too simple a solution then as I stood in the quick vacuum I had created. The gradual inevitability of my departure contrasted with an inner wrestling spirit (my heart) that wanted to remain firmly rooted to the spot, to lift the guitar strap over my head and throw off a costume drenched in sweat at the end of each night. But the resistance from my soul (my head in fact) was too deep; my weary being was battle scarred and desperate for home.

I knew one thing for sure though: the times I had shared with this crazed bunch had created an extraordinary web. For five years, 287,000 miles, 112 stages and seven studios I had walked the earth with these men.

Neil arrived on April 5. Completely free of any expectations and happy to take whatever circumstances he found himself in, Neil was in a state of high excitement from the moment he set foot on English soil. The combination of his suddenly achieving member status of the band with his instant ascension to the hallowed playing fields of London town was almost obscene in its idealistic totality. Whatever was going to happen was all right by him. He was quickly given a tape of all the new songs that had been demoed at E-Zee Hire. The next day he went to Denmark Street to buy his first electric guitar, a Yamaha. The third day, he spent grappling with this newfound electric thing and working out parts to the new songs. And then it was into rehearsal.

A few miles away I boarded a plane to Auckland.

Geoffrey Emerick had agreed to record four tracks as a starter and time was booked by Chrysalis at Air Studios. The four tracks were *My Mistake, Crosswords, Charlie,* and *Parrot Fashion Love.* Emerick had contributed little to the pre-production sessions in E-Zee Hire, just making occasional comments such as, 'That's great' or, 'It's really good.' There were no musical guidelines proffered.

Emerick, either side of 40, was living with his mum and would drive to Oxford Street, catch the lift to the Air floor and kick off around 9.00 am. Enz would be ready to go and the rhythm tracks went down without a hitch. Then Emerick would shoot off for lunch, return with a red nose and sweat all afternoon. This didn't seem to upset his engineering skills and the results were to everyone's satisfaction. In the producer's chair, he was intent on good feels and an emotive richness. With this in mind he insisted on Tim's out-of-tune vocal on *Charlie* being kept.

'Geoffrey, I want to do it again.'

'But, Tim, listen to it. It's got emotion ... passion.'

'All right then ... but, Geoffrey ...?'

'Yeah?'

'Why are you sweating so much?'

While these tracks were being recorded, Hoppy had secured a 14-date tour through the UK to try to bolster the very insignificant coffers. Consequently, when the tracks were in the can and Emerick had committed himself to producing the rest of the album at a later date, the lads returned to E-Zee Hire for a few more days' practice. As well as this emotional stirring within, Tim was having to confront without. After a week of visiting Liz Malam he had decided he shouldn't invest too much in the relationship and that he should leave. As he was walking down the street, she walked out and screamed: 'You come back here!'

On April 27, Split Enz drove up to St Albans for the first show with the new line-up. To a passionate response, the lads revelled in the new members and in a highly spirited display launched a whole stash of new material. Neil knew exactly what to do. Wearing a pair of specs and Noel's new costume with pride, he jumped, leapt, grimaced, and hopped in his own distilled impression of how a Split Enz member should behave. He was the 'Ant', tripping over, broken legs, broken neck. Denis the Menace. It slotted in perfectly. His guitar playing was tentative but he was kept judiciously low in the sound mix.

Nigel was the one to be jolted. Having never seen the band perform live or on video, he was handed a costume by Noel.

'Here, Nigel, put this on and some make-up and you'll be right.'

As the band kicked off, the whole stage erupted around him with a whirlpool of motion.

His immediate impression was simply: 'Jesus, fuck, no one told me about this.' A quick squizz at his mate Mal told him all would be right and he started to strut his stuff slowly but surely. The Enz persona gradually sank in.

After the show, there was a collective sigh of relief. The reception had proved that the effort put into touring the UK in late 1976 had provided a solid foundation on which they could build. And this first show proved to them that they had the muscle to do it. Now all they needed was to release a new single from one of the four tracks that Emerick had just mixed while they'd been on the road.

After the third show in Middlesbrough, Eddie wrote to me: 'Who are you? I'm waiting for Hoppy the slagheap to wake up so we can get on the road back to London ... We've done three shows and they've all been very successful. Seems as if we've lost nothing after being away for so long. There is a black cloud descending on the room. Mal has just walked in and farted. Aaaarggghhh.

'Geoffrey Emerick was entrusted with the four songs to mix as he was a God to us as you know. He crapped out. Badly. So no single for the UK as he's now in the Virgin Islands recording McCartney. We can't continue till he returns ... Neil is fitting perfectly visually as you can well imagine but of course he has a fair way to go before his playing etc. is up to scratch.

He's singing a lot to thicken out Tim's sprightly poppish voice!'

The tour highlight was a sold-out show at the Victoria Palace in London.

Noel wrote to me on May 19: 'I hopeyor newbyill littill frayim iz in azgooda shayp azwen we last spent ... oh i kan hard harder hardlee kontroll myself ... The Viktoreea Paliz woz full an went lyk a bom ... Ow hard kor following haz inlarggd konsidaribbelee. Pitee we onlee do wun sekkind thoorts trakk. Ha ha. Still manijj 2 kill it. Sooooo.'

Word was spreading about the new Enz line-up and the word was good. A certain number of fans were following the group from venue to venue and adopting the guise of various members of the band, principally Noel. This fluid group was quickly named the Frenz of the Enz. It didn't seem to matter that all the material save for *True Colours*, *Woman Who Loves You* and *Time For A Change* was new. The heightened 'punk' movement was now spawning huge numbers of bands and the new material, which was so different from the Judd epics such as *Nightmare Stampede*, *Under The Wheel* and so on, fitted neatly with the 'new wave' ethic of short, sharp three-minute songs. Noel's new costumes were also a nod to punk fashion, which was very particular. Tim's suit was slashed and torn; the others, while still distorted and coloured, harked back in style to the original pastels. They were certainly a sharp contrast to the 'medievals' from the New Zealand tour six months before.

Come June 1, Enz went back into Air Studios to continue recording. Once again Emerick was in the chair, sweating and buying red noses for lunch. The results of the *NME* magazine readers' poll came out a few days later. Split Enz took 13th place in the Most Promising category with Joan Armatrading and AC/DC either side. Not to be sneezed at.

Eddie wrote in mid-June: 'In between eagerly received narrations about *Sgt Peppers* and brief encounters with Air owner George Martin, we have managed over the last week or so to lay down the rhythm tracks. The album is tentatively *Dizrythmia*. As from tomorrow, we will start overdubbing although time's a bit tight. We lost a week with six of us down with Pommie flu. Today we're shooting the cover of the album. It's Noel's idea.'

In the last week, the rush was on. Emerick had been showing increasing signs of excess sweating and nervousness and he left before the album was mixed. It was presumed he had a breakdown but the conclusion remains loose. Pete Henderson was brought in to mix it all in a rush as the band was readying itself for another tour ... in New Zealand.

On July 12, Split Enz flew into Auckland and immediately, as usual, disappeared. Neil, Tim and Liz Malam sped down to Te Awamutu; the house was empty at the time as Dick and Mary were overseas. They set up a drum kit in the front lounge and with Tim whacking the skins and Neil on guitar, they started to write. In an almost primal way they thrashed out jam after jam, throwing in the urgency they had been absorbing from all the punk music they had heard in the UK. Two songs materialised, the first being the first Finn/Finn composition ever titled *Best Friend*. (Best of luck trying to find it!).

A few weeks later in Auckland they all materialised again and rehearsed the new songs. Tim was taken aside to be interviewed for New Zealand's new rock mag, *Rip It Up*. He was asked about the visual side of the new band: 'The whole visual side has taken more and more second place with us. We're far more interested in the music, so I think we'll tone that whole aspect down a little. It's not that we want to change – I think that what we've done has been good quality entertainment and if we didn't do it we might as well change the name of the band because it wouldn't be Split Enz any more ... But at the same time, it's a sort of trap in a way because people expect it of us now. It's quite a tricky dilemma really.

'I've put a lot of work into the band and I just want to take it as far as I can go. The new (songs) are much rockier. We've always told people that our roots are in The Beatles, The Kinks and so on but I think that's becoming more obvious now.'

At the same time, Neil took the opportunity to catch Mark Hough's new band The Suburban Reptiles, who were deeply immersed in the punk ontology. Hough was now calling himself Buster Stiggs.

The tour of New Zealand kicked off in Dunedin on September 7 to full houses. There was an enormous curiosity about the new line-up. *Dizrythmia* had been released two weeks before, which gave the punters time to familiarise themselves with the new batch of songs.

There were those who refused to accept the band without Judd and bemoaned the lack of old material in the show, but they were in the definite minority. Generally, with the memories of the almost staid *Courting The Act* tour of 1977 fading away, the public relished the vigorous presentation. Tim had shaken off his twittering master of ceremonies stance and was more aggressive. He sang from the heart and he projected his own songs as if to press home the belief he had in them.

The musical aspect was also vastly improved, with Neil's guitar playing developing quickly, and Mal and Nigel welding the bottom end to Eddie's keyboard work. While Neil's After Hours material was deemed not suitable for the new up-tempo Enz, he was given a solo slot on the tour and performed on stage alone with his mandolin – as he had done 18 months before as the support act. The song was *Platform Three*. This break in the concert gave the others the chance to retreat side-stage and smoke reefer.

Out front, Raewyn Turner continued to shine lights on everyone's heads in her increasingly talented way, while Geraldene Gillies manned the merchandising stall in the foyer. Buttons were the rage and the public were able to buy plastic spoons and learn to 'play in a day.'

The review in *Rip It Up* summed up the new momentum: 'Split

Enz were this time bouncier and brighter than they've been since the Pantamonium concerts of 1974. Entertainment it was before theatrics, energy before aura.' Aware of Neil's past in After Hours, the reviewer also commented: 'Tim Finn's stage manner is now as evolved as Neil Finn's musical resources are still to be tapped.'

As Enz flew out of Auckland for the Australian leg of the tour, they took with them the satisfaction that they had retained their status in New Zealand as the nation's top draw.

Coupled with that, the single from *Dizrythmia*, *My Mistake*, had spent nine weeks in the national chart and reached number 21, making it the first Enz Single ever to go into the Top 40. While airplay had been reasonable, it was the song's video clip that drew the attention.

In Australia the news was just as good. *My Mistake* was receiving solid airplay in all states and had reached number 12. Complete and utter relief set in as the lads savoured for the first time the reality of their conviction, the conviction that they now had music that would have mass appeal.

Twenty-eight shows were performed from Tasmania to Brisbane to Perth, once again to good houses. As in New Zealand, reaction was positive to the new line-up, the new sound, while in Australia, Noel and Rob conceived and directed a video clip for *Bold As Brass*, which was planned as a follow-up to *My Mistake*. The director of photography (DOP) was Chris Lofven, who went on to DOP many Enz clips in the future.

By mid-October, they were back in the UK where *Dizrythmia* had been released to positive reviews:

'... I play it a lot, it's a great improvement, a step closer to what the Enz are all about, it's confident and it's entertaining. Frenz of the Enz will already have bought it ... you at least should try it.' — *Sounds*.

'... *Dizrythmia* is deliberately more accessible than the wayward *Mental Notes* though Split Enz haven't forsaken their quirky arrangements ... *Dizrythmia* should please those who like *Mental Notes* and intrigue those who didn't.' — *NME*.

Although *My Mistake* had failed to make any impression radiowise in the UK, media approval in the all-important music press further convinced the lads that they were on the right track. With the line-up now finely tuned after hours of rehearsal and 60 odd live shows, they were ready to drive home the *Dizrythmia* album with a 28-date tour of the UK. Hoppy put the tour together with an appropriate start date of November 5. Chrysalis had managed to persuade the BBC's *Sight and Sound* show to feature Split Enz for the full one-hour programme on October 22 which would be beamed live to around 10 million people. The show was a massive promotional coup and gave Enz the chance to foist their new material on an enormous number of people. They threw in *Best Friend* as an appropriate closer.

The next day, Tim and Neil dropped by Abbey Road studios at the invitation of Geoffrey Emerick, who was finding the reaction to *Dizrythmia* much to his liking. He was working in Studio 2 with a chap called Paul McCartney who had made many records in that room over the years. One could say he and his band, The Beatles, had turned Abbey Road's Studio 2 into a shrine of mythical proportions.

The brothers found Emerick taking a break; they were introduced to Paul and Linda and Linda's daughter, Heather. McCartney had seen the *Sight and Sound* show and said he liked *Charlie*. This put Tim into glowing mode, comfortably delirious at his appreciation. Heather mentioned she was going that night to the Roundhouse to see The Stranglers. Tim said he'd like to see them as well so that night they went together. While at the show, talking to Heather, he decided she was a lonely 16-year-old kid and he started humming a song on the spot, turning over in his mind how, on meeting McCartney who was a god, he had found him to be just human. It turned into a song and he called it *Famous People*.

The tour started in Birmingham and from the opening chord of *Bold As Brass* to Noel's ubiquitous spooning climax, the reaction was magic. As it was for the whole tour, although the facilities were a far cry from the carpeted green rooms of the Albert Hall. At one North

England polytech, someone, about to run onstage, had to clamber into the rafters above the stage and leave his nervous pre-performance movement in a cardboard box. There were no rest rooms in sight. In the dark, he hadn't noticed his proximity to Noel's spotlight and during the show Noel, usually completely deadpan, was visibly twitching and squirming as the hot lights cooked up a vicious mist of steaming odours.

Once again the music press was spotlighting the band and, while the stage presentation was still paramount, the urgent vibrant musical delivery was noted.

'Musically, the stopper came at the ending of *True Colours* when the instrumentation unwound through the visitors from outer space syndrome and entered a brief phase of very eerie atmospherics featuring free-form sorties on synth, bass, percussion etc. with Finn lurching around in some anguish from player to player trying to end the number. As the lights dimmed, he stood behind the drummer staring at the audience with a chillingly melancholic look of disbelief on his face, the whole band frozen in a strange set-piece.' — *Sounds*.

The London show at the Roundhouse was particularly triumphant:

'The Split Enz musical variety act extraordinaire. Their ridiculous hairstyles have become somewhat modified so that now, apart from the makeup, they look almost normal ...The warmth of the band has transformed the crowded punters into a seething mass of swaying bodies who sing along to the final almost music hall number. A totally successful evening.' — *Record Mirror*.

At the same show, Phil Judd was in the audience. Shortly after he wrote to Tim and implied that 'if Bob is ever a problem, consider me as a substitute ...'

Tim thought immediately, 'Oh yeah ... Good. Maybe it will be like it was.' He had visited Phil at his house in Surrey and listened to the demo tapes of new songs that Phil was putting together for Hoppy to try to sell to publishers. Hoppy hadn't got his teeth around that one and nothing had happened. A pity because there were some incredible pop songs *So This Is Love* being one of them. And there was *I'm So Up*. He had one that was in the throes of being put together. It was *No Alibi*. He had written the lyrics from a sheet of paper littered as usual with a long list of what he called at the top of the page 'physical ideas'. A selection: '*Stuff and Nonsense; Betrayed cheated; retaliation; stab in the back; clean-cut man; clear-cut case; scapegoat; put up job ...*'

As much as Tim was now struggling to shake off Phil, Phil was facing up to his sense of being the victim. Phil was putting his side of the story down in a cathartic gesture and making it clear that he felt he had been hounded out of the band. His lyrics pointed to a determination to carry on and his writing in Surrey was proof that his creative talents were anything but dulled by the past six months of isolation. In the quiet of Surrey with Amy and Julie, Phil found the energy to write and it was a burst. But nothing was happening with the songs. Phil thought of forming his own group and even came up with some possible names:Judder Band/Philander Band or The Philistines. But the reality quickly dawned on him and he saw his re-entry into Enz as the best vehicle for his new material.

On hearing the demo tape, Tim was enthused. He took the demo to Eddie, who was also impressed with the new short 'n' snappy material. He felt with Phil writing songs that fitted the new Enz format, it made sense to give it a go. Neither Tim nor Ed spoke to the other members about this as they boarded the cross channel ferry to Holland, where they were about to embark on a 15-date tour. On the same day, Chrysalis released *Bold As Brass* as a single and to save your waiting in anticipation – yes, it stiffed.

The Dutch tour was akin to the UK sojourn. Crowds were hefty and the response excellent.

At one of the shows near the end of the tour Phil was there with Hoppy although no one quite knew how or why, particularly Rob Gillies.

'Perhaps he got there in the boot of the car', mused Robert.

By the end, they were ready for some rest and recreation so they hired a boarding house at the holiday resort of Burgen aan Zee, which had closed for the winter. (I know what you're thinking: *The Shining!*) They set all the equipment up in the dining room, surrounded by stacked chairs, tables, and a musty post-summer season air in which they started to rehearse. There was a dull silence in the place as if the echoes of the previous summer should be still rocketing through the now-dead corridors and rooms. Outside the sky was full of mist, and low clouds slid through the tall trees lining the shore. A few days into the stay, the wind came up and a storm raged along the empty beach and whipped up the steel-grey sea.

Tim went to see Rob in his room: 'Rob, we want to have Phil back in the group ... I'm sorry but ...'

'Aha ... it's come full circle,' Rob replied.

Later Hoppy came to talk to Rob and qualify the decision. In one of his lengthy, convoluted explanatory sessions, he said: 'With Phil back in the band, Split Enz will be bigger than The Beatles.'

'Hoppy?' said Rob.

'Yes ...?'

'You're next.'

Rob accepted his dismissal, although he was privately enraged at the stealth and subterfuge that had preceded it. He saw precisely the reason for Phil's presence at the Amsterdam show and the generally quiet, reserved air of the other members over the past few days. He was particularly disappointed that Noel, his old cohort, had said nothing to him.

The next day, under a wild North Sea sky, he and Geraldene drove out of Burgen aan Zee, the others stood at doorways and windows waving goodbye, an almost pathetic gesture in a setting of tempest, dark skies and gusting winds fit for King Lear.

Hoppy and Tim were convinced Phil should be back and Ed was in general agreement.

Noel was dead against the decision but the votes were against him and, in keeping with the continuing fear of confrontation and communication that still crippled the band, did not battle it out with

Tim nor have the heart to warn Rob. Neil, Mal and Nigel were outside the scenario and watched from a distance.

With Rob on his way back to Auckland, Phil appeared out of his hiding place and the band started to rehearse his new material. Tim was particularly excited at the prospect, although when a few days into it a certain number of Phil's songs hadn't worked in the Enz environment, Tim was disappointed. Those that did come together were good, however, and the mood was quite spirited.

With Tim spending his time off with Liz, Phil befriended Neil and they would go jogging in the mornings through the freezing sand dunes. Phil's practical-joker thread was still active, and he and Neil would go upstairs to Tim's room, knock on the door and stand there spooning hot food into their mouths while exclaiming 'Mmmm ... Ooohhh ... Yuummmm ...' Little did they realise that Tim didn't give a shit. Phil's ostentatious attempts to get in on Tim's intense relationship with Liz (using Neil as a willing disciple) fell short. Phil was still in need of the 'boys' club' scenario within the band as had been in the past. But times were changing.

Christmas Day rolled around and they drove off to shout themselves a meal out, but all they could find was a cafe with sausages and soup on the menu. 'This is like Oliver Twist,' Tim thought to himself.

Ed was now more vocal at rehearsals and a submerged bond of suspicion developed between he and Phil. Ed was less inclined to give Phil free rein and would question more. This was new for Phil and a little uncomfortable.

During this adjustment period, Hopkins was in the process of putting together a British tour to kick off in February, and the band returned to London in late January to find houses.

Tim, Liz and Neil checked out an amazing 14th century house in the country where the woman owner would be living for a month while they settled in. She purported to be a brilliant cook. On their first night she served them meat pies that she had bought from the corner store; during the night, her Irish wolf-hounds shat all through the house. It was tentative steps to the bathroom in the morning. She was still in the house three months later so they scarpered.

The British tour was particularly successful, more so than their last jaunt. Playing bigger venues and to better receptions, Split Enz could best be described as 'hot' at that stage in February and March 1978. Noelmania was rampant and Phil's new songs merged well with Tim's *Dizrythmia* catalogue. As well, the twin guitar attack of Neil and Phil gave the group extra body.

London's Roundhouse was again sold out and *Music Week* focused on the re-emergence of Phil: 'Phil Judd's new song, *Play It Strange*, is surely bound for singles chart honours – a classic in the mould of *Whiter Shade Of Pale* in terms of atmospherics.'

The attention on appearances was now fading and Tim, in an interview for *RAM* magazine, was clear: 'We're sick of reading about how we look.' And on the continuing progressive rock comparisons: 'Our main influence is The Beatles and always has been. That's why the King Crimson/Genesis tags have always puzzled me – we're far more interested in songs than they ever were. We're more in the mould of bands like The Kinks, The Move – and I think the next album will prove that once and for all.'

The subject of albums was pertinent. Chrysalis had come to Hopkins and made it clear that it needed a hit single desperately and the next step recording-wise should be with just that in mind. When Hopkins came to the group with this, it was rejected outright. Enz had just completed their most successful tour of the UK, they had plenty of songs to constitute an album and if Chrysalis didn't want to finance an album then it should let the band go. Coupled with this direct plan of attack was the thought at the back of their minds, particularly Ed and Tim's, that they were over £150,000 in the red to Chrysalis and if they were dropped then this debt would disappear.

Chrysalis refused to budge and in March Split Enz found themselves, to their satisfaction, without a UK record company. At the same time, they finally realised that although Hoppy was committed to the band, he was toothless on an industry level, particularly with record companies. The decision was made to fire him. (And yes, Rob was right). This would free the lads to pursue top level English management, which could secure a quality recording contract with a top level English record company. Then they could get into the studio and record a new album while the band was cooking.

By the end of April 1978, Tim and Liz were living in 13 Osborne Road, Palmers Green; Neil and Noel were ensconced way up north at 1 Appletree Dell, Dog Kennel Lane, Chorley Wood; and Ed and Raewyn, Mal and Nigel were in Radlett. Collectively, they were ready to get the whole administrative side of their careers in place, make the album they had always wanted to make and capitalise on their solid foundations in the UK, Australia and New Zealand. By now, they were having little communication with Mushroom in Australia and decided to leave them out of the future decisions. Gudinski was distracted anyway. His promotions company, Evans-Gudinski Associates, was about to collapse and he had plenty to think about on Australian soil. Split Enz were still officially signed to the label so Gudinski would get his cut, and that would be that.

It was not to be. The following months were awash with frustration, wasted efforts and meaningless to-ing and fro-ing between noncommittal managers and record companies. Enz plummeted to financial despair and their whole live momentum was lost. But there would be a sweet irony. Against this sweep of poverty, loneliness and inaction, Enz forged a creative surge. They were about to write and rehearse songs of enormous power, emotion and insight – and no one would hear them.

11

BUT SCREW YOUR COURAGE TO THE STICKING-PLACE

Post-Hopkins and Chrysalis, Tim and Ed set about garnering interest wherever they could. Tim recalled Ray Davies' 'Look me up some time', and he and Ed spent awhile talking to the man at his Konk studios. Davies gave them a lift back to town in his limo and that was that. Tim and Ed decided that his support was encouraging but he would be of no direct help.

They approached a chap at a management company by the name of Ron Wright who thought he was on to a good thing; on hearing of his interest, Tim proclaimed to the others:

'We have to sign with him. He's Mr Wright!' When it came time for the paperwork, Mr Wright tried to cut his partner out of the deal. Unimpressed with his underhand methods, they walked away. Other managers and agents were approached; in fact, anybody they thought could help them. All to no avail. Demo tapes were sent out to record companies and nothing was heard. The band immersed itself in a complacency that masked the reality of life as a group without a record company or manager.

The weeks started to roll by. With Hopkins gone, the communications with Mushroom deteriorated to nothing. While the band was still officially signed to the label, Gudinski had reduced his flow of financial support while he assessed just what Enz planned to do next. He knew it would be foolish to embark on the recording of a new album with no UK management in place. He'd been there twice already.

Consequently, all of them were on the dole and feeling the pinch ... especially Phil who was in dire straits. Isolated by virtue of his country residence in Surrey and facing financial ruin, he had no option but to leave the band. This time it would be his final exit. He rang Tim who could do nothing. Immersed in the searching and planning for managers and record companies, Tim had no answers. He had found Phil's contribution of new material a boon and had been hoping that he could stick it out, but realised it was impossible.

Shortly after, Phil returned to New Zealand where he joined the ranks of the Suburban Reptiles. At last, Mark Hough was playing with Phil Judd and it wasn't long before vinyl was released. Their debut single, *Saturday Night Stay At Home*, credited to Hough, featured a mass of Juddsy's electric guitar.

During this time of empty promises and silence, Tim and Neil had an unbelievable writing spree. For weeks on end, flat broke, with no work and winter hanging on, they would spend hours in their respective flats writing and writing and writing. The collection of material is staggering. At nights, while Liz worked in Soho, Tim sat at the piano in Palmers Green. During this period he wrote about 20 songs. *I See Red, Semi-Detached, Hermitt McDermitt, She Got Body She Got Soul, Next Exit* ... However, there was a strong subtext to all these songs – Phil Judd. Tim was still unable to shake off his subconscious feelings for him, which poured out onto the pages of his lyric book.

In essence, he was sensing Phil's isolation and these songs were a response to that. He wanted to reach out and help him; despite any evidence to the contrary, he believed Phil to be an innocent victim, more sinned against than sinning. In many respects, he matched Phil's own view of the situation as if there had been some telepathic synergy. He had a shining image, a memory that he held on to with a grim determination.

Neil was also on a roll. Finally, with the confidence to present his own material, he would offer songs and half-finished pieces during rehearsals at Radlett. *Carried Away, Evelyn* and *Holy Smoke*.

Two songs were completed with help from Tim: *Give It A Whirl* and *Mind Over Matter*. While Neil's material was more narrative and less introverted than Tim's, his lyrical command was improving and his melodies were starting to be more hooky. As well as his own stuff, he and Noel would jam away in their flat. They called themselves the 'Ninnies' and would have Ninnies jams. At times the others would join in. Presumably if they jammed when pissed, it was a Ninnie knees-up?

As April rolled out, the financial situation suddenly plummeted. Mal had gone to the dole office for his obligatory interview:

'Mr Green, it seems we have a vacancy for you at the Neasden launderette ironing smocks. Start date is next Thursday.'

'Sorry, I can't start then I've got band rehearsals.'

'I see, Mr Green, you bludger. Just who exactly is in this band of yours?'

'Oh ...'

Just a week after Mal's faux pas, the members of Split Enz had their dole cut off. No more jellied eels, pie and mash down at the greasy spoon. Desperate situation! The isolation that had been slowly threatening them now closed in. Tim decided that sitting around watching his already slender cohorts waste and wither was not in his best interests (he was surviving on Liz' fat wage packets from garment divestment), so he wrote a pleading letter to Ray Columbus in New Zealand. Ray had been one of the judges on the *New Faces* show in 1973 and had gone against the general negative stance of his fellow adjudicators, claiming that he felt Split Enz had the potential to achieve international success.

This thought was still logged in his head when, as chairman of the Projects Committee of the Queen Elizabeth II Arts Council (a council of the NZ Government providing assistance to the arts), he took the QEII chairman, Hamish Keith, and Executive Director, Michael Volkerling, aside and read them the letter in which Tim, on behalf of Enz, requested some (any) financial assistance. They all agreed instantly that Enz should be funded and the next day, sweeping aside the usual red tape, Columbus made an impassioned plea to the Council board for the grant to be given.

It was passed unanimously; the Council's generosity was noted in the hallowed chambers of Parliament when a backbencher applauded them for their quick foresight. Enz were moving towards national treasure status! Very soon, $5,000 was winging its way to London, allowing the skinny ranks of Enz to fatten slightly. In essence, mind you, they were still broke.

In the nick of time, one Barry Dickens, an agent who had been sitting on their tape for a while, came back to them with the offer of a management contract. His lack of management experience didn't really matter as they had no other offers on the table.

On May 15, Tim wrote home: 'Well today ... we did it! We signed with Barry Dickens ... it's with a mixture of relief, excitement and a little trepidation, that we face the next step. The trepidation is based on the twice-bitten-thrice-shy factor but the overwhelming feeling is one of great gladness. I really think we have done well to come through it all ... Now all we have to do is find a record company and a record producer.'

Enz quickly got into forge-ahead mode and booked time at a small studio in Luton called Quest, with engineer Dave Cook. As well as developing a competitive taste for pool, they recorded around 15 tracks. With the management problem out of the way and a batch of songs of which they were particularly proud, Split Enz put down music of brute force.

Following months of frustration and adversity, with a collective will and spirit of enormous proportions, and an almost natural sense of being up against the odds, they found the drive.

This internal vigour was enhanced by the influence of the punk movement. As the new wave artists such as Elvis Costello, the Jam, the Clash and so on started to give punk a more melodic perspective over its driving musical foundation, so too did Split Enz in corollary. Having mastered the melodic aspects of pop music over the past five years, Enz shook off the meandering, stop-start arrangements of the past. Mal, Nigel, Ed, and Neil found themselves, with Tim's encouragement, driving the songs at full tit. Neil would send his guitar picks spinning out across the studio floor as he tried to match Tim's cries for more speed; his playing full, beefy and adept. The others were amazed at how much he had improved over the past 12 months. On top of this rush of energy, Noel relished his role as basher extraordinaire. He whacked, thrashed, bonged, and shouted along.

With the tapes, now known as the 'Rootin' Tootin' Luton' tapes, safe in their possession, Enz had the ammunition for Dickens to secure that magic record deal. But it was not to be.

Within a month of signing Split Enz, Dickens was gone. The band, in their naivety, had expected Dickens to not only find them a record company, producer and live work but pay out wages on a regular basis in the meantime. Dickens had parted with some cash but very soon it dawned on him that he was looking at a financial vacuum cleaner and he closed it all down. The band, sensing his lack of managerial experience would lead to just another protracted waiting period, weren't overly perturbed.

Split Enz were back to square one. A week later, Ed called a meeting of the band at Radlett.

'We have no choice, whakkos. I think we should get Hoppy back and we should go back to Gudinski and get a new deal. At least that way, we'll get a commitment and have something happening.'

They talked it over; it was agreed that Tim would write to Michael Gudinski and ask him to come over and sort out the recording situation. As far as Hopkins went, they were split. Noel and Neil were most unimpressed with the prospect. But they decided that if Hoppy could just get them enough work to pay for their flights home, it would be satisfactory. Hoppy was contacted and came back to the fold.

Shortly after, in early August, a Manchester fan, Brandon Liam, offered them some time in his recording studio. He had an 18-year-old engineer who was a whizz. His name was David Tickle.

'Oh yeah ... what a fuckwit,' went everybody. That's just what they did. But the studio time was free, and on the day it became immediately obvious that this engineer kid was brilliant, wringing big drum sounds and a fat rhythm track for *Next Exit*. *I See Red* was tried but didn't click and was left. During the sessions Tickle mentioned that he had applied for the job as head engineer at Ringo Starr's Startling Studios. 'Is that right?' thought the lads.

By the time the next session at Manchester was due, Tickle had secured the Startling job and was producing Sham 69. He contacted Ed and said: '... Sham 69 are taking the weekend off. Come up here and finish the songs.'

Startling Studios are set on Tittenhurst Park near Virginia Waters near Ascot near all sorts of places. Tittenhurst had been John Lennon's home from 1967 to 1971, and he sold it to Ringo Starr on his departure to New York. Lennon recorded *Imagine* there, and as Tim and the boys drove down the long driveway to the house, the occasion loomed large with opportunity. The famous Lennon grand piano was still there. (Google images will take you there too). With Nigel sitting on the lawn, Mal in the hallway, the others in the small studio, and Tickle directing the proceedings with confidence, the tracks went down. (Yes – Nigel was playing bass while sitting on the lawn).

Unfortunately, they were unable to practise their pool as Sham 69 had whacked all the pool balls into the trees with golf clubs.

'Dickheads ...' said Noel.

Back in Auckland, I had settled back in. I was in a band with brother Geoffrey. We were called Citizen Band. One day I opened the letterbox and there was a letter from Tim with an English stamp on it.

'We've been doing some serious recording of late. We used an engineer called David Tickle and he's something of a boy wonder in that he's 18 and has already worked on quite a few successful albums (The Knack & Blondie). He's very good at getting sounds and maybe we've found the guy we've been looking for. The recording has been going well: a short version of *Next Exit* ... and a socked-out version of *I See Red* which a lot of people reckon to be a single. We'll try and get that one out before we start the album. Michael Gudinski comes over next week to discuss things and if we can squeeze a good deal out of him, we should get the money to do an album. We've booked Startling from September 19 for just that, otherwise, my time is spent jogging, reading, writing, visiting, eating, sleeping, gnashing, gnawing, and weeping with the odd chuckle here and there and, despite the setbacks, a growing determination governs all. The "scene" is lulled at present and there is more than ever a gap for us.

'Hoppy is back amongst it. Dickens was indeed a turd posing as a stool, and after six months of looking around for Mr Right, we decided better the devil you know. I mean with Hoppy at least we get to direct things. He was always good at some things and the others are the same as ever.'

Tim sounded bright and the tone was positive. He was shaking off his frustrations and moving on, and Liz was there right behind him. Her support was always solid and she backed every move Split Enz made. And while the yin and yang of their own relationship was steeped in a little more mystery and tension than either of them might have wanted, they were hanging in there.

Gudinski arrived and met with the lads. Tim's letter to him had struck a chord; he was happy to have Enz wanting to talk to him about a future together. To his credit, after watching an enormous amount of money fritter away over the past few years, he still believed that the band had the core talent to pull off international success, although he sensed quickly just how close the band were to being torn apart by the lack of industry support. He committed Mushroom to another album as well as advancing money for wages against future royalties.

At long last, after months of scrimping, Split Enz were receiving regular money: £35 a week each. If only the English made prawn sandwiches.

Gudinski thought the album had to be done with an experienced producer and recorded at a top-class studio, if the record was to have a real chance of being picked up. Consequently, when the lads pushed for the album to be done with Tickle at Startling, Gudinski wouldn't buy it. Tickle was an unknown. While reluctant to let the Tickle contact slip, Enz went with Gudinski's directive and started to consider other producers. Gudinski returned to Australia with the master tape of *I See Red* in his suitcase and it was immediately scheduled for release in Australasia in November. *Hermitt McDermitt* and *Message Boy*, from the Luton tapes, would be on the B-side. Gudinski put up money for a film clip and in late October a video was filmed for *I See Red*, which summed up 1978 in a quick three minutes of energy. Like caged animals let loose after months of solitary confinement, the performance on the *I See Red* video still stands today as one of Enz' most infectious. There is an incredible unity there ... a cohesive and monolithic sense of delivery.

Hoppy was ferreting around trying to find work and putting the word out to producers.

He had managed to secure an appearance for September 13 at the *Time Out* magazine 10th birthday bash. The show went well, but yielded little tangible results. Otherwise there was nothing, apart from a request from New Zealand to return in January and play at an outdoor festival. They sat on that one for a while as other more pressing matters were at hand.

The real problems were just the usual: who was going to produce the album and which record company in England would release it? By mid-October, there were two producers lined up: Eddie Leonetti and Mallory Earl, both Americans. In the end, the job went to

Mallory Earl, who was fanatical about working with the band and who pumped up Hopkins and Tim.

He talked about their 'being the next Beatles' (a recurring theme it seems), and his time as a tape op on some Hendrix and Fat Mattress sessions was somehow enough of a credential to seal the deal. He was available from early December and time was booked at The Manor studios.

During one of his many days off in Palmers Green, Tim was interviewed by *Rip It Up*: 'I think we've been out on a limb in the UK. We don't see ourselves as part of any new wave movement ... It's certainly helped more than hindered though, in that there's an emphasis on new things that there wasn't say a few years ago. When we first hit England, punk was just starting and there was a desperate need for the public to be reassured that rock 'n' roll still had some life in its veins. Hence the return to a very basic, raw rock with an awful lot of energy ... The management hassles made us more aggressive in some ways. You have to take note of what's happening around you, business wise, and get the best deal you can ... You've got to go through it all. We've always been totally ambitious in Split Enz. We're writing the music, we're deciding what happens on stage.'

In preparation for the album, the lads booked the month of November at Rockfield rehearsal studios near Monmouth in Wales. Once again the band clicked; with album sessions booked the mood was optimistic and charged, and they spent the four-week period in a positive state. Nigel would stay up till all hours of the night (into the morning) piecing together the best takes from the various rehearsal sessions on tape and moulding the songs into shape.

He would then play them back the next day and provide a tee for that day's first hole. Nigel was now deeply immersed in the Enz way and had brought his own style to bear on the music.

His melody and rhythmic stability made a quite unique combination. And each member of the band played over 600 games of pool during their one-month stay.

Once again, Tim had found his quiet night at Palmers Green to be productive and new songs were rehearsed. *Stuff and Nonsense, Master Plan* and *The Roughest Toughest Game in the World*. (A bunch of key indicators if ever there were).

Eddie had also found the past months of waiting a creative opportunity. He presented his *Marooned* instrumental at Rockfield, as well as two other pieces to which Tim contributed lyrics and the odd melodic interjection. One was *Abu Dhabi*, the other *Frenzy*.

Mallory Earl would come along to the odd jubilant rehearsal and lavish glowing praise on the lads, which was lapped up. While they had little idea of what the results might be with this loquacious West Coaster, they decided that, with the songs they had in the pot, this new album stood a real chance.

Once again, it was not to be. In the lap of luxury at the Manor Studios (where they were able to utilize a full size pool table), the sessions started slowly. After a few days of rhythm tracks, the only one in the can was *Master Plan*. The songs that had been recorded on the Rootin' Tootin' Luton sessions were tried but virtually all failed to match the intensity and spontaneity of the originals. One by one they fell by the wayside, to be overtaken by the newer tracks like *Frenzy, Roughest*, and so on. While these might have been bettering the sound of the originals, they weren't bettering the feel. After a couple of weeks, Tim, in particular, was showing signs of stress from the less than expected results. As had always been the case, Tim's irritations were contagious and Eddie suggested he keep them to himself.

'Go write your own fucking hit singles,' was the reply, and Tim disappeared for a while.

After three periods at Luton, Startling and Rockfield, where the band had performed to an astonishing standard, the opportunity had now arrived to do it just one more time and have a brilliant album to release, It failed to transpire. Once again, Split Enz had bumbled through, failing to choose a producer with any real careful thought. Why they had not insisted that Frenzy be recorded at Startling is still a mystery to them all. They knew what could be achieved there. But they failed to convince Gudinski of this.

By mid-January, the album was in the can with only one song, *Give It A Whirl*, being regarded as a possible single. Copies were sent to the various UK record companies who had shown interest and were waiting to hear the finished product – amongst them Virgin, Warners and Nick Mobbs' new label, Automatic. Mobbs had been the most interested throughout the latter half of the year. In the end, it meant little as the album was turned down by everyone.

This time the cover was not in the Noel domain. Raewyn Turner showed her talent for the paintbrush and oiled a New Zealand landscape, featuring a portrait of the boys in the foreground. And some sheep as well.

Hoppy had confirmed the appearance of Enz at the Nambassa Festival in Waihi on January 28 so the boys now had a free trip home. They drove back to London from the Manor and packed their bags. With around $8,000 worth of debt still hovering over their heads, Ed bravely wrote to all creditors and suggested they direct their vitriol at him. He might have thought twice about this had he known he would be arrested at Heathrow airport on departure date. Swift talking saw him catch the flight.

On the day he and the others left Radlett, a Pakistani family moved in to find the place flooded from burst pipes. The others too closed down their flats and they boarded the plane for Auckland not sure exactly what they were in for, or if they would ever come back.

1978 had been a year in which their development in the UK stalled and slid back down the drain. There was not one record released in the UK the entire year. Australia and New Zealand had only seen the *I See Red* single; in Australia, this was starting to gather airplay and the news was warmly received by the intrepid minstrels. In New Zealand, nothing.

Giving Chrysalis and Hopkins the heave after their successful February tour highlighted the exaggerated status Split Enz felt they had; or, more to the point, their naivety in concluding that they had the chance to secure top-flight management and record companies

because of it. Essentially, Ed and Tim didn't have the energy or negotiating skills to get the good deals.

And the financial destitution just ground them down, until they
had no option but to call back Hopkins and re-acquaint themselves
with Mushroom.

But against all this dreary administrative confusion, we must
assess the creative output: there is no doubt, with the tapes as proof,
that in 1978 Split Enz achieved a musical high.

The Rootin' Tootin' Luton tapes and the Tickle Startling sessions,
coupled with the hours and hours of tapes from Rockfield, are
witness to this magnificent era. As a unit, their struggles and setbacks
gave them incredible strength and they bonded together as one
powerhouse unit, resolutely refusing to give up.

If ever, sometime in the future, they were to achieve success on a
grand scale, then 1978 would have been the year that set it in motion
on the wheel of fate. No doubt. It was just sad that they had to return
to New Zealand and pretend they had an album they were happy
with. Because they weren't.

12

PERSEVERANCE KEEPS HONOUR BRIGHT

The Nambassa Festival of 1979 was held on sprawling fields a few miles from Waihi on New Zealand's East Coast. While the Great Ngaruawahia Music Festival had been little more than a large mass of people listening to music through large sound systems and showering in a communal tent, Nambassa was a defined alternative event.

Completely devoid of hamburgers and hot dogs, the fare was of the brown rice and tofu variety; while the hippie fashions of the early seventies had faded somewhat, there was still a general flow and swish to everything with accompanying wafts of incense. The Hare Krishna group were giving away free food: Hare Bol would traipse through the dust-laden tent cities around 7.00 am, chanting 'Hare Bol' to loud cries of derision. During the day the tramping of bare feet kicked up a dust haze, and a trail of local bands came and went on the big stage. There were no dressing rooms or caravans, and fingers and throats glued with dust and sweat as their owners threw out songs to the moving shifting mass.

By now, there were two threads of musical style in the country, battling with each other.

The younger bands were nodding heavily to the 'new wave', although within that infrastructure was a myriad of trends from hardcore punk to lightweight pop to power pop to mop and pop kettle. All of this shambolic adventure resting still and intent on a reasonably credible and contemporary base. (Get my drift?) The number of New Zealand artists performing in the disco mould was virtually nil. The other side of the coin were the acts that continued from the early to mid-seventies, still entrenched in musical expertise and minimal display. Only the likes of Dragon had taken an r'n'b base and added a performing style they could call their own.

Fashion-wise, the long hair, beards and beads were starting to look decidedly humorous although the legacy of the Tim Shadbolt years was still prevalent in the incense-laced house trucks and buses that parked off in the distance. But they were outnumbered. Whether the organisers thought such an event might have a uniform appeal in terms of lifestyles and alternative forms was irrelevant – no one cared about brown rice. They drove in with crates of beer and tolerated the bland food. They all came for some loud music and a chance to score.

Two days before their scheduled Saturday night headline slot, Enz set up their equipment in a hall in Waihi for rehearsals. The next morning they turned up for a bash to find the hall burned to the ground and $30,000 worth of amps, gats, percussion and so on reduced to ash. Noel suggested they rehearse a cappella. Ed scoured the ash and rubble for remains of his precious keyboards and found nothing. Tim scratched his head. Neil got on the phone – 'we need gear!' Theft followed by arson was suspected, as Eddie's metal keyboard frame should have been poking out of the cinders.

Hopkins put the word out and, in a matter of hours, Split Enz had a full complement of gear courtesy of a number of bands in town for the festival. As was usually the case when Enz faced some calamity (by then a regular feature of their history), they steeled themselves and come Saturday night, took the stage with a hook-or-by-crook stance. Citizen Band were booked to play later that night so I was there watching the proceedings. Eddie's keyboard rack was being nailed together out of bits of two-by-four seconds before they walked on stage and the dust was all over them.

The 45,000 punters sitting in the dust out front knew this was something special. Decked out in a new set of costumes, Enz once again summoned their resources and threw it out with style. They took the crowd up with *I See Red* and took them low with *Stuff and Nonsense*; crazed them with *Frenzy* and made them laugh with *True Colours*.

Back in Auckland for a few days before flying to Oz, Tim was asked by John Dix of *Rip It Up* whether the time would come when the band concentrated solely on the music.

'Look, we don't concentrate on anything but the music. The costumes are just the cream in the coffee ... but I don't think there'll come a time when we'll say we're not going to have an image anymore. If that happens it just wouldn't be Split Enz.'

When Mr Dix asked him about *Frenzy*, the veneer was thin: 'We're very happy with it. I think it sounds better than our previous albums. Also, it's got 12 tracks, which is good because the others only had nine.'

While the Nambassa show had charged those that were there, New Zealand at large was still ignorant of Enz' new music – radio stations had steered clear of *I See Red*. FM Radio was still five years away and the AM relics were pumping out disco on high rotate. Toppermost of the poppermost was Rod Stewart's *Do You Think I'm Sexy?* In every New Zealand city there were dance classes for the New York Shuffle, and disco clubs had opened up hither and thither with dance floors showered in flashing coloured lights. The guitar-driven energy of *I See Red* was deemed unsuitable against this current trend.

As Enz flew into Australia for their 26-date tour for Premier Artists, the situation was quite different. With a strong FM rock base, Australian stations were on to the record and the single was charting. This posed a problem for Mushroom, who found itself with a potential hit single and an album about to be released that didn't have the song on it. Tres sillois. Enz had decided that because *I See Red* wasn't recorded at The Manor and sounded a little rough, it would stay off the album. Unfortunately, they hadn't envisaged it would be a hit although Eddie, months before, did have a hunch that the single would set them up back home. Edward Rayner complemento. Consequently, when Frenzy was released in Australia on February 19, it was decided by the band and Mushroom that *I See Red* would be added to future pressings.

Five days after landing back in Melbourne, the lads were on the road and there was no looking back. Australia had certainly not forgotten the band and they had excellent houses everywhere they went, from Newcastle to Tamworth, Sydney to Byron Bay. The consistent airplay of *I See Red* continued to focus attention on the band and the single slowly climbed the national charts to number 12. Halfway through the tour Mushroom announced that Frenzy was gold with sales of 20,000 copies.

Even though the band had only played twice in the past 12 months, the intensive rehearsals in Radlett and Rockfield coupled with a new intensity of purpose found them blending consummate musicianship with a new, streamlined and energetic stage show. Just what punters were after in 1979.

At the completion of the tour, Mushroom found the sales of Frenzy and the general industry 'vibe' on the band to be to its satisfaction, and moved to schedule another album towards the end of the year. Enz quickly seconded the motion and it was passed unanimously. Someone brought the gavel down.

This time the band were adamant that they take up where they had left off with David Tickle. Gudinski, now convinced from the success of *I See Red*, approached Tickle's management.

Tickle was busy engineering for Mike Chapman on the Blondie sessions but would be available later in the year. Enz would have to wait. Waiting, however, was anathema to the guys and they were unhappy. The Australasian tour had reintroduced them to Australia but failed to swell the bank balance. Eddie was still under duress from UK creditors and the prospect of paying high rents for accommodation while they had no work was ... shall we say, a piss-off.

The decision was then made to return to New Zealand, tour the country again, settle in for a bit, rehearse, write, find a new manager, and return for a major tour of Australia. And that is exactly what they did.

Ian Magan's Concert Promotions company put together the *Whirlwind* tour of New Zealand and on March 29 in Timaru they set about confirming the positive rumours that had spread through the country after the Nambassa show. The reaction was uniformly positive:

'Gone are the epics ... Split Enz have moved with the times and are now closer to being classified as a mainstream rock band than at any time in the past. *Frenzy* and the all out, danceable, live Split Enz spells the beginning of a new era for the band. I think it's their best yet.' — *Rip It Up*.

Climaxing at their old haunt, His Majesty's Theatre in Auckland, to two full houses, Enz sealed the lid on the past. With a now huge catalogue of material to draw from, the shows featured little pre-*Dizrythmia* material; on the *Whirlwind* tour it was only *True Colours, Maybe* and *Time For A Change*. At His Majesty's I was invited to play bass with them on the latter.

The previous year had shown them the strength they had in themselves – a strength of conviction and creativity – and, now with the continued support in Australasia, they realised that they had lost nothing on the live circuit. In fact, with the success of *I See Red* in Australia, they were positioned well to take the whole country by storm. New Zealand still harboured a virile core of fans but *I See Red* had failed to expand that.

Frenzy, while eventually maintaining a chart slot for 18 weeks, only peaked at number 13. *Dizrythmia* had peaked at three. The reviews for *Frenzy* were varied: Gordon Campbell in the *The Listener* described the lads as 'hysterical spinsters'; *Rip It Up* said, 'If there's a better New Zealand record I'd like to know about it.' But there was still a general consensus that Split Enz had yet to make that one major album that wasn't faulted by weak production. And they were running out of time.

Martin Phillips (The Chills)

In 1977, the only rock concert I had been to was The Hues Corporation before I found myself alone – at fourteen easily the youngest person at Dunedin's Regent Theatre – in an audience of Ian Anderson's in army surplus greatcoats waiting to see Split Enz on their Courting The Act *tour. Some of the hippy women looked at me in a concerned and motherly way while I nervously wondered how strange the band would really be and what I would do if one of them came off-stage towards me.*

Split Enz finally came on in something like long white robes and did a cleverly choreographed aimless wandering about the stage, arriving at their instruments on cue and WHAM! The first chords of Stranger Than Fiction. *Such glorious volume for young ears. I was transfixed and spellbound. Songs like* Another Great Divide, Time For A Change *and later it was time for that old* Nightmare Stampede. *At some stage the singer introduced the rest of the band finishing with himself ... and I'm Tim – full of vim ... and vigour!' It was a memorable show and a true revelation that this band were as good as any of the overseas music I was listening to at the time.*

After the show I tried to meet the band but got too nervous and ended up pulling gaffer tape off the stage for the crew. The next Split Enz tour I went backstage and got autographs and asked Noel Crombie a question and made him speak. But it was the following tour, backstage again, where I had a real learning experience. A small group of us diehard fans surrounded Tim and one guy asked him if he could remember his name from the previous tour. When Tim did, it was open season. Each of us in turn asked the poor man if he knew our names but it wasn't until my turn came and I saw the bemused looks on the faces of the other Enz members and Tim looking concerned as he rattled off random names that I realised he was making it up. That moment made quite an impact. He could have more easily just told us all to bugger off as I know many others would have done, but some sense of loyalty to his fans made him go through with the whole charade.

To this day I feel the only album to at least partially capture the strange and unique surreal qualities of New Zealand was Mental Notes *and its disturbing cover art but over the years Split Enz became many different things. The audience changed – I was definitely no longer their youngest Dunedin fan. Their epic songs, tempo changes and crazy rhythms later inspired me to compose tunes of my own like* Green-Eyed Owl *and* Dream By Dream *and in 1984, my group, The Chills, supported them on their final* Enz With A Bang *tour of New Zealand. I never once saw a less than inspiring Split Enz show but for sheer majesty and imagination it is those early concerts that will always remain among my most treasured musical memories.*

By mid-April, the New Zealand tour was over. With 10 weeks before the start of their extensive Australian tour, they decided to camp out in Auckland and write, rehearse and do as much promotion as Festival Records wanted. That didn't amount to much. Festival didn't have much of a handle on the band, although the lack of airplay didn't make it easy for them.

Enz didn't relate to the Festival general manager and there were murmurings of trying to get Gudinski to allow them to shift to another distributor. There was still the release of *Give It A Whirl* to come, so they decided to see what happened with that.

One aspect of their careers couldn't wait and it was decided unanimously that Hoppy would be released from the payroll. While his history with the band was one of loyalty and commitment, the lads felt that this wasn't matched with results – and in the cold, bleak winter of Auckland, 1979, they were still unsure of what the future held. This continuing uncertainty was rubbing them raw; they wanted new blood, exactly as they had done 12 months before.

They said goodbye to Hoppy (presumably Rob Gillies was aware of this) and contacted Gudinski with regard to finding a tour manager to handle their affairs in Australia.

They then split off in various directions, gathering at Harlequin Studios for regular demo sessions. Various new songs were brought along and shaped up by the band. Neil had one that was considered suitable as the next single titled *Things*. The punk syndrome was now fully operational in Auckland and Enz were pretty much held in low regard by the vocal short haired rock 'n' rollers for their past theatrical meanderings.

It seemed that the powerhouse Split Enz unit of 1979 wasn't going to be allowed the privilege of a fresh start. Tim had written another ballad at his Titirangi base. Juddsy was settled back in town and, on the dissolution of The Suburban Reptiles a few months before, had formed a three piece with Mark Hough on drums and Bones Hillman, also from the Reptiles, on bass. They were calling themselves The Swingers. Tim was by now in a state of real frustration: again they had no management, and the failure of *I See Red* in New Zealand was preventing the group's expansion in this country. He rang Phil one night and was told by Julie that Phil wouldn't talk to him. That night he wrote *I Hope I Never*.

Give It A Whirl was released in late May and failed to penetrate. The toppermost of the poppermost was ABBA's *Chiquitita*. This lack of single success ran parallel, as usual, to continued success on the stage. Flush with the success of the *Whirlwind* tour, Ian Magan put together a short three-centre tour in late May with shows in Auckland, Palmerston North and Wellington. Once again the houses were full with an added attraction. For the duration, Enz were supported by The Swingers.

Tim may have been moved to write a song as a reaction to Phil's reluctance to speak to him in Titirangi, but the moment was now forgotten; he was happy to give Juddsy the opportunity to spread his new music.

Duncan Campbell from *Rip It Up* was in the crowd: 'The audience gave the Swingers a warm reception. A very promising debut and a welcome return of one of New' Zealand's most uncompromising and most distinctive artists ... Split Enz could do no wrong ... A grand farewell it was indeed as the Super Six give it a whirl once more before winging it away again.'

I was in the audience too, and found Phil's pop songs quite remarkable. His time with the Suburban Reptiles had given his material an appealing mix of melody and edge. Very promising stuff. Mark Hough and Bones Hillman were a perfect, understated foil. Both had rollicking, rolling styles that wormed around Phil's craggy chords.

This trip was followed by a few more weeks in waiting mode. Then, with five days left before the start of the Australian tour, a one-off birthday gig was arranged post-haste at Auckland's Mainstreet club. It was June 25, 1979; Tim was turning 27, and there was a full house of course.

Give It A Whirl had by now officially stiffed; the band had decided that *Frenzy* was over and resolved to get into the studio back in Australia to produce a one-off single themselves.

Neil's *Things* was chosen.

On their arrival in Australia, Michael Gudinski met up with the band. He was setting up November as the month for the new album sessions with David Tickle. In the meantime Split Enz had a few months of work lined up courtesy of his 'Harbour Premier Agency'. For this it was decided that they needed a tour manager in place. A young man was recommended by Sam Righi (manager of the Sydney Harbour/Premier office). His name was Nathan Brenner.

Nathan Brenner and Michael Gudinski first met as kids at school. In time, they went their separate ways but with Gudinski's entry into the music business they met up again. Gudinski threw Brenner odd jobs as a 'bum boy', selling drinks at a few dances and taking photos at concerts (Brenner was subsidising his Bachelor of

Arts degree from behind a camera). He was, in fact, hired to shoot Split Enz at the Reefer Cabaret in 1975. Gudinski then put him in as manager for Dave Warner, who had a hit with *Suburban Boy*. A while later Warner and Brenner parted company and it was then Sam Righi suggested he shoot for the Enz tour managing position. Gudinski thought it was a good idea; the band met Brenner, and he was in.

They kicked off a seven-week tour in Canberra and, once again, the crowds were packed in – although it was very much a virulent cult status that was keeping them aloft Brenner had to come to grips quickly with the band's debt burden. His attempts to book equipment, travel and so on were met with demands for debt clearance arrangements and his personal guarantee against further credit. He also had to come to grips with Tim's high standards of stage presentation. At the third show, at Sydney University, Tim asked Brenner to lead them out onto the stage because it was pitch black and no one could see where they were going.

He did this and when they got there, Tim pushed him off stage into the audience where he landed on his back.

Tim's later reasoning to Brenner was: 'It just wouldn't have been very professional to have you up there when the lights went up.' There was no way Enz were going to be caught with their tour manager on stage. Brenner, however, was a whole new step up as far as the band were concerned, as he encouraged the lads to stand back from themselves and fully believe they had it in them to crack Australia wide open. Here was a new objective voice, a new face, and as the tour wound on money was set aside for the UK and Australian debts. By the end of the tour, they were in the black.

This six-week stretch was the uplift that the band needed. Australia was still obsessed with seeing Split Enz live and flocked to the concerts. I happened to be in Sydney on July 10 and saw their show at the Pitt Street Gardens. With a huge core of fans mouthing every word, it became clear to me just how much the phase-two unit had achieved. The Split Enz of Judd, Crowther et moi was an open and shut case; the Enz of 1979, while a tangential embodiment of the original, had developed a musical intensity all their own. Eddie had spent his early days displaying an incredible technical and melodic expertise allowing, at times, his majestic arrangements to work outside the rest of the band. By 1979 he was in there amongst it – striding, surging to an extraordinary extent. There was magic in the air again and it seemed obvious that with this level of public support and the musical expertise of the band, it was just a matter of time.

Immediately following their final date in Hurstville, the lads booked into Richmond Recorders in Melbourne. They recorded *Things* as a single, with David Cohen engineering. For a while it was a toss-up as to whether in fact the proposed B-side, *Semi-Detached* from the 1978 Luton sessions, should be the A-side. But they stuck with the original plan, and *Things* was scheduled for release on October 1.

While in Melbourne for the sessions, Tim cranked out a couple of songs in the confines of his Diplomat hotel room in St Kilda. Charged with the successes of the tour, Nathan Brenner's encouragement and glad to be free of the futile waiting game he had been playing in Auckland for those endless weeks, Tim wrote in a spirited fashion with one eye on the singles charts. Songs popped up like *Shark Attack*.

He was piecing together another song from a scribbled list of possible phrases, lines and so on in his book from which he could mould the verses. He may even have called them 'physical ideas'. A selection: 'I'm gonna try and trace; I'm training my telescope; the crackle of the radio; between us there's too much space; I was a wireless whizz kid' and so on. It wasn't long before he had the whole song in place and he called it *Poor Boy*.

Tiring of writing on guitar, the young buck booked a rehearsal room down the way and hired a piano. It was delivered by an attractive female roadie by the name of Snow and the muse drifted in his open window. That song was called *How Can I Resist Her*.

Soon after, the band gathered together under the direction of

Noel for the video shoot of *Things*. In a similar fashion to the one set, brilliant dips for *Bold As Brass* and *I See Red*, *Things* succeeded on a powerful eye-to-eye performance from Neil with Tim hovering close by. With moments of intensity and humour, the clip enhanced the song greatly. However, it made little difference: the record set off on a trip to nowhere and plummeted out of sight. The toppermost of the poppermost at the time was something like Patrick Hernandez' *Born To Be Alive*. (Google it).

The record label spelled the B-side *Semi-Detached* as *Semi-Datached*; perhaps an omen that no one was expecting much out of the exercise.

In New Zealand, *Things* wasn't released at all. By now, Enz had decided they wanted out from Festival Records; when *I See Red* finally did chart in June (seven months after release) it entered the national chart at 43 and dropped out again the next week. This didn't equate to the ecstatic response the song was getting at each and every live show. Something wasn't adding up and it was deemed to be Festival. As Mushroom were contracted to Festival in New Zealand, it took a long impassioned plea from Tim in the form of a handwritten letter to the Festival Records managing director in Sydney, Alan Healy (Tim and his letters!) before they were given the go ahead to look for another record company in New Zealand. It was decided to just let *Things* fall through the cracks.

After the *Things* sessions, the band travelled to Sydney where they settled in, Tim and Neil, with Liz and Neil's partner Sharon, moved into a top-floor flat on New South Head Road, Rose Bay. Neil had met Sharon through Paul Pattie during an Auckland stopover and they were intent on pursuing each other. During the day, Liz and Sharon would take off to work; Tim and Neil would write. Separately. Occasionally, they would give each other titles then split off to their respective rooms and strum something out. One title that Tim gave Neil was *What's The Matter With You?* Neil was happy with that. Then *Missing Person* arrived. Another was unfinished and he wasn't sure about it. The verse seemed okay but he felt the chorus could probably do with some work. He sang it to Tim one afternoon as the Sydney traffic swished by outside.

'What do you think of this one, dear sibling Tim?'

'Sounds good, Fang. Finish the thing!'

Neil took it to rehearsals where Nigel convinced him it should stay as it was; nothing should be changed. No one really knew what they had when they started to learn the song which Neil titled *I Got You*.

Tim was also finding Rose Bay a haven for writing. He quickly finished off two songs. *I Wouldn't Dream Of It* and *Nobody Takes Me Seriously*.

Another popped into his head as Liz flew out the door after a fight. That was *A Fraction Too Much Friction*.

While Tim's songs were still a little fraught with angst and potential disasters, there was a light-hearted vein in there. It seems certain that away from the cold environs of Auckland and London, with the aforementioned new resonance running through the band and a sense of anticipation, the elder Finn's Phil Judd sub-text was now completely gone. Having seen Phil's commitment to The Swingers and realising for certain that the two of them would never team up again, he had shaken the mantle of his former hero figure and walked off into the sunset ready to go it alone. The stylistic changes in the songs clearly indicate that shift. In 1978, in his world of intensity and self-immersion, Tim would have been incapable of writing *How Can I Resist Her?*

Neil's writing was also changing. He had found a real knack for the melodic hook and was littering his new songs with sharp, snappy phrases that logged in the brain instantly. He was finding the answer to the eternal pop question, when is a hook a hook?

By mid-October 1979, David Tickle had arrived and the band went into pre-production in Sydney. Tickle stood in the room and cajoled, encouraged and charged them along. He saw very quickly the potential of *I Got You* and suggested they strip it to its basics. *What's The Matter With You?* and *How Can I Resist Her?* were also focused on by Tickle. Coming from a long stretch with Mike Chapman and the honed-down power pop of the Knack and Blondie, Tickle was into the band achieving more space over resolute drum tracks. This led to Neil's guitar cutting down on sustained overdrive and chopping and chunking a lot more, Mal and Nigel held the rhythm section down in a basic sense; the flourishes and tumbling fills that Mal had scattered liberally through the songs of the past two years were cut down considerably.

Eddie's keyboards were even more streamlined, with single melody lines to the fore. Tickle thought the piano was an instrument that just cluttered the sound spectrum, and Eddie kept to synthesisers.

Virtually all the new songs were working well with the only exception being *Fraction Too Much Friction*, which the band failed to get a grip on. Tim put it in a bottom drawer. Still brimming with the confidence they had found from the successful tours and delighted to be back with Tickle, who had, after all, produced the band's most successful single to date, they found themselves walking into Melbourne's Armstrong Studios in a state of real expectation. Tickle meant 'success'.

The sessions were done with a unanimous air of confidence and a concerted intensity. Neil recalls standing in the control room and being simply amazed at the sound he was hearing.

It was make or break this time, and as the tracks went down on tape they thought more and more: 'This time we've got it.' While they were recording the new album, tentatively entitled *Take One*, Mushroom released a retrospective *The Beginning Of The Enz*, which featured all the tracks recorded in New Zealand in 1973 and 1974. Gudinski had leased the tracks off Barry Coburn and the record went straight in as a catalogue item. It bore negligible resemblance to the group working away in Armstrong Studios. By now the novelty of pool had worn off; this time the sport was slow bicycle races around the studio corridors.

By the time mixing came around, Noel suddenly realised where

Tickle stood with regards to percussion. In order to keep the stripped-bare production he wanted, Tickle mixed out virtually all of Noel's percussion tracks. They just weren't there. Eddie had contributed a funky, synth-driven piece entitled *Double Happy* and there was another instrumental patched together in rehearsals called *The Choral Sea*.

As far as potential singles went, there was no shortage although in the final tally it came down to either *I Hope I Never* or *I Got You*. There was a general to-ing and fro-ing between the two, quite divergent, songs. In the end, with Tickle and Mushroom all lobbying for *I Got You*, it was chosen and scheduled for early January release in 1980. This would be Neil's third single in a row. He was poised for a hat trick of flops.

With the album in the can, the band took off on an *Enz of the 70s* tour of the Australian east coast, kicking off in Tasmania. At the first show, they tried *I Got You* for the first time live and it felt good. Moving north, the full house sign was generally outside before the show began. On the Gold Coast, David Tickle turned up to mix some of the shows. Tim walked in on one sound check: they were running through *I Got You*, and Tickle was pumping it out loud into the room. It seemed very clear to him, at that moment, that it was all going to go according to plan.

After the tour, all the lads bar Tim went to live in Melbourne. It made sense with Brenner, Mushroom and Premier Artists all there.

Brenner put together a promotional campaign whereby posters were pasted all through Sydney and Melbourne proclaiming: 'The Enz is now!'

Tim remained in Sydney at Rose Bay where I would drop in occasionally. Citizen Band was now in Sydney trying to climb a few rungs on the ladder of fame and fortune.

Tim gave me a copy of the new album: 'Chunn?'

'Yes, Tim?'

'Here's the new album. This time I think we got it.'

I returned to where we were all staying in the one flat (my wheel had come full circle!) and played the album through. It was immediately apparent – they had got it!

A few days later, Tim and I were down on Bondi beach taking in a spot of UV and a wave or two. He told me they'd thought of a name for the album.

'You should be able to guess it. It's the name of one of our old songs that we played with you. One that we never recorded.'

I embarked on a deep thought process.

'Wise Men?'

'No.'

'Buffs?'

'No.'

'Prophecy?'

'No,'

'Fascination?'

'No.'

'Lawdy?'

'No.'

'Nightmare Stampede?'

'No.'

'Hermine?'

'No.'

'Blankets?'

'No.'

'Eugene?'

'No.'

'City Of Dreams?'

'No.'

'There's A Way?'

'No.'

'I don't know, Timmy boy. What is it?'

'True Colours.'

13

LIKE WE NEVER DID BEFORE

Two weeks after our swim in the sea on that quiet Sydney day, all hell broke loose.

True Colours and *I Got You* were released in Australia on January 21, 1980, and Split Enz commenced their glorious ascension to the upper reaches of notoriety.

The album cover, which was available in various colour combinations (red and green, purple and yellow, blue and orange), was designed by Noel and encapsulated in a graphic sense the new Split Enz: angular, structured, precise, appealing, and varied. Noel had also conceived the film clip for *I Got You* and, as usual, it set tongues wagging. Its clarity of image and perfect relationship to the perception of Enz was further proof of the man's importance to the Enz ideology.

The transfer of Split Enz' music from the introverted, romantic ideals of 1978 to the commercial, hooky imagism of *True Colours* was mirrored beautifully by Noel's shifting costume designs and promotional graphics. This design aspect was of course matched by his masterful stage presence and increasingly competent percussion work. The only irony being that while his cover design for *True*

Colours was universally praised, his percussion work on the album was nowhere to be heard.

Within minutes of release, *I Got You* was added to the playlist of every radio station in Australia; within hours, the video clip was on every music programme. The entire Australian music industry knew in a flash that Split Enz were about to scale incredible heights. It had always been on the cards; now it looked inevitable.

The band travelled to New Zealand for another outdoor festival, this time titled Sweetwaters. With a new bunch of promoters, Sweetwaters was a different kettle of fish to Nambassa. Sporting hamburgers and soft drinks, this was one huge rock 'n' roll concert and much more akin to what people were after. The line-up featured Enz and Elvis Costello as headliners, and an abundance of local bands in support. With a crowd of around 45,000 and a new set of colourful costumes, the band, aware that back in Australia *I Got You* had been received with unanimous approval, couldn't hold back the euphoric surge and whacked every New Zealander in that huge crowd right between the eyes.

Nathan Brenner had secured a distribution deal with Polygram Records. Polygram had handed out cardboard sun-hats to virtually everyone on the site, which proclaimed the impending arrival of the *True Colours* album.

Expectation was rife and in the dead calm of the Saturday night headline slot, Split Enz triumphed. While the Nambassa show the year before had allowed them to shake off the previous year's frustrations and kick start themselves back into gear, the Sweetwaters show was a culmination of hard touring and a defined, new sound. It found them less urgent and more streamlined. Tickle's production had fostered a less frenetic, more layered and ordered musicality on the band; people who were new to them or who had been unable to assimilate them previously found the space and economy much easier to digest. The hooks were now prominent, almost naked, and the sparser rhythm tracks allowed lyrics to be heard. The show received an ecstatic reception and was the perfect introduction for the New Zealand tour that followed under the title *Trooping The Colours.*

As the tour kicked off, word came through that both the single and album were number one in Australia. Split Enz were finally at the toppermost of the poppermost. New Zealand would follow a short time later. In the next few months, *True Colours* would spend 10 weeks at the top of the Australian chart; in New Zealand, eight. *I Got You* was number one in Australia for eight weeks; in New Zealand, five. The huge rush on the album coupled with the media focus on the band sent all previous albums (except *Second Thoughts*) back into the New Zealand national chart. Every member of the public who had enjoyed Enz live but who had failed to buy their previous albums jumped at the opportunity to purchase *True Colours* with its massive hit single. And more. The album quickly rocketed to multi-platinum status in both countries, leading to Noel instigating new colour combinations for the re-pressings. The two new combos were lime green and pink, and hot purple and burnt orange (very Noel); the sheer weight of sales was celebrated with a gold and platinum cover.

In hindsight, the *True Colours* golden age was a natural consequence. The seven years that had built to that moment had a natural, almost predestined flow to them and, in many ways, it was only by 1980 that Split Enz were ready for massive success. The fragility of the esoteric Judd/Finn era and the lack of suitable singles prior to 1980 prevented chart successes. It would be fair to say, however, that without that isolated, creative stance of the mid-70s, the unique concepts Enz were able to mould with the development of Neil's songwriting talents and the commercial ears and fingers of David Tickle, the *True Colours* story might have been less gigantic.

As each year unfolded, changes and distillations slowly transformed Split Enz in a continuous evolution. Looking at the initial music that was so purposefully outside the times, it had to take seven years to achieve the final, ambitious result. This applied directly to Neil's writing as well. By 1980, Neil had come to grips with the intuitive songwriting talent he had within him. In the past two years he had moved closer into the band; he was now in line with the rest of them, and had the confidence and intent to not only write more but to present his material to the band. He was confident that it would be on a par with the material Tim was delivering. Tim's encouragement was paramount in the process. In the manner of the big brother/little brother, Tim was happy to see his brother's writing flourish; there was certainly nothing of the complicated emotive leanings that had racked him when Phil was in the band (or without, for that matter). Split Enz now had two writers on a par although Neil had pulled out 'the big one'.

Coupled with the band's progression were the changing foci of the music industry. The punk era of 1976–78 had injected a fervour and urgency into the band that had not been there before. This combined with the confidence gained from a string of successful pub dates in Australia, and they found in themselves a pure, pop strain that was the ideal musical foundation for Tim's new songs.

At the time this failed to translate to major success, as while Tim was happy to pour his frustrations and Phil Judd sub-texts out on vinyl, the industry, particularly radio, wasn't interested in pleading, convoluted songs. While we can say now that the broadcasters were the losers, the disco craze of the time must also be considered as another hazard in the band's path, making it easy for radio to put them in the too-hard basket back in 1977 and 1978.

By January 1980, however, the new wave had blossomed into a myriad of pop forms. Acts as diverse as Tubeway Army, The Knack and The Pretenders all claimed a punk birthright but rested comfortably on an almost sixties beat boom, pop edifice. The particularly healthy state of local music in Australasia was another factor. In the late seventies, the touring circuits in both countries became sophisticated. While touring had been a part of the Australian industry for many years, the number of venues multiplied enormously in the late seventies as the local music quota on radio led to a huge number of bands becoming popular.

In sharp contrast to 1975 – when Skyhooks and AC/DC were it – 1980 found The Angels, Cold Chisel, Dragon, Mi-Sex, and so on drawing huge crowds and selling many thousands of records. While on a smaller scale, New Zealand also had a major focus on local music. Hello Sailor, Th' Dudes, Streetalk, Toy Love, and Citizen Band were touring consistently; as in Australia, there was a healthy focus on local records although, without the quota, there was not a lot heard on radio. US radio consultants were being brought in by commercial radio and if they didn't know a record they didn't put it on playlists. They all knew about *I Got You* though!

Television New Zealand was seemingly unaccountable to its accountants and offered studio facilities to dozens of New Zealand bands to record video clips. In a 12-month period between 1978 and 1979, brother Geoffrey and I with our fellow Citizen Band cohorts were able to record no less than 28 different clips for our various songs! In 1979, TVNZ flew Split Enz to Wellington and filmed five different songs from *Frenzy* in two days.

With this bubbling activity and the consequent spotlight on all things local, the stage was set for the *True Colours* success. All the band had to do was compose to their usual standard and record with a producer who had a fix on what the public were buying at the time as well as what the band were capable of musically. The rest was already in place.

Following the success of the *Trooping The Colours* tour in New Zealand, Enz hit the stages in Australia on a double bill package tour with The Sports. The tour was called *Sporting True Colours* and ran for most of April. Gudinski planned the tour as a double bill but recalls Brenner resenting the inclusion of The Sports in the tour title. In the end, it wasn't much fun for The Sports. While their new album *Suddenly* was hovering in the middle reaches of the Australian chart, Enz were sustaining their uninterrupted run of number ones and the full houses quickly made it clear who they had come to see. Ever the gentlemen, Enz handed the headline slot over to The Sports one night but the streams of people leaving during their set gave Enz no option but to take the top bill from then on.

The press saw the slightly tragic aspect: 'The cheers to which Split Enz took the stage demonstrated it was they who the fans had come to see.'

Virtually ignoring The Sports, the vast majority of press reviews heralded the arrival of Split Enz to the apex of the Australian popularity ladder; noting the final shedding of their progressive rock label, while still appreciating their unique qualities.

'I hope no one will ever compare Split Enz to Roxy Music or Genesis again. With their new musical maturity – contributed to admirably by Neil Finn – the Enz show themselves to be a uniquely modern band ... Split Enz are a very original outfit.' — *RAM*.

By the end of the tour, *I Got You* was starting to slide so *I Hope I Never* was released. With another, rather eccentric video clip from Noel's eclectic brain, the single was swept up in the speedy momentum of the whole Split Enz scenario that now enveloped Australia. It received massive airplay and climbed the charts rapidly, although failing to match the peaks of its predecessor.

The lads took a short break before a West Australian tour. Tim was still in Sydney and he grabbed his guitar and thrashed out a couple of new numbers. *Hard Act To Follow* and *Walking Through The Ruins*.

While *Ruins* was another slice of internal wrangling {whereby Tim was perhaps forecasting his eventual separation from Liz), *Hard Act To Follow* was an almost humorous piece of irony – as if Tim was trying to cut expectation of their new album by making a joke out of it. There was certainly a feeling that even with the huge success they now enjoyed, it wouldn't take long for the sense of joy and satisfaction to slide away as other factors came into play.

One was Tim's yearning for success in the northern hemisphere. Brenner and Gudinski were of the same inclination. To that end, once the *Sporting True Colours* tour had ended, they both headed to the UK where A&M records were particularly interested in the album, courtesy of the A&R chief Mike Noble. A&M had a history with Gudinski: they had licensed Mushroom's *Ayers Rock* album for US release in 1976, and label boss, Jerry Moss (the '*M*' of A&M. Who was the '*A*' I hear you ask? That was Herb Alpert!), had become a personal friend of Gudinski's.

With a 'commitment' from the London office, Gudinski and Brenner then travelled to New York where Moss had been charged up by Noble's enthusiasm and was ready to sign a deal. It was inked by early May and a release date set for early August, to coincide with the end of their summer recess. A&M planned a major campaign. Taking a literal interpretation of the album title, they planned to release the *True Colours* album with a lazer-etched design of the cover symbols engraved on the actual vinyl. This would be a global first and the pivot of the promotional activities.

Gudinski also pushed for Brenner to have a sub-licensing deal with North American management and introduced him to a few possibilities. In the end, Brenner went with Champion Management, who represented Hall and Oates amongst others. A neat twist. Darryl Hall had come backstage after one of our shows in New York in 1977. Champion was headed by New Yorker Tommy Mottola.

While the administrative chaps were sorting out their global releases, the Enz travelled to Perth for a 10-date West Australian tour. Greeted with general mass hysteria, crowds outside hotels and young females clutching and grabbing (particularly at Neil), the tour was huge.

Graffiti started to appear on walls: *'I lust for Neil's Finn!'* Based in the same hotel room each night, Neil found little stability to write. Life on the road didn't suit his concentrated, laboured methods and he was unable to complete anything as he skipped from hotel to hotel.

In Perth, the solid base, if only for a couple of weeks, was enough and he pulled a few ideas together ... reworking them and kneading them into shape. Not unlike Tim's *Hard Act To Follow*, Neil's song had a similar theme although he claims it isn't specific. The title – *History Never Repeats*.

He would later describe the song as 'about the way people make resolutions. Some people tend to think of themselves as losers. This is how easy it is to be ridiculously optimistic, to learn how to balance your pessimism and succeed.'

On completion of the tour, some of the lads stayed on. Neil returned to Melbourne and the Murphy Street apartments in St Kilda. In seclusion again, he had the time to concentrate on writing. Enz had planned to keep the recording process rolling with the anticipated trip to the USA and the UK; in order to have an album ready for the New Year they would have to record it in August/September. This meant that songs had to be found almost immediately.

The Murphy Street environs must have provided the right stimulus. *One Step Ahead* came to be.

Up in Sydney, Tim was writing as well. He recalled some gothic Enz fans he'd met in Christchurch earlier in the year. Females with pale, pale skin and dark hair. He called that song *Ghost Girl*.

He followed that with a virtual nonsense piece of biographic intent, regarding his far from graceful faculties – *Clumsy*.

This led neatly into his fable of loneliness under the flashing lights of the nightclubs. While the Tim of the past had steered clear of nightlife, 1980 and the lifting of the shroud of failed records put a spring in his feet and he was out and about a lot more. I guess. The song is *I Don't Want To Dance*.

By now, Neil and Sharon, with Noel and Mark Hough (still under the moniker Buster Stiggs), were living in Glen Iris, Melbourne. The Swingers were in town and while Juddsy and Bones wallowed in poverty and squalor in St Kilda, Hough grooved away with the boys in their new relatively spacious house. This divergence of living standards in The Swingers' camp proved unhealthy for Buster's tenure.

In June, Enz went back on the road, this time in major venues such as the Hordern Pavilion in Sydney and Festival Hall in Melbourne. With sold-out houses and a huge contingent of teenagers adopting the band (after years of ignoring them), the receptions were once again ecstatic; a far cry from the 'Go back to where you came from' chorus that had been hurled at them in those same vast halls five years before.

In many ways the lads found this ironic. The teenage-phenomenon syndrome that had been foisted on Skyhooks when the band were first in Australia was regarded as tawdry and almost distasteful. Five years later, exactly the same thing was happening to them and there was a sense of detachment from it all. It hadn't taken long for the eruption of joy at the success of *True Colours* to settle into a self-regulating forward momentum. Each week that the album and single sat perched on their respective number one slots, Brenner would announce the new chart as they gathered in some hotel foyer by putting the index finger of both hands in the air ... another double number one. The band's reaction was virtually unanimous: 'What shall we have for breakfast?'

Sitting back and watching the frenetic goings-on was very much a part of the day-to-day lives of Noel, Ed, Nigel and Mal. They had weathered so much in the past few years. Yet, free of the responsibility of providing the material, they had kept an even keel, a stable foundation for Tim and, most importantly, a consistent, unwavering musical effort.

For Noel, in particular, each year had been a considerable creative progression. The success of 1980, while relieving the burdens of debt and allowing them substantial weekly advances, didn't change them. They had no illusions. There was still a lot of hard work strung out in front of them, and a lengthy stay at number one wasn't going to solve everything.

Tim and Neil found themselves in the firing line of endless press and media interviews.

While Tim had grown almost immune to the probing and questioning, Neil found it all rather tedious. But it was only just the beginning.

With the northern hemisphere looming, and the album and single about to be released in Europe and North America, the band went back to Armstrong Studios with David Tickle to record the follow-up. This was a different situation to *True Colours*. The previous album was recorded by a band and producer both poised to crack their respective, mid-level reputations wide open and that is exactly what happened.

And while Split Enz, then in their late twenties and quite ready for huge success, had absorbed the attention and heady acclaim in an orderly fashion, the same can't be said for David Tickle. As the sessions kicked off, the lads quickly sensed Tickle's shifting attitude. He was more dogmatic and less communicative; his ego seemed to have ballooned with the success of *True Colours* and the media fixation on Tickle, 'the boy genius'. In addition, the songs, more convoluted in themselves, had been rush-rehearsed. Neil had had trouble finishing lyrics in time and Tim's contributions hadn't quite matched the quality of his previous efforts, leaving the selection of singles very much in Neil's camp. The mood in the studio was generally more workmanlike and functional, although they felt they were progressing musically and, in fact, putting together a record that in the end would be quite different to *True Colours*.

After five weeks the 11 tracks were all on tape. Once again, Eddie had two instrumentals on the album.

The last track, *Albert Of India*, featured a beautiful piano arrangement. While *True Colours* had lacked any piano parts (apart from *I Hope I Never*) as a consequence of Tickle's thirst for space, this time Eddie insisted.

During the latter half of the sessions, Brenner came in with reports that *I Got You* was starting to get airplay in the UK. Dates were being booked in September and the promoter was keen to take a gamble on the Hammersmith Odeon venue in London.

Tim harked back to those 1978 days, when he would drive past the Hammersmith Odeon and imagine what might be. The image was turning into fact.

As well, Brenner brought down copies of the American *True Colours* with the lazer etching. The Americans had considered putting *I See Red* on the album but found it didn't match the rest of the material. Instead, feeling they had to change something 'cos they could, they put *I Got You* as the lead track. The lads were excited by the arrival of the discs. Here was the proof, the physical embodiment of the potential successes before them. It was a pleasant distraction from the stilted recording sessions.

During the odd day off from recording Enz, Tickle would work on a new project he was doing for Gudinski: The Swingers' debut single for Mushroom. The A-side was called *Counting The Beat*. One day Tim dropped by to check on his old partner's progress. As he walked in on Messrs Judd, Hough and Bones they greeted him with 'Oooohwee ... pop stars, eh!'

'You'll be next,' replied the Finn.

When it came time to mix the Enz material, Tickle insisted on working in England at Rupert Hine's Farmyard Studios. The band weren't prepared to see this huge recording bill debited to their royalty account with Mushroom, so Tickle agreed to cover the costs himself. He packed up the pile of two-inch tapes and left for London in September for 10 days of mixing. The band would be touring the UK at the time and set aside a few days to visit the Farmyard.

In the first week of September, Tim and Neil were flown to the USA, via New Zealand, for a promotional trip under the direction of Champion Management and A&M. The album and single were at an early stage but the confidence was there. Both of them were interviewed to the hilt and were quick to disassociate the band from the line-up that had disintegrated in the States three years before.

Tim spelt it out during an LA talk session: 'Back then a lot of people hated to think of us as a genuine band. But then, how can you sing out a love song when you look like a parrot?'

Nathan Brenner was also in on one interview and he focused on Mushroom and Gudinski in particular. The story ran:

'... Nathan Brenner, Split Enz' manager, says that when he delivered the completed *True Colours* to the head of their Australian record company, the executive 'went white', He said, 'It's not even going to go gold, and there's no single.' So the company only printed 6,000 copies. But then a popular Australian rock TV show, *Countdown*, ran a video clip of the group performing *I Got You*. Bang. Off it went,' says Brenner. 'Those 6,000 copies were sold in three days.'

After a week of chitchat, the three of them flew to London brimming with anticipation. This time, they felt America could actually come through for them. They left behind them a nation full of good album reviews.

On arrival in London, they met up with the rest of the band. *I Got You* was already charting and the reviews for *True Colours* were running very much on the positive side:

'The Enz' original assault on Britain was buried beneath the New Wave explosion. The silly make-up also obscured their undoubted talent. But they've forgotten that gimmicky nonsense now, concentrating wholly on the music which is rather splendid.

'The songs here speak for themselves – wacky, witty, intelligent pop-rock that hook you around the aurals and won't let you go.' — *Swindon Evening Echo*.

'The band, long recognised as outrageous and rather eccentric, appear now to have concentrated much more on their musical performances and the result is an album of lasting qualities.' — *Grimsby Evening Standard*.

The tour dates were filling fast as airplay for *I Got You* went on the increase and A&M started to put the foot on the accelerator. In the lead-up to the tour, Tim and Neil hit the interview trail. Once again they put the lid on the past. Tim went on record: '(The Chrysalis years) was part of the evolution of the band, an organic thing – and we're proud of it all. Attitude and presentation-wise, we were probably a little ahead of our time, but the thing about that period is that everybody remembers the way we looked rather than the way we sounded. The image was provocative, but turned out not to be a selling point, which was the obvious intention. We're more human now – we used to be completely asexual – but we still have a strong visual identity. We KNOW our craft.'

Neil was, by now, sick of the continuous harking back to early Enz manifestations: 'This line-up has been together for three years and that's as old as the band feels. The past is irrelevant now ... A critic once said that Split Enz was a band a guy could take his girl-friend to see without any danger of her fancying the bass-player (*presumably this was Nigel!*). Well, I think the image we had did isolate us from the audience. There was a barrier. We've realised that we don't have to be so extreme to be different. Split Enz is now just simpler and more effective.'

The rest of the lads went out to the Farmyard Studios where Tickle was mixing the new album. On walking into the gloomy control room at the Farmyard, they didn't like what they heard. Tickle was mixing in a room dwarfed by huge eight foot speakers that he drove at such a volume no one could stay in the room for longer than a minute or two. 'Ooops!' was the general comment.

Eddie and Nigel were particularly distressed. When they asked Tickle for cassette dubs of the songs he had mixed, he wouldn't hand any over; when questioned, he wouldn't discuss the mixes. It was obvious that Tickle had decided that mixing was totally his domain and that he would prefer the band to stay away. This particularly rankled with Eddie, who found the possibility (probability?) of a less-than-satisfactory album too much to bear. He suffered an anxiety attack, with a dose of scabies for good measure. Ed was not well. He literally ran off down the road. In the final analysis, with the UK tour about to commence, there was little they could do. It was decided to wait for the finished songs to arrive in toto, then take it from there.

The English tour kicked off in Bristol and ran for four shows, climaxing at the Hammersmith Odeon Theatre. That night *I Got You* had just slid inside the Top 20 at number 19, and the band had performed the song on the BBC prime time music show *Top Of The Pops* to around 15 million people. As the lads drove up to the theatre, the huge flood lit sign above the entrance read: 'SPLIT ENZ – SOLD OUT.'

In a night of sweet vindication for all the years of strife, endless rehearsals, record company rejections, priggish agents, laboured waiting sessions, dud albums, fobbed managers, dole queues, burst pipes, dark nights, freezing dressing rooms, managers with pungent armpits, disparaging comparisons, loneliness, radio nihilism, and the occasional tendency to further their own destiny by rotating in ever decreasing circles till they were ensconced in their own rectums, the concert at the Hammersmith Odeon on September 27, 1980, was a crowning achievement. It was the crest of the wave that was hurtling Enz into a future that everyone was telling them would be nothing less than supreme.

As they walked on stage to a huge, warm welcome from 3,500 fans they sensed the moment's glory and played a magnificent show. Tim was 'in the zone', zooming and reaching out; Nigel and Mal were enthused at this conquering of the home town. It was effortless, sublime, unstoppable. The very essence of what that year had meant to them. Rewards, acclaim and a debt free bank account. They were called back for three encores and, in the usual tradition of the unexpected, finished the night with *Charlie* which Tim had fashioned a few suburbs away one heady, crystal clear morning not so long ago.

After the show there was jubilation in the dressing room. Mr and Mrs Griggs drank the majesty of their son's achievements with this crowd of colonial twits. A reporter from New Zealand, John Hudson, was covering the show. He asked Tim about the new material.

Tim replied: 'We have some very nice rayon and some lovely silks for the next season.'

Neil was asked about the upcoming American tour: 'I'm sure the cowboys will love us, especially our rural approach.'

Tim would later describe it as a perfect, perfect night. As he strode off stage, having slaughtered the Pommie assemblage with a super eminent and peerless keyboard display, Ed was heard to mutter, 'Conquer Shmonker!'

As the band checked in their baggage at Heathrow airport for their flight to the USA, Neil rang the A&M office in London for the new chart position of *I Got You*.

'Tell me, you whacker, what is our chart position today taking into regard its dated position of number 19?'

'Number 10, parvenu!'

It was champagne all the way as they rolled in the glory of their first Top 10 UK hit.

Unfortunately, the next week it slipped away. There were those in A&M who felt the band's image on *Top Of The Pops* was too extreme and had gone against the momentum created from the heavy radio play. Brenner felt A&M had hyped the record too soon and were left wanting by the time the single had climbed to its peak.

In New York for the first time together, they craned their necks and lapped it up. Tommy Mottola clocked in and asked them what their particular fancy was: Chinese, Black, French?

He introduced them to the Champion man-on-the-spot Randy Hoffman, and that night they took in a Talking Heads concert at Central Park. Buzz buzz buzz. By now *I Got You* had reached number 40 on the Billboard Hot 100.

The next day they met up with the A&M promo chap. He spurted: 'You guys will be Top 5 in four weeks.'

Neil: 'Oh well, that's it. Top 5 ... four weeks. Okay. What's for lunch?'

Noel: 'Chart schmart.'

The band crossed the great continent and kicked off the tour at the Whiskey in Los Angeles. By now, they had received a tape of the new album mixes and were generally dissatisfied with the results. Noel once again had been mixed to insignificance.

'This won't happen again,' he resolved.

One Step Ahead was deemed good enough, however, and was immediately scheduled as a single back in Australasia for early November release. A few tracks would have to be remixed but this could wait till the lads were back in Australia. The album would be held over for a few months as its release in Australasia could lead to imports flying to the northern hemisphere before the scheduled release there. After all, in the grand scheme of things, *True Colours* had really only just got going.

However, the concept of releasing more singles off *True Colours* in Australia and New Zealand didn't seem to occur to anyone. Had *Poor Boy* and then *What's The Matter With You* succeeded *I Got You* and *I Hope I Never*, who knows how long that album might have hovered in the Top 10? But it wasn't to be, and *One Step Ahead* was put down for a November 17 ship date. The film clip for the single was filmed while the boys were in Los Angeles.

This time Noel designed a set that surpassed the (by now) slightly nonsensical stagings of the previous two clips; with the band dressed in black turtlenecks on an angular, oblique stage, a sophisticated slick video was put in the can. The Enz never-stand-still ethos was still very active.

The first show at the Whiskey in Los Angeles was packed and a crowd of curious celebrities showed up. Tommy Mottola was there and he took a table near the front with a group of cohorts. Nathan Brenner arrived with some acquaintances to find Mottola sitting at what he believed was his table and insisted they shift. An argument ensued and neither would back off. As far as Mottola was concerned, Brenner was small fry and could sit somewhere else. Eddie felt uncomfortable when he heard about it.

Bette Midler was one of the celebrities there that night. Backstage, she was introduced to the band and struck up a dialogue. Midler talked of her fondness for *I See Red*, which had been particularly rousing on that occasion; a discussion ensued about the possibility of her recording it. Although nothing came of it, the sheer enthusiasm of the woman was a bolster to the lads. Donna Summer was also on hand, raving about the show and asking for songs.

As the tour continued, word came down from A&M Canada that *I Got You* was exploding on radio, and the single and album were climbing the charts steadily. In the USA, however, *I Got You* had stalled at number 40. Gudinski took to the phone at 5.00 am Australian time for a conference call on the matter with Nathan

Brenner and key A&M executives. While Gudinski was not happy with the hitch, he knew that certain factors hadn't come into play such as the penetration of the AM radio market – and his intention was to discuss these issues and convince A&M to bolster their troops for a more concerted effort to get the single back on the upward path. He had continued faith in the label and certainly did not see the problem as irreversible.

As far as Gudinski was concerned, the means to the end of a hit single in the USA was a complicated game of chess. Perhaps A&M had let a week slip by without investing in independent promotion, which had pinned the record to its number 40 slot. Maybe something else ... It had to be resolved but before he had a chance, Nathan Brenner spoke out.

Brenner was concerned at what he considered to be a major lapse by the Americans in their timing of the UK Squeeze album, which they had released a few weeks before *True Colours*. Brenner was sure that A&M were marketing the UK Squeeze album on radio at the expense of *True Colours*. In his opinion, the push for Split Enz was diluted. Brenner insisted that Gudinski come in with Mushroom money for independent promotion, to bring in the pop radio stations that were not playlisting *I Got You*. As far as he was concerned, Mushroom had made good money out of the advances from A&M and could afford to cough up. Brenner told them all just what he thought in no uncertain terms.

Gudinski recalls this torrent, hurled at both the A&M people and himself, as the moment A&M turned off the juice. While Brenner had certain A&M staffers who were with him, Gudinski found that after that session on the phone he no longer sensed true commitment from the movers on the label. In fact, the next week *I Got You* started its descent to oblivion.

The foolish thing was that A&M had been talking about Split Enz as the next Supertramp; nothing would have pleased Jerry Moss more than to finally do something in the USA with one of Gudinski's acts. But the business in America doesn't work like anywhere else. People take offence and pull plugs. The claims foisted on Mottola and Champion Management in what many thought was an early stage in the life of the album, let alone the proposed life span of the band, were unnecessary even if they had some truth. No doubt Brenner had nothing but the band's interests at heart. But with this, his first foray into the almost absurd methodology of the US music industry, he had made a declaration that some in the A&M and Champion camps regarded as a threat.

Meanwhile, Split Enz crossed the continent, garnering excellent reviews as they had been doing all year. Their show at the Ritz in New York was noted by the New York Post, no less:

'Split Enz is an entourage whose musical stance hovers somewhere between New Wave and Vaudeville. Currently enmeshed in deceptively melodic pop, the group manages to conjure up quite a few vivid word pictures in their tunes.'

When the band flew into Canada in late October, the situation was nothing less than splendid. *I Got You* was Top 10 and *True Colours* was almost platinum. They were receiving massive airplay across the country and the shows were all selling furiously. By the time they reached each city, most shows were sell-outs. The reviews were laudatory, particularly as no one in Canada had seen the group before:

'Certainly, the world has never before experienced a group quite like Split Enz. Their image was one of glorious excess and unrestrained oddity.' — *Trans FM*.

From there it was back to the UK, where *I Got You* had bottomed out but *True Colours* was still selling steadily. A&M UK had decided to release *Nobody Takes Me Seriously* as its second single, but it didn't stick and sloped off fairly quickly. Next up they were planning on *Poor Boy* in a four-colour picture bag. Surprisingly, this beautiful song failed to ignite the flagging singles situation and that was it. A&M would wait for the next album.

After three shows Enz flew to Belgium for concerts in Brussels, Amsterdam (back to the Paradiso and those hash blocks!) and Maastricht. Zippadee-doo-da, they were then back in the UK, touring England and Scotland with two superb nights at the Apollo Victoria in London; then skedaddle-a-do to Paris; zim-zam to Hamburg; Viola another quick show in Paris; then 24 hours of absolute stillness as they flew to Melbourne.

On arrival, they found *One Step Ahead* on all the airwaves. This jolted them into the realisation that they had better do something about the new album. In the northern hemisphere their whole focus had been on *True Colours* but now, with the first single from the new album getting saturation response, they had better get the it shaped up. It could also do with a title.

Unfortunately, though, they would still be unable to ship it out as virtually all northern hemisphere territories wanted the album held back owing to their continued concentration on *True Colours*.

Tickle flew out from England to do some of the remixes that the band were insisting on.

The lads performed three quick end-of-year concerts in Melbourne, Sydney and Brisbane, and found themselves recipients of various radio station awards for 'single of the year', 'group of the year', 'performance of the year' and so on. As well, Mushroom released the lazer-etched *True Colours* album, with an ultra-bright yellow, blue and red sleeve, in time for the end-of-year sales rush. It quickly sold 22,000 copies. Split Enz then broke for Christmas, put their feet up and kissed 1980 goodbye.

What a year! After being a solid, mid-level live act with two reasonably successful but short-lived singles and a clutch of eclectic albums to their name, the band had rocketed to the pinnacle of success in Australia, selling over 200,000 albums. Nearly one in ten homes had a copy of *True Colours*, and they received celebrity status wherever they went.

In New Zealand, the situation was virtually the same – although their live work had always sustained the largest concert venues and, in fact, while their following may not have blossomed much during the 1975–79 era, it certainly hadn't reduced in the slightest. Once again the album was multi-platinum.

Twelve months before in the northern hemisphere, Split Enz were has-beens. *Frenzy* had been rejected by all the record companies and with the departure from Chrysalis, it was assumed they wouldn't be heard from again. The previous UK and USA attempts had left Split Enz with a small cult following. Twelve months later, on close inspection and with an eye on what real success in those major territories means in terms of chart longevity and position, Split Enz were still only cult status, although on a much larger scale. Instead of reaching the heights that bands like Men At Work were about to achieve, they had set a merry pace that definitely required more touring and an album of equally commercial material ... as well as continued effort from A&M Records and, presumably, US management.

Champion Management, however, wasn't to be part of the equation as far as Brenner was concerned.

He had found Champion interested only in the band's US mission and of little assistance in the Canadian climb to success. As well, the strong focus on Tim and Neil (being the singer/songwriters) and general lack of attention to the other band members wasn't to his liking.

For 1981 Brenner wanted change. As he had a term deal with Champion, Gudinski had to negotiate with Mottola on a personal level to extract Brenner from the agreement. Brenner, who had now signed a full management agreement with the band, was going it alone.

14

SURRENDER TO THE SKY

The band readied itself for another Sweetwaters extravaganza. It was over 10 months since the last New Zealand show, the longest break from New Zealand shores in the band's history.

Tim and Liz flew into Auckland in mid-January and headed south to Hamilton, where Dick and Mary were now owners of Claudelands Motel. While there, they were married. The ceremony was very small and very quiet, and Tim woke the next morning wondering what he had done.

Back in Auckland, Tim was interviewed for the *Auckland Star*. When asked who was on the up and up in Australia, he put in a plug for The Swingers. He suggested their new single, *Counting The Beat*, which was about to be released, would go really well. Might he be right?

The next day he checked into Steelbox rehearsal rooms, where he had a drum kit set up. He was determined to knuckle down and learn how to play them. Liz was keen on jamming along on bass. I wondered at the time just what Tim was trying to do. I was aware (always had been) of his major focus inside the musical machine of the band being the drums. But, aside from the absurd prospect that he might be thinking of playing drums for Enz, I could only think that he was searching for more in his life.

By the 25th, the rest of the clan had gathered at Steelbox to shape up the Sweetwaters set. It soon became apparent that Mal was out on a tangent. He had shown a tendency over the past few months to indulge in the writing of his own material; he had recorded a solo single in Australia, entitled *Follow Me*, which was going to be released at an opportune time under the moniker of The Mal Green Sound. This extracurricular activity seems to have distracted him more than it should; he sat on his drum stool in Auckland, tapping out a hi-hat beat while gazing into space.

The others, particularly Noel, noticed Mal's lackadaisical air. After a few half-hearted whacks, taps and pocks, Mal went off into another room and started to play out a tune on the piano – presumably something that he was piecing together. In the course of history its working title has become a moot, minor point. Noel looked at his whizzers, bangers, cymbals, tintinnabulum, castanets, rattles, tocsin, xylophone, maracas, jew's-harp, and military bass drum. The kazoo and the conch looked puny compared to the huge, vacant drum kit with its lone stool, kick pedals, hi-hats, tom toms and cracking whiplash snare. While Mal doodled, much as Nero fiddled, Noel picked up the sticks. As the band kicked off into *Hard Act To Follow*, Noel thudded, thumped, pounded, and whacked those drums in the manner of a whirling dervish; a manic rhythmic pioneer, cleaving Mal's now-loosening bond to Split Enz and sending the recalcitrant Pommie stickman to the far reaches of some other place. As the rest of the band grinned at Noel's fresh, tumbling, and deft drumming, Mal's fate was sealed.

With the completion of the Sweetwaters concert, he was released. His single was also released but failed to go far.

The Sweetwaters performance was sublime and kicked off with *Albert Of India* rippling out into the still Waikato night. Split Enz were now so in tune with each other and possessed such a spontaneous communication that they were faultless. Raewyn's lighting rig was extravagant and glorious, and she utilised light and shade, colour and monotones brilliantly. If I remember rightly, there was also a mirror ball. This time the festival was a double bill with Roxy Music although the posters featured Split Enz first up. A pleasant contrast to that Hordern Pavilion show in 1975.

I was on site ferreting around as manager of local groups The Crocodiles and Pop Mechanix, who had charged up the power-pop ladder over the latter half of 1980 and who were both on stage that weekend. I had hung up my bass and crossed the fence into the bun fight that is the music industry. The mood backstage was relaxed and informal as the lads savoured the laid-back air that only New Zealand can provide on occasions like this.

Having spent the past six months travelling the planet on the back of an album that had sent them spiralling northwards, surrounding them with record company and management staffers rattling on about this interview, that radio station, this venue, that celebrity, this journalist, that television show and so on, they found the contrast to their liking. For myself, it was good to catch up with the whakkos and meet the ever-charming and elegant Phil Manzanera again. It seemed an eternity since anyone had called me Jonathan. After the festival, Eddie took some time off to produce a single for Pop Mechanix entitled *Jumping Out A Window*. The track went Top 20 in New Zealand a couple of months later.

On their return to Australia, the new album title was decided on. The long-player would be called *Waiata* in all countries except Australia, where it would be called *Corroboree*.

Waiata was a Maori term for 'celebratory song'; corroboree was the aboriginal equivalent in a broad sense.

Down in Albert Park, Gudinski was trying to get a fix on this new album. He had two major problems: the album cover and the title, neither of which impressed him. Noel's black, brown and white 'musical notation' design didn't get a great reaction in the USA either. A&M was prepared to stick with the title, even though they had difficulty pronouncing it, but decided to do something about the cover design. As Noel would later say 'They didn't like brown. It's after all the colour of shit.'

Noel had actually hoped to have the cover shaped like a shield however Mushroom was unable to achieve that in the lead time up to the album release.

Tim was not happy and later told *RAM*: 'We are constantly forced to make these sickening compromises ... It's all part of the challenge. It's all part of life. But when you end up not getting exactly what you want, the taste of defeat is entirely sickening.'

This seemed rather harsh. Knowing Tim's propensity for wanting instantaneous action, it was not surprising that he might feel this way but it was unlike him to rant about it in the press.

He knows as well as anybody that there are two sides to every story and is generally steeped in diplomacy. I suspected at the time that the band were becoming increasingly isolated from the Mushroom office for a smattering of reasons and were, in the self-confidence that their success brought, feeling they had the right to put the boot in.

Meanwhile, as *History Never Repeats* was released on March 9, Enz kicked off more dates. The video clip was extravagant, featuring past costumes and an array of props and garb. A literal interpretation of Neil 'telling himself before he goes to sleep' had him miming to the song in bed, with Tim on the edge as if he were about to tuck him in. The final 'a cappella' chorus at the end of the bridge found them wind-blown and grim. In time, the viewer might be tempted to conclude there was a prophecy in this intense, tightly knit proclamation.

History Never Repeats, in the manner of the previous three singles, crashed onto the airwaves. The single was soon Top 10 in Australia and New Zealand, although spent less time on the chart than *One Step Ahead*; *Waiata* was just around the corner and the fans were prepared to wait. The number-one slot wasn't up for grabs anyway, as Mr Judd and his Swingers had a hold on it in both Australia and New Zealand with *Counting The Beat*. The single had made the quickest ascension to the toppermost of the poppermost since *Daddy Cool* many many years before. Tim had been right and he was happy for Phil; nothing pleased him more than to see Juddsy achieve that kind of major success.

Enz kicked off a 'rural' Victorian tour in March, with Pop Mechanix as support. The first show was at Shepparton, they wore the 'polys' and Noel debuted on drums. He had been hitting things for so long now he had developed a keen sense of timing and a reasonable coordination.

The new line-up worked a treat. This time *The Woman Who Loves You* was shelved, and a Tim sing-along track, entitled *You Can Lead A Horse To Water*, was sung in an acoustic arrangement allowing Noel to come out from behind the drums and continue his spooning activities.

At the annual Rock Awards in Sydney a few days later, the band were up for a variety of categories. An hour before the show, the band were doing their pre-awards warm-up tomfoolery in a dressing room when *RAM* magazine brought in a proof copy of a huge four-page article on the band. It consisted of separate interviews with each member. Pens were handed out and the guys asked to scribble over it, commenting on the quotes in the article.

Tim took the opportunity to espouse his philosophies: 'The Humimal Theory: Each person is an animal. At heart, in gesture, and particularly in face. Try it. It's easier for some reason to find the male animal correlative. Tim – Bull; Neil – Ant; Eddie – Horse; Noel – Goat; Nigel – Turtle.'

In his interview, Eddie had been asked if Tim might take over production duties one day.

His reply was: 'No. He (Tim) reckons there's no way he could ever produce us. Tim tends to change his mind very often ...'

Next to this Tim scribbled with his pen: 'That's not true. Last week I thought Eddie was a histrionic shrieking tool and I still do.'

Eddie then scribbled: 'That's OK, Tim, I'd rather be a hot tool than a cold chisel.'

Elsewhere in his interview, Eddie, generally ignored by the media, was probed alone: 'I've no idea how I am perceived publicly; I try to keep myself incredibly low profile – deliberately. I'm really only concerned with the music.' He talked of recording a solo album but eschewed any talk of existing outside the band: 'I've been dying to take full control for once – just to prove to myself that I can't do it.'

In his interview, Nigel referred to a growing frustration with the lack of control in their day-to-day lives, if not their destiny, particularly in regard to their female companions. By this stage most of them had partners who had to say goodbye to them at regular intervals (although Ed had it sussed with Raewyn being the lighting operator): 'Their life is the band's life – and in that situation, they always come second to the band ... it's very hard for the girls. If things keep going well for us, in a year or two we might have a bit more control over our lives. At the moment it's pretty manipulated (though that's our commitment and we're happy to do it) – and we could afford to take them with us ...'

Noel was asked how he sewed flies onto all those costumes: 'Sowing fliez kan be bothasurn but swot them ferzt. Thiz maykz it e.z.a.'

Tim talked about solo possibilities: 'There are a lot of songs I write that aren't used by the band for one reason or another; and it would be a release for me to play a lot of instruments. On the Split Enz albums, I mainly do just vocals.'

This was interesting. With the huge success of *True Colours*, the tight bond that had kept the band breathing life into itself through the previous years was becoming more elastic. This was most obvious with Tim, Noel, and Eddie; with Tim teaching himself drums in Auckland and his talking of solo projects to the press, one could sense his growing tendency to look for outside activities in order to keep his hyperactive brain boiling. Noel and Ed to a lesser extent. The future would tell, no doubt.

Later in the auditorium, *I Got You* received the Single Of The Year award. Neil had planned beforehand to trip up and fall flat on his face should he have to collect this prize and this he did with remarkable aplomb. As he lay there, his nose flattened on the polished wood and his heart pumping with the joy, not from winning the coveted trophy but a keen sense of mischief, the usually loquacious emcee Molly Meldrum was struck dumb. The television directors and so on ran around in circles, trying to fashion a visual remedy. After a fair few drawn-out seconds, young Neil, in the manner of the ant, clambered to his feet and lugged the trophy back to his seat. He hadn't had a hat trick of flops after all.

The following night, Neil's party trick had not been conceived in advance. At the Palais Theatre in Melbourne, he was hurtled from his microphone stand by an electric shock during the second encore. The concert was immediately cut short and the following day all activities for the band were cancelled. In many ways, Neil's 'buzz' reflected the general shattered nature of the lot of them. For the past 12 months they had either been touring or recording and their batteries were running low. This interruption shocked them into the realisation that time was screaming by. The ladder they had doggedly clambered up all those years seemed to be going in a circle.

Tim, however, knew that the imminent release of *Waiata* in the northern hemisphere meant they had to press on regardless. He took time out to have a full-on day of interviews, while Neil got the blood back in his veins and the rest of them took a rain check.

One of Tim's many chat sessions was with *Rip It Up* magazine in Auckland: 'Corroboree is just a word – like Waiata in New Zealand. There is a celebratory aspect to Split Enz because we have survived through thick and thin and there is that ecstasy of being a young band whenever we play together ... Malcolm was a very good rock drummer; Noel is a better swing drummer, he's more imaginative. Now it's more of a band. People have said they don't miss Noel as front man, weirdo-on-the-left etc. and the stage line-up and look has changed so much, anyway. Ultimately, something is missing but something has taken its place.'

April was spent capitalising on the success of *Waiata*, which was released on April Fool's Day. The album quickly shot to number one in New Zealand. Enz toured Queensland, with Pop Mechanix in support, and then crossed the Tasman Sea for the *Waiata* tour of New Zealand, with supports from The Penknife Glides and Blam Blam Blam. The first show in Christchurch featured a taped intro of aboriginal music, which confused the crowd. Ed later told a journalist: 'The tape was meant for Australian concerts and we didn't have time to get one for here – we'll have to get the sound of kiwis mating or something.'

Back home, the reception to *Waiata* by the critics had been glowing. Roy Colbert, who had reviewed the Dunedin University concert more than nine years previously, was still pen-in-hand:

'Split Enz are still moving forward, sounding healthier by the album. On the one hand they've tossed out a drummer on the eve of releasing an album ... On the other, stronger hand, the band's real musical ace-in-the-hole, Rayner, is playing an instrumentally larger role all the time. Meanwhile, the two Finns are beatling down the home straight, shoulder to shoulder, hurling diamonds at each other as they run. The race is a delight to watch.' — *Rip It Up*.

Phil Gifford who had reviewed Enz in 1973 was also still active on the typewriter and writing for *The Listener*. He interviewed the lads who, glad to be back home, were in ebullient moods.

The subject came around to *Mental Notes*.

Ed: 'What's this about me screwing up *Mental Notes*?'

Tim: 'We succumbed to all this tricky British art rock.'

Ed: 'So I wrote all those little parts that made such good songs?'

Tim: 'We were all guilty.'

Ed: 'I wasn't guilty.'

Tim: 'You brought a heavy Yes influence to bear upon us, Rayner.'

Ed: 'Who bought the mellotron?'

Tim: 'I know. I went off and bought it. Phil and I were gullible enough and naive enough to get sucked into the whole thing. We were ripe for the plucking.'

Later, Neil was interrogated. Gifford queried the current role of Tim in the band.

Neil: 'Certain people always take on leadership. He's good at motivating others. He can be a negative force within the band sometimes – he's quite moody and subject to bouts of depression. But in other ways, because he's such a tempestuous person, he inspires everyone else. We tend to sort of drift along. Tim can come into a rehearsal in a bad mood and suddenly we're all working. He's good for us. When Tim's up everybody feels it.'

Neil was then asked about the songs and the thread of anxiety that some critics had perceived: 'I think it might be a New Zealand thing. If you've got ambitions beyond New Zealand it can be a very frustrating place. I've never dug beneath the lyrics too much but sometimes I see things there six months later I didn't realise at the time. It's also a very unnerving way of life being in a band. There's a constant battle between being a public or private person. You can become very obsessive about success.'

A final session with Tim pointed to his continued commitment: 'We've always seen past New Zealand. We want to make it in England and America.'

So America it was, and they flew into LA to kick off their *Waiata* promotion tour in the second week of May. They took with them an assortment of water pistols. Over the past few tours, Eddie had garnered a vast arsenal of pistols, rifles, machine-guns, and so on, all capable of a good torrent. It paid to keep out of Eddie's way when the battles raged.

The band met up with A&M executives, who were readying themselves for the *Waiata* onslaught. Jerry Moss had a chat to Tim about the failure of *I Got You* to crack the Top 40 the previous year. 'I guess that's what you call paying your dues, Tim.'

Tim thought to himself, 'I've already paid my dues.'

A&M were taking on *Waiata* in very much the same way as the previous album. They wanted another *True Colours* and they wanted another *I Got You*.

'Give us another *I Got You* and we'll get it this time, boys.'

Much to Noel's horror, they set about issuing the *Waiata* cover in its own colour combination: pink, black and white. Only on extremely rare occasions would shit be pink, black and white. To further link the new album to the previous one, they issued the first single from the record, *One Step Ahead*, with lazer etchings on it.

Eddie noted this. 'Lazer Schmaze.'

This time, however, while the crowds were on par if not greater than the year before, the album and single failed to match the 1980 chart positions. Brenner was the management spearhead this time and it appeared A&M wasn't overly enamoured of this scenario. Brenner had hired a tour manager, Lars Sorenson, to take over the day-to-day organisation, while Brenner concentrated on the broader picture. Back at Mushroom in Melbourne there was concern as to how Brenner would cope, considering the general state of irritation he had left A&M in last time he was there. As well, there was no major US management support.

Sometime later, as they all gathered in some forgotten lounge or foyer, Brenner threw a coin at Eddie in jest. Eddie then shot Brenner with a burst of water from whichever pistol he had tucked in his belt at the time. They ended up grappling on the floor and the mood went dark between them. During that day, Eddie bought himself a brand-spanking-new cashmere jersey; as they gathered in readiness to board the bus to that night's concert, Brenner let Ed and the new jersey have it with his water pistol.

On the bus, in an irate mood, Eddie produced his supreme gun, the 'power-soaker' and drenched Brenner. Later, in the dressing room before the show, Brenner once again produced his pistol and let Eddie have it. Ed snapped, as he is wont to do every five or 10 years, and lunged at Brenner, landing a solid punch. As the others held Ed back, Brenner went white. Suffering some kind of heart fibrillation, Brenner was driven back to the hotel for the night to recuperate. Eddie went on stage and from that moment on felt he and Brenner were on other sides of some strange no-man's land.

Once again, much as they had done in 1977 in the UK, Enz had to stare at ecstatic crowds while the airwaves ran cold. From the first time he heard the mixes, Eddie had not had complete faith in the album, and as he shifted from city to city he sensed they were backing a horse that had no chance of winning.

As usual the press were dragged in by A&M to overload Tim and Neil's spare time. This time Neil was a rogue:

Neil: 'This whole business of the band being coined "avant garde" is a lot of wank!'

IN: 'What does "wank" mean?'

Neil: 'Are you joking?'

IN: 'No.'

Neil: [pause] ... 'Well, I don't know whether or not you can print this but "wank" is a term which has to do with some naughty thing little boys aren't supposed to do in the bathroom.'

IN: 'You mean shit in the basin?'

In Baltimore he was asked about the album title: 'It's just a word; an idea. We like the sound of the word. We like having titles that don't relate to anything else.'

In Florida, he qualified the use of make-up: 'We still highlight our faces so people 100 yards back can see us. I always hated not being able to see the faces.'

While Neil was divesting himself of witticisms, Noel found himself with a drum roadie who was a coke fiend. He burst into Noel's hotel room: 'Hey look at this man! It's pure [sniff] blue. Pure blue, man! Pure and fresh! Hey ... (sniff).'

'Fresh schmesh,' mumbled Noel, willing the goon to evaporate.

Eddie was becoming more and more oppressed by the air-conditioned air that seemed to continually envelop him. Hotel after hotel featured windows that wouldn't open. He wanted to know why fresh air was barred from his rooms and went to the reception desk.

'Excuse me, you American Wally. Why is it that the windows in this hotel are permanently sealed?'

'To prevent suicides from the upper floors.'

'I guess I'll just have to go to the bathroom and slit my wrists then!'

The next day Eddie was in the foyer waiting for the gang to materialise. The only other member there was Nigel, who had a blue haze around his head. Nigel found the mornings anathema, preferring to sleep to around 4.00 pm and then start the day. Consequently, whenever he was forced into consciousness to catch buses, he would check out and foist a large dose of crabbiness on the hotel receptionist. Late afternoon saw him surface to normality.

This particular morning the foyer was full of Japanese tourists; Nigel, still desperately short of blood sugar, decided to advise them of their wrongs. He called out 'don't stay here, it's a shithole!' After repeating himself a few times as would a revivalist sandwich-board preacher on the footpaths of Oxford Street, the hotel security guard approached.

'Excuse me, sir. You are uttering a profanity. Please refrain.'

'Okay then ... this place is a fuckhole!'

It wasn't until a gun was pulled on the irritable bass-player and he was bundled outside that the proclamations ceased.

Tim was very much the focus for A&M by virtue of his lengthy tenure and diplomacy under stress. He would be dragged off here and there, and this time he was in the mood for it. His marriage to Liz had jolted him and he found himself reacting to the situation. A situation he was regretting. His solution was to live the rock-star life as a means of escape; for the first time in his life he was anybody's, drowning his shaky foundations under a sea of flesh.

While in New York, Split Enz appeared on a nationwide television talkback show. They performed *One Step Ahead* and *Hard Act To Follow*. One of the other guests on the show was Sandy Allen, the tallest woman in the world who checked in at 7' 7".

When asked by the host, Tom Snyder, how she coped with being stared at all the time, being the subject of wonder and almost ridicule, she replied: 'When you're number one, you don't have to try so hard.'

Neil was impressed by the woman and her positive attitude. He later put his thoughts down on paper with his song *Sandy Allen*.

The band flew out of the States just as *Waiata* peaked at number 50 on the Billboard album charts. Over the other side of the pond, in the summer haze of London, the A&M UK branch had decided to bypass the American option and release *History Never Repeats* as the lead single. It too was resplendent in lazer-etched vinyl; the album was resplendent in the wrong colours.

A 20-date European tour had been put together under Brenner's direction, with Gordeon Troeller's Worldchief as tour co-ordinator, Wasted Talent as Agency and Lars Sorenson continuing the tour manager role from the US trip. This tour was designed to tackle territories previously uncharted, such as Germany and Switzerland, and was shaping up to be an expensive exercise as many of the venues had smallish capacities. The intention was to spread the Split Enz net wider throughout Europe; with this in mind, they flew into Geneva airport on June 7.

The tour kicked off in Lyons. Almost straightaway the lads found it tough going. The crowds varied in size from place to place and there were few fans. By the time they got to Paris on the fourth day they'd driven 1,100 kilometres and were testy. Before they took off to the show, Tim, anticipating hunger pangs upon his return, ordered toasted sandwiches for a midnight delivery. The show was fairly lack-lustre. Layered in dried sweat, Tim sat in his poky Paris room waiting for the sarnies, hot, steaming and tasty. They failed to materialise and the desk clerk was approached.

'I ordered toasted sandwiches, kind French person, for the midnight hour and they have failed to materialise. How come?'

... 'Monsieur! Just because you pay money, don't expect service!'

A short while later, in the romantic stillness of Paris 2.00 am, they gathered in the stairwell, their hushed tones echoing and spiralling down the marble walls. Noel gently lit the match, put the fizzing stick to the fuse and tossed the wad of firecrackers down the stairs. The hotel shook to the loud retorts and ricochets of the exploding thunder-crackers. Tim was heard to comment: 'Got 'im.'

Next it was Holland, where the lads squeezed a fire hose under the door of Tim's hotel room. He managed to find a corner of the room where the vicious spray wouldn't rip his skin off.

Six days later, after winding their way through another 1,500 kilometres, they were in Berlin. At the Kant Kino nightclub, as they played on in a virtual monotonous haze, a front row fascist hurled abuse and Eddie snapped. He ran from his keyboard and lashed out with his boot at the nerd's head. At the same time, the fire alarm went off and the room filled up with firemen. There had been a bomb scare. The scene transposed into a nightmare in miniature. Something about Berlin and bombs it seems.

Three days and 1,200 kilometres later, they were in Munich. Munich was not the tourist centre Berlin was. Here the Germanic nature was cast in chiselled heads and stern eyes.

Having spent nine hours that day on the bus, the guys were robotic and dishevelled. The CBS promotions people (CBS Records were distributing A&M through Europe) seemed to have little interest in the band and the lack of any progress with *History Never Repeats*, not to mention the album, ground the Enz down.

Tim took to the pavements and wandered unknowingly into a Munchen brothel, thinking it was a bar. He ordered a drink and then decided the mechanical, dense atmosphere was not to his liking. As he went to leave, he was handed a bill for $80. He turned to the fraulein who had delivered the docket. She stood rigid and alert, framed in hard muscle and a jaw that was made of concrete. Her tight, solid head sat squarely on slabs of granite. Her grandmother had been an SS Kommandofrau.

Tim: 'I'm not paying this just for one drink.'

The woman glanced across at a burly, Aryan monster who had materialised out of the gloom. His grandfather had been a ... well, you get the picture. He came over and stood beside her, his eyes on Tim, his hand on the gun in his pocket.

She reached out, grabbed Tim's jacket and hoisted him into the air, his purple brothel creepers a few inches off the ground: 'You vill pay!'

That night, back at the Leopold Hotel, Tim snapped. He ran from the dreary insipid place, throwing his clothes off one by one until he was running down the street virtually naked, screaming 'Arrest me!' Lars Sorenson, ever the intrepid tour manager, chased after him, picking up his clothes piece by piece much as Diana scooped up those golden apples.

The record company sent out a press release shortly after the Munich show. It is an extraordinary, almost insane read conjuring up images of *Cabaret*, *The Night of the Long Knives* and Peter O'Toole staring at Van Gogh in *The Night of the Generals*.

'... The European leg of the (Split Enz) *Waiata* tour 1981 required a group performance on a day-to-day level, so bitterly abstract, involving varying intensities of endurance, that all rewards, henceforth, became gruesomely small and hollow ... SPLITEN-HEIM ENZENN? Do not pass go, do not collect a sacful (sic) of platinum awards en route.

'Maybe next time, no? West Germany punks hung-up on imported attitudes, black nail polish, and kraftwerk, huddle together in tribes. Then you get the German couples – the guy studies the band, strings together bloated mental notes while his girlfriend freaks out to the quasi space-age watusi of *I Don't Wanna Dance*. Jah, itzt goooooot ...'

No wonder the guys were going mad.

At the same time as they were driving thousands of kilometres through the European motorways, service stops, autobahns, Kaiser Willhewillhenotz, bridges, off-ramps and roundabouts, Mushroom released *I Don't Wanna Dance* in Australasia. It attracted reasonable attention but fell short of the peak of *History Never Repeats*, particularly in New Zealand where the song failed to chart. It wasn't helped by a rather mundane video clip, which featured a quasi-disco nightclub scene with Tim wandering around under a mirror-ball. He really looked like someone who didn't want to dance.

Two days later the band were back in the UK, kicking off yet another English tour. The venues were around the 2,000–3,000 capacity; the fans were still out in force, although the press were showing signs of backing off from the unanimous laudatory praises of the previous year.

By this time, *History Never Repeats* was deemed to have failed and *One Step Ahead* was on the shelves in lazer etchings.

'... by all means marvel at the lazer-etched super spectrum that appears before your very eyes but whatever you do keep the volume way down low, or you may just find yourself, mere moments later, snoring on the carpet to the naff new sound of numb New Z-z-z-z-zealand.' — *Melody Maker.*

To put a focus on the A&M thrust at this time it is worth mentioning that the above review was sent out by the A&M publicity department in a press release, along with an equally bad single review and a good live review from Record Mirror. Just what were A&M trying to do? Some of the guys wished all this lazer-etched bull-shit would just go away.

Without the 'hit' single in place, or even looking like happening, the mid-echelon status of the previous year wasn't moving upward. Enz found themselves letting the odd performance slip through the cracks, unable to muster their usual commitment to excellence.

Winding through Guildford, Nottingham, Liverpool, Manchester and so on, the endless flicker of white lines on the motorway and the hangover from the frustrating European dates were getting them down. Even their second London Hammersmith Odeon concert failed to pull them up and, as they moved closer to the last concert in Portsmouth, they set their sights on a break.

After the final show the band drove back immediately to their hotel in London, the Kensington Hilton in Holland Park. They arrived about 2.00 am and woke at 7.30 am as the hotel shook to a fire alarm test. The camel's back strained and shuddered under the ringing siren until it finally collapsed; the lads started to ring Reception, screaming and shouting at them to explain this absurd commotion at such an ungodly hour. Nigel didn't get a satisfactory reply and threw his telephone through the window. Neil went downstairs and demanded an explanation.

'I'm sorry, sir. We have no option but to test the alarm at this time of day as this is when the flight crews arrive and if we tested the alarm later on, we'd wake them.'

Neil laughed as he realised, yet again, that they were really just musician scum. Nigel, looking over Neil's shoulder, found the explanation particularly outrageous and in the middle of a foyer brimming, as usual, with Japanese tourists and the odd American visitor in long socks and leisure suit, he shouted out at the top of his voice: 'Don't stay here. Don't fucking stay here; it's a shit-hole!'

Once again a burly security guard bundled him out of the reception area, although this time he wasn't looking down the barrel of a gun. The rest of them sloped back to bed.

Later, dragging their dinged, battered and messy suitcases behind them, they split in different directions, signing off from six years of hard graft in a country that saw them evolve from total unknowns to the dizzy heights of the Top 10 and *Top Of The Pops*. Neil flew to Amsterdam, Brenner to the Bahamas, Tim stayed in London, and the others can't remember what they did.

While in London, Tim finalised the arrangements for the producer of the next album: Hugh Padgham. Before *Waiata* had been finished, the band knew they wouldn't be working with Tickle again. Consequently, as the time drew near for scheduling the sessions and finalising a producer, they focused on Padgham who had shot to fame since his time on *Frenzy* as the button pushing tape operator. He had produced albums by The Police and Phil Collins and established a very strong reputation. He remembered the lads as a hearty, talented lot and was available from the end of November. He and the band were booked in by Mushroom at Paradise Studios in Sydney.

But before the band could dive back into the studio for some creative dabbling, they had thousands more kilometres to cover. They eventually gathered back in London and flew to New York for the first of a series of shows in the USA and Canada as support for Tom Petty. Petty had grown aware of the band and enjoyed what he heard. He asked for Enz to come on the tour and Brenner took up the offer. The shows in Canada would in fact be double bills although Split Enz would open the show.

The New York concert on July 27 was outdoors and attracted a huge crowd. From there, the shows wormed across America. The stuffing was pretty much knocked out of the lads by now, and the day-to-day librettos, intermezzos and melodramas of the road faded into one sweeping spiralling routine.

The only refined activity was the dropping of coins. With their now no-longer-$3-a-day status, the band were receiving reasonably substantial day-to-day allowances ('per diems' in the trade) and the coin change in their pockets would start to build up. In the relative quiet of the baggage carousels at airports, the lads would alleviate the boredom by dropping coins onto the hard floors. Feigning a disinterested air, the band member responsible for this would stare straight ahead as if this discharge onto the floor had never happened.

Slowly but surely the more foolish members of the public, flitting their eyes from side to side to ensure no one was watching, would scoop up as many of the coins as they could and stuff them in their pockets. It was the perfect Split Enz window on the world: watching the scurrying plebeians ferret around for cash.

Tim was particularly wild. He never took the time to find the correct amount when buying something and would hand over a $20 note for a banana. Not that he was into buying bananas any more. Way back in a distant tour of New Zealand (in Palmerston North, to be exact) he had bought himself a banana and an ice-cream at a corner store. As the rest of us clambered back into the Toyota Hi-Ace for the journey north, he looked at the banana ... at the ice-cream ... back at the banana ... and so on. The whole rigmarole of deciding in which order to eat them flummoxed him and he found it easier just to throw them both in the rubbish bin, which is exactly what he did.

However, back to the airports. This continuous breaking of large notes led to a huge build-up of coins in his ever-trusty satchel. Standing motionless at the baggage carousel, adorned with dark glasses and a great coat, Tim wouldn't discreetly tumble a few coppers onto the floor but rather thrust his hand into the morass of dimes, quarters, nickels and so on and turf a handful over his shoulder. The public would scurry here and there picking up the spoils.

A&M was now struggling with *Waiata*. They had released a 12" of *I Don't Wanna Dance* in the hope of achieving a groundswell at club level but this failed to materialise. There was ill logic there anyway. Why play a song in a dance club about NOT wanting to dance? By the time the band were worming their way through with Tom Petty, *Iris* was on release. This single had no video clip and in those days, with the explosion of the music video channel MTV, no clip was a shot in the foot. *Iris* didn't happen. A pity. Such a neat chorus! As well, the band weren't able to perform the song live as Neil had written it with his guitar in an open tuning. He didn't have the luxury of a roadie to pass him a specially-tuned guitar just for one song.

There was little opportunity to organise anything much on the Tom Petty dates as far as on-stage machinations went. Never once did they have the opportunity to sound check. Petty and his boys would spend all the time leading up to the show doodling, fiddling and occasionally tuning their guitars on stage. Twing, twing, ping, plonk, plonk ... twang, twing, kang.

Some of the dates featured Stevie Nicks who must have had some contagious disease as Enz weren't permitted backstage when she was there. Neil shot some super-8 footage of her tu-whit tu-whooing away at soundcheck, only to find himself being ordered to cease by her bouncer. 'Mmm ... pathetic woman,' Neil thought to himself.

As they crossed the border into Canada, however, the pace hotted up. A&M had continued to build the band and *Waiata* was a platinum success; coupled with solid showings on the chart for all singles. They performed a few shows with Petty to round off the tour and then, shaking Petty off, they did some dates of their own in major venues in the second week of August. By now, it was obvious: Split Enz were HUGE in Canada. The receptions to their shows were excellent:

'In a faultless performance of uniformly good material, Australasia's gift to pop led 2,700 believers to the meaning of state-of-the-art last night. Intelligence without pretence, solid musicianship and vocals without overkill, colourful stage presence – undoubtedly one of the events of the year.' — *Calgary Sun.*

'Aided by the best sound mix that has probably been heard in Winnipeg and an immaculate understated light show, lead vocalist Tim Finn and his five (sic) flawless cohorts cast an unbreakable spell that was just this side of miraculous ... every song was almost obsessively appreciated.' — *Winnipeg Free Press.*

Tim, however, was having problems. Still rankled by insecurity over his marriage, he copped another load of irritation on the Canadian tour. Two women (one a mother, the other her daughter) started to follow him. At every venue, just as Tim would charge on stage, thinking and wanting every show to be different, he would find these two women standing right under his nose. The daughter was obviously completely fixated by him, her eyes never shifting from his. Later on, they would hang out in the foyers of the hotels the band were staying in. They couldn't be sent packing as they were staying there too.

After a few shows Tim decided he'd had enough, and bent over and screamed in their ears, 'Fuck off.'

The mother called out to him: 'You can't stop us loving you!'

As far as she was concerned, Tim had obliged them with a Byronesque tantrum.

The next night Brenner waded into the crowd to remove them.

Later in another town, in another foyer, Tim went up to the

mother and suggested she was irresponsible for allowing her daughter to be so obsessed.

'She's a better person than you'll ever know, young man.'

Tim was full of rage and frustration at this. There is the possibility however that he was just frustrated and raging, full stop.

Soon after, the band, except Neil who flew to Auckland, flew to Australia. While Neil was in New Zealand he tripped to Wellington to receive a special award from the Minister of Broadcasting, Warren Cooper, for the contribution of Split Enz to the nation's music. *The Dominion* newspaper wrote: 'Finn casually dressed in black trousers and an open-neck shirt with a black and light blue cardigan said he hoped New Zealand would soon become synonymous not only with lamb, butter and the All Blacks but also with fresh and exciting music.'

They forgot the colour of his shoes.

Back in Sydney, Tim was facing a maelstrom. He knew it was curtains for him and Liz. Awash with the jealousy and neuroses that had plagued their relationship from day one, she said to him: 'Look, I'm going to go out and if you're not here when I get back, I'll assume it's over.'

As soon as she was out the door he was gone. While this release was exactly what he had yearned for, he was suddenly crippled with massive guilt for closing her world.

His attraction for her had been based on opposites whereby her street-wise persona, nightclub career and association with the London underworld appealed to him. In her company he came across the wild underbelly of society – semi-criminals, transvestites and so on – and he found comfort in her loyalty and unquestioning commitment to his talent and ambitions for the group. Even though he wanted out, her manipulation of his guilt kept him bonded if only in a superficial way. However, by October 1981, he couldn't keep it up and it was over. Tim then slid down a long chute to despair. His health disappeared like that gambler's lucky streak.

In a state of acute clinical anxiety bordering on a nervous breakdown, Tim left Melbourne where he had been camping at Brenner's home. He travelled with Neil to Philip Island, ostensibly for a session of songwriting for the coming album. But they hardly touched their instruments and spent the five days going for walks, climbing cliffs like they had done as kids and just talking. Tim stripped himself bare with Neil and, in a way, destroyed the conception Neil had of Tim as some kind of hero figure.

Channelling emotional energy into Tim, Neil found his brother vulnerable and afraid. His encouragement helped Tim clamber back out of his hell. The upshot of their time together was that Tim burst forth and channelled all his pent-up energies on a songwriting spree; Neil was left bewildered and confused by the whole affair.

Back in Melbourne, with the album just a few weeks away, the lads put some demos down at Richmond Recorders. During the breaks they would discuss the new album. They were tired of the commercial angle, the slightly frothy pop songs and the relentless pressure to come up with *I Got You* after *I Got You*. The choice of Hugh Padgham seemed inspired: he had obvious, major engineering skills but wasn't domineering. They had found him pleasant, cooperative and creative during the *Frenzy* fiasco. All they had to do now was come up with a bunch of songs that mirrored this new philosophy. They wanted an album that was a coherent, Split Enz album ... almost a collection of songs for themselves to savour and enjoy.

They (those that ever had them in the first place) had virtually given up on their grandiose schemes for international success once and for all. They still had a vaguely purist approach to their music although that purity had taken a battering over the last year. This album would be the album to bring back that clarity and homogeneity.

Shortly before the sessions began, Neil was sitting in the sun-drenched front room of a house he and Sharon were looking after in St Kilda. He had a riff of Nigel's going round in his head: a jumpy, resolving thing that demanded a song. It all came in a rush and he called it *Giant Heartbeat*.

Later, Neil would discuss the song with Helen Collett of the *NZ Times*: 'I wanted a song that wasn't totally obvious. It's basically about seeing the world as one. The giant heartbeat that binds us all. People seem to be becoming more and more separate, country to country. Other people have said it before and it's probably a total impossibility but it would be nice if the whole world was one big country.'

While Neil's expose has a global reference, the last line of the lyric excerpt might be more microscopic than macroscopic. The mouse and the elephant ... the bull and the ant?

Back at Domain Road, Neil fashioned out another song that was inspired by a phrase they had heard while touring Canada *Log Cabin Fever*. The theme of flight and escape came to the fore in his next composition called *Take A Walk*.

He later talked about the song to *Juke* magazine. 'It's about looking back, not so much remembering things that were but how you felt when you were young and the idealism you had back then. Try to conjure it up and relive it.'

While Neil was shaking off his poppy lyrics of the past and delving deep into the more serious side of life, Tim, sensing an album that would meet his expectations and coming to grips with the positivity he had reaped of late, presented the band with songs in a more relaxed vein. He had the thread of one, but was stalled, unable to complete the beast. For inspiration, he crossed the road and lay down in the botanical gardens listening intently. It fell into place and *Never Ceases To Amaze Me* was born.

The band travelled to northern New South Wales for a session of demos at the Music Farm. Songs such as *Lost For Words* were finished.

The second of the three was, in fact, written by Tim in 1978. It had a working title *Savage Lament* and in a literal sense depicted the arrival of the Europeans in New Zealand as seen through Maori eyes. The haunting mix of conquest and defeat was wonderfully portrayed; the melody came from the same era as *Stuff And Nonsense* and *Semi-Detached*. It was finally called *Remember When*.

It would later surface as the B-side to one of the least successful singles the band ever recorded.

The Music Farm was located in the bush and there was a primeval air to the place, an attractive wickedness. This green sensuality was enhanced by the mushrooms that grew nearby. *Remember When*, with its chanting, soaring vocal and pounding drums, (You-Tube that baby) points in a most definitive way to the feel and undercurrent that was to permeate the new album and, in particular, one song that Tim had been thrashing around with for months. He'd meshed a few chords with a melody that Nigel had written years before and had a couple of lines ... nothing else. He didn't know what it meant. But the completed song was very clear. It was *Dirty Creature*.

With his head rolling around in a mushroom cloud, Tim found himself thinking about the song in various contexts, the high awareness of nature almost enveloping him and pricking his imagination ... what might be lurking beneath the surface, under the simple facade of wind, earth, and water?

As the band walked into Sydney's Paradise Studios on November 30, 1981, they knew, in their hearts, that this was going to be a celebration. From the first note struck, it felt good. Padgham was superb in his creative expertise, encouragement and willingness to let the band explore their own devices. This time Split Enz were a band in the truest sense, and the sessions developed in a state of harmony and altruism. As well as recording songs that had been written by more than just the Finns, the musical framework burgeoned into a fantastic three-dimensional superstructure. Eddie, Nigel and Noel came out of themselves and were able to improvise and explore, knowing that Padgham was ready and willing to utilise anything they could throw at him.

Dirty Creature was one of the first tracks to be tried. They quickly stalled on it, much as they had done in the past. But Padgham prodded them, and over a period of three days they finally got it to work. By stripping the song back, Noel and Nigel utilised a sparser, more simple arrangement, with Nigel's bass almost ignoring the chord changes. This gave the song a firm, tight foundation. Once that was in place Tim was ready to put together those jigsaw pieces from the Music Farm.

In one burst of lyric writing back at the apartment he finished the whole thing. He poured out pages of phrases and physical ideas, slowly homing in on the final realisation: *'Have me back on dry land; save me from myself; animal magnet thug; I don't wanna stay (swim) in the ocean of madness; sunless deep; binds and gags my wits.'*

Dirty Creature was the perfect embodiment of the album's mood. Led by Tim's songs of replenishment and courage, built on arrangements that far surpassed the almost pop confections of the Tickle years, Split Enz, once again, bonded good and strong. Gone were the stripped bare rhythm sections and fruggy guitar arrangements. Noel and Ed combined to create a percussive kaleidoscope that pushed songs like *Dirty Creature* to superb heights around Nigel's fluid bass. Noel recalls his spine-tingling euphoria during the recording of the rhythm track for *Make Sense Of It*. Without Tickle, he knew he was going to be heard and not just on percussion. This time he and Nigel were the engine room.

Nigel, too, was excited by the spontaneous nature of the sessions, He had been hoping that this album would find them relaxed, unpressured and instinctive, and it was happening before his eyes, He was always looking for material from the old tapes that should be tried out in the studio, and would spend his spare time back at the hotel listening to old rehearsal tapes. One particular demo had existed as a melody for around three years and had been roughly assembled at a rehearsal. He thought it was perfect for the new album and suggested they work on it in the studio, shape it up and record it. It was called *Six Months In A Leaky Boat*.

Tim had conceived the song a while back after reading the book *Tyranny Of Distance* and looking at old folk music scores that harked back to the pioneer days and the quest for new lands. He wrote a set of lyrics that had a nautical flavour and highlighted Tim's boyhood fantasies about the sea. This salty imagery merged beautifully with the new found spirit he had enveloped himself in. During a game of golf, Phil Judd would later tell Tim that as a marriage of words to music, *Six Months In A Leaky Boat* was the best song Tim had ever written.

Eddie may have only come up with one instrumental track, but *Pioneer* segued beautifully into *Six Months In A Leaky Boat*. It proved yet again that when it comes to playing the piano, the man is a master. Once again the concept of merging the two pieces was devised and constructed in the studio with Padgham's overview guiding the process.

Split Enz forgot about A&M, Mushroom, American charts and Tom Petty supports. The whole carousel of the past 18 months was shunted away and found them clear-headed and dedicated. There was a magic internal chemistry and a belief that they had it in themselves, collectively, to create music that said more about themselves and their new-found strength than they had ever done before.

In parallel with his outpourings in the weeks leading up to the sessions, Tim wrote out his life story in simple verse. A song whose form was again inspired by the ancient folk music songs that he had been perusing. He forged the lyrics from a page of random bits and pieces: *'round the world; knew nothing of the world; football and musk; friendship and laughter; young men are waiting; haul away; smoking and punching; everyone has their own little story.'*

In an almost sea-shanty style, perfectly suited to his story of quest and struggle, the band created a unique song. There is nothing quite like *Haul Away*.

By February 1982, the album was in the can and they called it *Time And Tide*.

15

A WALK ON GILDED VINYL

With the release of the *Dirty Creature* single on March 15, 1982, Split Enz set about educating the public as to their musical progression from the Tickle era to this more mature stance. The track received an immediate, positive response from radio and media alike and hit the Top 10 in New Zealand, Australia and Canada without a hitch.

Meanwhile, waiting for the album release, Neil married Sharon on February 13 at Glen Iris. The occasion saw the whole Finn ensemble flying over from New Zealand only to be greeted by a 40-degree heatwave. Mary Finn couldn't find the church and arrived seconds before the service. She almost collapsed from heat exhaustion but the sing-song hooley back at the house allayed her distressed physical condition. There is little in the way of malady that a Finn brothers sing-along won't fix!

Neil, however, being a slight lad and in an excitable condition, couldn't hack the pace and after a couple of champagnes and a bit of beer on an empty stomach had to go and lie down. He had time to recover before the busy year began.

As a lead-in to the album's release date of April 13, the group planned a few dates through major centres. A press release announcing the tour went out with a photo of the band naked from the waist up. Neil later explained this to the *Perth Independent*: 'The current photo with us all without shirts was done very quickly and we had such horrible shirts on we decided to take them off. We just did it because it made us laugh ... Nigel looks totally cracked.'

The press release also contained a quote from Tim indicating the band's willingness to get out there and play. 'We're straining at the bit to unleash our tumescent desires, to play new music to the people who matter most. Yes, to present a musical striptease that will reveal the glistening body of Split Enz.'

What Tim probably didn't anticipate was that every newspaper in Australia thought his summation so eccentric that they decided to print it and then ask him exactly what he meant.

By the time he'd been interrogated on the subject by 20 journalists he was dismissive: 'Yeah, I was drunk when I wrote that.'

The endless probing by the press again found the Finn brothers at the forefront, although by virtue of the large number of interviews all members of the group were roped in to answer questions, tossing up a wild mix of warranty and wit.

Tim in the *South Australian Advertiser*: 'I suppose every person's Irish mother is a poet or a drunk and mine was a poet ... Having Neil in the band is great too, not only because we only have to write one letter home instead of two. *Time And Tide* is our seventh album. I suppose it's a bit like the dance of the seven veils and this is the last veil coming off ... We have run up the flag. Now we will wait and see if it is saluted.'

Neil was asked by *Scene* magazine about *Dirty Creature*: 'Taniwha is a Maori demon who lives in a lake. Every now and then he rises up and creates havoc. The funny thing is, Taniwha is better known in New Zealand as a brand of soap. Maybe it's got something to do with bubbles rising to the surface.'

He was then asked about Hugh Padgham and Noel: 'He (Hugh) has worked with some great people but he's as much a whacker as we are so we don't feel in awe of him ... Noel's a cult figure for us in the band as well as for people outside it. He's worked so hard and has to be the most together person I have ever met. Apart from all that, he's a bit of a twit.'

On the subject of the album's title in *Juke* magazine:

'Backwards it says "Edit Dna Emit" and that's fantastic. I like it anyway.'

'What does it mean?'

'I don't know ... look in the mirror, that's what it's about.'

Tim told the *Sunday Magazine*: 'My image of Noel from the (*Time and Tide*) sessions is him walking around in his underpants. You don't know how good Crombie can look! He'd make a wonderful wife, he can cook and sew.'

At times they were more serious. Neil told *Rolling Stone* just where *I Got You* stood in his perspective: 'It's quite a vacuous thing having a number one hit, because suddenly one song takes on the importance of ten years' work and you have to keep telling yourself that it was only ten minutes' effort. When I wrote it, I didn't even think it was a very good song and I was a bit embarrassed about it. You've got to keep reminding yourself of that otherwise you get to think *I Got You* – it's supreme, there's something magic about it. But I don't think there is. I think it's just a particularly catchy little song and we did it quite well and it was thrashed on the radio and it was a hit and that's all there was to it.'

Tim told *Juke* magazine just where the Tickle albums stood now in relation to *Time and Tide*: 'The thing with Hugh (Padgham) that really came out in the album is that he encouraged us to take a lot of risks, to play what we felt and to leave the mistakes and rough edges in. So in the arrangements there's a lot of strange notes floating around ... His sounds are just as big but he doesn't fuss with them ... We were very streamlined and poppy on *True Colours* and less so on *Corroboree*. This one is much more open ended and less rigid.'

Tim also put one in for his mates: 'In the studio, (Noel's) drumming really affected us all. He's got such a good feel and he's so adaptable. Also, Eddie came up with some things on the keyboards which I couldn't believe. His playing just gets better and better. And Nigel. The bass is the best it's been and he really came through with the songwriting too. And Neil. He's got some great vocals. He sings half the album. And ...' For possibly the first time, Tim was very much in love with his fellow Enz. They were all that mattered to him.

During the interview days, word came through from A&M Canada that pre-sales on the album had taken it to gold status with over 50,000 copies on order. A&M in America was impressed with the album, although they quickly came to the conclusion that they didn't have another *I Got You*. By now, they were probably thinking they would never get one. They decided to market it as a double package with a free *Frenzy* sleeved inside the *Time and Tide* cover. Rather than see them use *Frenzy* as released in 1979, the band, particularly Eddie, wanted that album recharged.

To this end Ed had the Rootin' Tootin' Luton multi-tracks sent out from England and proceeded to mix a selection for A&M. In the end, side one of this bonus *Frenzy* contained Mallory Earl tracks; side two was all Eddie's remixes of Rootin' Tootin' Luton songs.

There was no word from the UK about anything in particular, except that they were going to open with, *Six Months In A Leaky Boat* as the first single.

During an interview with *RAM*, Neil put the Split Enz attitude to the northern hemisphere on the table: 'We're only going overseas for about eight weeks this year and then coming straight back. Instead of touring places we hope to break we'll sit back and wait. We'll go to Canada because the album is gold on pre-sales and then to America. England we're going to leave unless it really happens.'

This was a new one. In the past, the band had seen touring as a means to achievement; now the philosophy had deviated to one of touring as a means to capitalise on a record's success. No one is quite sure where this dictum came from. It would appear though that the guys had quite simply grown tired of Europe and the struggle it had been. As well, the success of *I Got You* hadn't been matched by the

Waiata release; it looked probable that *Time And Tide* wouldn't happen there either, so why bother? Unfortunately, things don't change overnight. When a record company is told they won't get a band to tour until they sell a whole lot of copies of a new record, the company starts to think about the horse and the cart and the chicken and the egg.

In the squall of activity before the tour, young Eddie found himself under the microscope as well. He spoke to *Roadrunner*: 'Sometimes I feel it's a little futile what I'm doing. I guess as you start to get older you start thinking "Well, why am I doing this?" I'm making money, okay, and I'm becoming a bit famous but, you know, I don't feel any happier for it. The world's not getting any better for it and I should be doing something to help ...

'Over the last couple of months, I feel like I'm returning to normality. Just through getting to bed earlier and eating home-cooked food – getting a grip on what it's like to be a human being again ... It makes you realise how bad you've been feeling, healthwise. I wouldn't say the word insane, but it's a really unusual existence being a musician in a band. With all the travelling and things, you tend to get very disorientated. In fact, there's not many aspects of being in a band that I enjoy ... Playing live sometimes, playing in the studio and rehearsing. I think rehearsing would be my biggest joy. But everything else, the touring, the travelling, mixing with American rock industry people, is a pain in the arse really. One of the most important things we're trying to do when we play live is to play as we do at rehearsal, when we feel relaxed with no pressures. Just to try and capture that essence of friends playing together.'

There was the rub – another rub. Encapsulating the new Split Enz ethos, Eddie spelt out the changes that were now set in motion, changes that had been in the air the moment the band left America in August the previous year. *Time And Tide* was the musical experience they had yearned for and they had achieved it.

Now they wanted their day-to-day lives back for themselves. All the lads, except Tim, were living in homes with partners; the prospect of global travel in the pursuit of some dream that had nearly materialised two years before and was now retreating seemed a particularly daunting task. As far as Tim was concerned, now that he had hovered close to the brink of personal collapse and been pulled back by the strength and support of his fellow Enz members, he found himself questioning his blinkered aspirations. The others sensed this shift and found themselves able to realistically modify the level of commitment to touring, promotions, wheeling, dealing and grovelling that they had previously endured. Having shown they could make records that received unanimous critical praise, they had proved a point and now just wanted to go out living their lives.

In an interview with *Rip It Up*, Tim summed it up: 'After the success of *True Colours* and *Waiata* I realised that success wasn't what I was chasing all those years. It's a piece of shit, really; it doesn't make any difference to anything. What I'm chasing more is my own brand of perfection in what I do. I haven't come near to reaching it yet. *Time And Tide* was a great victory for me personally to be able to come up with what I think are some of my best songs ever. For everyone else it was a time of learning and a time of great joy. We had a very happy time making it.'

This sense of fulfilment with *Time And Tide* didn't alleviate their short-term responsibilities as far as touring went, and they flew off to Western Australia for the first show of the year.

The tour was by now called *Take No Chances*, which none of the band knew about until they saw it on a poster. In their typically reticent fashion they thought, 'Stupid title. Too bad.' However, having not played live for five months, they had other priorities. There were many thousands of people out there with concert tickets and the anticipation was high.

It had been two years since they had performed out West (12 months since their last performance anywhere in Australia!) and the reaction from the full house at the Perth Entertainment Centre was enormous. The rest of the dates through Victoria, New South Wales and Queensland were equally successful with the full-house sign out virtually every night. While in Melbourne, the lads filmed the video clip for *Dirty Creature*. Underwater scenes were shot in Channel Nine's swimming pool and the land and surface segments at a lake near Woodend. Once again, Noel's ideas were to the fore and the clip received a noble reception when it went to air a few days later. There was little emphasis on costumes. The sets and personal performances carried the show.

The tour finished with a huge show at Melbourne's Festival Hall and they then prepared for another film shoot. The second single had been chosen; it would be *Six Months In A Leaky Boat*. Noel built a rollicking nautical set in the confines of a Richmond furniture store and they shot the clip under his direction.

The day before the shoot for 'Six Months ...', the album was released worldwide. The reaction from the global press announced to the public the band's musical renaissance.

'The mad, eccentric and jokey Enz have been overtaken by the forces of maturity. This former teenager's band has proved through endurance and growth that it has a future of adult proportions.' — *Sydney Morning Herald*.

'*Time And Tide* is what we, who unlike time and tide, wait in hope, have all been waiting for.' — *Newcastle Herald Leisure Guide*.

Poppy sweet and Beatleish, (*True Colours and Waiata*) took the Enz closer to global success than they'd ever been, so what happens now? They check out of the hotel and start on the next leg of the journey.' — *Melody Maker, UK*.

'Perhaps their most honest LP, certainly their darkest ... Introspection and revelation. A lament for lost innocence and hope to find a future.' — *Rip It Up*.

'With *Time And Tide*, Split Enz presents a remarkable collection of tunes that take full advantage of studio technique while retaining the crisp, melodic lines of fresh pop at its most engaging.' — *Music & Media, USA*.

'The songs on *Time And Tide* are sophisticated and unpretentious, and full of the kind of aware, concerned humanism that has been missing in pop since the days of The Beatles.' — *Vancouver Free Press*.

On April 29, all bar Nigel flew into Auckland for a promotional visit. On arrival they found *Time And Tide* had entered the rational album chart in the numero uno position, with *Dirty Creature* perched at number four.

It was good to see the fools again although I was ambivalent about this number one album business. I was six months into my new job running Mushroom Records in New Zealand, and the whackos had just dislodged my number one album, *Cool Bananas* by Dave Dobbyn's DD Smash. Tim came round to my place and stayed a couple of days.

'Hey, Chang! I believe we knocked Dobbyn off number one. Too bad, West Coast Sucker!'

The next day there was an article in the *Auckland Star* telling us that The Swingers had broken up. Phil was going to be recording a solo album for Mushroom in LA with Al Kooper producing.

A few days later Split Enz were winging their way to Los Angeles for a sold-out concert at the Palladium. There were over 4,000 eager, ecstatic fans on site. *Juke* magazine was there: 'Instead of the polite attention and applause that greeted them in the past, the lads were continually enveloped in the arms of loving females rushing the stage.'

By now, the mechanics of Split Enz playing America had become highly sophisticated. Raewyn Turner and soundman, John Farrelly, were getting support from the best road crews and technicians. This quality back-up made for concerts with the best possible audio and visual presentation, and responses from the audience mirrored that. Once again, however, they found the airplay on the single lacking and the album bobbing around the 100 mark on the album chart. It was deemed, however, to be worthy of another shot. Brenner started planning some more American dates to follow the Canadian tour, which was about to start.

As they arrived in Vancouver, they quickly sank into the glory that was waiting for them. *Time and Tide* was platinum, *Dirty Creature* had been sloping around the Top 10 for weeks, and tickets for their concerts, booked in larger venues yet again, were selling like wildfire. In contrast to the States, Nathan Brenner had developed a positive rapport with A&M and the label was firing on all cylinders when it came to Split Enz records. In many ways, Canada, with its Commonwealth status and European influences, was quite removed from the way the Americans ran their music industry and it worked for Brenner. When *Rip It Up* travelled to Toronto, they got the low-down on 'why Canada and not the USA.'

Brenner: 'The whole music industry in Canada is less industry orientated; they are more open to new things.'

Eddie: 'Canadian radio stations offer much more space for new bands.'

Lorna Richards, of A&M: 'Split Enz are bigger here because Canadians have better taste!'

The truth of the matter was plain to see when the concerts kicked off: Split Enz were gigantic.

'Surveying an adoring crowd of 8,000, the look on the face of Captain Tim Finn told it all; Split Enz have circumnavigated the globe to find gold at a distant port-of-call. It's difficult to resist dubbing the Melbourne-based quintet as pop music's finest band. Intelligent, exciting, eye-catching, MUSICAL.' — *Edmonton Journal.*

'Synthesiser player Eddie Rayner is the fastest and most imaginative keyboard player in rock. Percussionist Noel Crombie is a light and frothy drummer, whose imagination also overflowed. Bassist Nigel Griggs anchored the band with a strong metallic bottom.' — *Edmonton Sun.*

'Split Enz can always be counted on to be colourful, musically, visually, lyrically, practically every pop dimension. They were in fine form on Saturday (to a sold out house of 4,000).' — *Calgary Herald.*

The consistent veneration heaped on the lads was tempered with the news from the UK that *Six Months In A Leaky Boat*, which had been receiving solid airplay on London's Capital Radio, had been yanked from the playlist because of the Falklands War crisis where, in essence, the UK was at war with Argentina.

The station manager was quoted: 'We feel it is a duty to our listeners not to go with the record. In view of the sinking of the (destroyer) *Sheffield* we thought the song would cause offence to a large number of our listeners.'

This ironic twist amused Tim in particular. It seemed absurd. His belief in that song and *Time And Tide* as an album of real credibility and substance flowed through to an anticipation that England might re-embrace the band after the virtual rejection of the extrapolated pop images that had found their way on to *Waiata*. With the expulsion of *Six Months In A Leaky Boat* from the airwaves, that prospect looked particularly remote.

That night on Vancouver Island the band, imbued with the sense of well-being that comes from full houses, glowing reviews and a wad of spare cash, took in a late night. Retiring in the early hours of the morning, they were awoken around 7.00 am by jack-hammers, pneumatic drills, chisels and thudding mallets as workmen started on the hotel renovations.

One by one each devitalised member threw open his door and screamed in the general direction of the cacophony: 'Fuuucckkk ooofffff!'

The racket continued, and Tim began to pace up and down the hotel corridor thumping on every door he passed: 'Come on, get up. The workmen have started. TIME TO GET UP!'

Eddie had opened his door for another bout of abuse when he spied Tim at the far end of the corridor, poised beside a maid's trolley stacked with dirty dishes. With a swift, dexterous flick of the wrist Tim sent it tumbling down the stairs to the floor below. As he sprinted out of sight, the manager walked out of the lift and knocked on Neil's door.

'Excuse me, Mr Finn, what is the meaning of this?'

'Well, Mr Manager ... Just try and see the lodge.'

With thousands of hours on the road notched on their belts, the 'boy's own' activities were now extremely sophisticated. The water pistols had a range, pressure and accuracy of lethal proportions. As well, the band had evolved their own language. Expressions pertaining to the negative such as 'no, not really, not too hot and not wonderful' were replaced by those from the 'pus' family, such as 'pus, pussy, heap of pus, heap of pie, pus-ridden, pus bags.' The morning after a vindaloo session would normally be described as the 'horse pours on the sauce', or perhaps 'monkeys' bumholes on toast.' When a member was trying to get a certain point of view across, the phrase designed to emphasise the issue at hand was 'see the lodge.'

This was also used to fob off irate hotel managers.

The continuing battles and rivalry with paper darts flourished unabated; the flights of these aeroplanes would be described as a 'stab the earth', 'check in' or 'Majesty' in ascending order. In recording sessions, the maker of the next cup of tea would be found by asking the pertinent question: 'Who's the youngest?' Eddie would always worm his way out of tricky situations by saying, 'No one told me,' or 'I wasn't there.' Persons accused of a 'selectiv memaree' would be showing an intentional thickness. And on it went.

With a nation full of ecstatic fans, the band tripped over the border to the wild and woolly extremes of the United States. Here they found plenty of interviews and some sold-out shows, but nothing to speak of as far as record sales went. Once again, they realised how singles-driven the States was; the fact that their *Time And Tide* album, as a whole, was a creditable, worthy record made little difference.

The band played shows in New York (at the Pier, supported by Duran Duran), Los Angeles and a few places in between, but with the records wallowing in Nowhereland and the general vibe a paltry comparison to the eminence bestowed on them in Canada, the shows pretty much came and went. When they flew out of Los Angeles on July 3 it might not have surprised them to know that they would never perform in the United States again.

Australia was still revelling in the musical greatness of *Time and*

Tide. The band kicked off a 21-date tour, this time climbing as high as Townsville on Queensland's northeast coast. It would be fair to say that the receptions were unanimously excellent and, with the public now familiar with the new album, the shows were able to focus on the *Time And Tide* material to the crowd's satisfaction.

At this stage, while the touring scenario in Australia was, on the face of it, a vista of adoring young fans, serious listeners and curious onlookers all in sufficient quantity to fill each venue, the overall picture was tending to stagnation. Having come from an arduous and varied tour of North America, Enz brought that stagnation and a healthy dose of tenacious fatigue with them.

Split Enz had been touring up and down Australia for two years now with the same level of intensity. As each show flicked up before their eyes, they started to merge into one long series of sound checks, interviews, dressing rooms, spotlights, screams, buses, road signs, and so on. The exhilaration of the live show was still there but in a milder, less sensational way and the lads found themselves hanging out for this merry-go-round to grind to a halt.

Raewyn Turner, who had lived every minute of this tour (and dozens previously), wrote an article for *Rip It Up* magazine which summed up the situation in a lyrical portrait:

'The past five months have been a variety show; the star hosts mingle with us, briefly, from their conveyor belts, flanked by the extras who are directed to have walk-on and bit parts for the day. The many famed and fabled buildings and cities roll on the big rollers past the car windows, and lots of people pass us in a hurry, to and fro, people with different accents and different smiles, clothes, lifestyles. While we sit and stand, walk and work, moving from car to aeroplane, airport to motel to theatre. The big rollers roll in the world's projection room, on to the screens which are our windows ... Split Enz the audience, the judge, in the van with the video surround windows. The selection committee, in a chartered plane, seated in rows until a kind man appears and opens the exit door, ushering us into another windowed room. We sit there breathing in the muted greens and browns and admiring the blue sky, until we're told to get out and into another room where soft muzak whispers that life is a breeze. Water flows from taps, milk is instant non-dairy whitener, food is but a phone call and an hour's wait away, all night television to lull to sleep and air comes from an air-conditioner.'

They were looking forward more and more to some time apart; a chance to find more of themselves and focus inwardly. A retreat. But this would have to wait a month or two.

By late July, *Six Months In A Leaky Boat* was ending its run on the Australian charts, having spent six weeks at number two, and Mushroom put their thinking caps on regarding the next single. After talking to radio people and the like, they chose *Never Ceases To Amaze Me*. The lads thought the decision a little dubious, but accepted the decision with 'Oh, well, you never know ... Could do okay I guess ... Can't really see the lodge but it might happen.'

It didn't occur to them that after the varied, mature and solid *Dirty Creature* and *Six Months In A Leaky Boat* singles, they were about to foist a lightweight song on an audience they had just converted from such ditties.

The film clip of *Never Ceases To Amaze Me* was put together by Noel and a director communicating on the telephone from various points on the Australian tour. This higgledy-piggledy planning process essentially guaranteed a less-than-satisfactory focus with regard to the end result. This was exacerbated by the extremely tight time-frame for filming. The band played their last tour date at an under-18s concert in the afternoon of August 15 at Melbourne's Festival Hall. At 10.00 am the next morning they were filming at the Melbourne zoo; the next morning (August 17) they were on a plane to New Zealand for their first shows in 16 months. Mushroom scheduled the single for release on August 30; put together too quickly, the film clip was victim to the schedules, vagaries and lack of detail.

The New Zealand *Time And Tide* tour was, in the eyes of the public, a chance to see Split Enz in their stripped down, finely-tuned musical state. The records were certainly trucking out of the stores: as the band flew in, *Time And Tide* was at number one again, *Six Months In A Leaky Boat* was number seven, *Dirty Creature* was 32. As usual the reception to the shows was ecstatic.

'As a visual spectacle, the concert was captivating. But it was the music that earned the adulatory reception. The five-piece were tighter and more technically accomplished than ever before.' — Wellington's *Evening Post*.

'The band is closer to its music than it's ever been. With a sound as near perfect as the Logan Campbell has ever heard and a brilliant light show, the band played with skill, intensity and real fire.' — *Auckland Star*.

But there was an irony behind the full houses and the multiple encores. The lads were tired and each night was a struggle. On the positive side, they were playing in New Zealand and there were friends and acquaintances popping up wherever they went. But that did not alleviate their clouded perspective and at each sound check they would stand around desperate for some clear thoughts and a stray thread of enthusiasm. Certain songs had driven them mad in the night after night repetition and they were trying to ferret out old numbers to replace them. *Hard Act To Follow* was summarily turfed. Ageing chestnuts like *Jamboree, Under The Wheel* and *In The Wars* were regurgitated and then thrown off like a scratchy, moth-eaten coat. It had been too long.

One night, Eddie, Tim and Neil started talking about the future. They decided that the perfect scenario would be a two-year break punctuated by spectacular one-off concerts. This would allow them to delve into different areas in the quest for something new. They talked about movies, perhaps taking a year off to make one. Or maybe a year to concentrate on nothing but songwriting. Since embarking on their six month touring schedule, they hadn't written a thing.

The New Zealand tour provided the odd distraction from the grind. The Dunedin show worked beautifully and the group took the southerners to an extreme musical height. The town was full of Miss New Zealand contestants readying themselves for the pageant the following night. So the lads had a sing-along around the piano at the hotel house bar and ignored them.

In Wellington, there was a reception put on by Polygram Records and Radio 2ZM for the lads to celebrate the impending 10th anniversary and *Time and Tide* reaching double platinum. Various Government figures were in attendance and Prime Minister Bill Rowling and MP Marilyn Waring gave speeches.

Waring hit the nail right on the head: 'We're all fans but we don't know how to tell you.'

The final show was in Auckland at the Mainstreet cabaret – sold out and hot on a cold, wet night. I was there when they kicked off with *Haul Away* and watched Tim carefully as he rolled through the years. They had it all; every eye, every ear was on them. Each note, beat and word spun out in a perfect sound mix under Raewyn's umbrella of light. The exhaustion and frustration were beautifully masked as, in the manner of the committed and the dedicated, they held that respect for their audience close to their hearts and made sure that there was not one moment of condescension, lethargy or cynicism. Another rollicking time was had by us all.

The next morning they rose, they packed and they boarded a plane. They were going home after having spent six months filling over a quarter of a million heads with their music.

As the lads arrived back in Melbourne, Mushroom released *Never Ceases To Amaze Me* in Australia and New Zealand. It failed to get anything more than a smattering of airplay or television exposure, and failed on the charts in both countries. They had *Time And Tide* poised in the Top 10 on both sides of the Tasman. The album had remained high from the huge successes of both *Dirty Creature* and *Six Months In A Leaky Boat*, and only needed another song of the calibre of those two to sustain its position.

In many ways, the *Never Ceases To Amaze Me* single was an indication that the Split Enz stumbling-along principle was now so entrenched it was never going to go away. In fact, from various quotes in various interviews it could be surmised that Split Enz took a certain pride in this bumbling approach.

On stage, the group were supremely well oiled and confident. But in the light of day, still reticent to confront major decisions, insecurities and aspirations with frank discussion, there was a tendency to roll with the punches and leave important decisions to the last minute.

As well, Gudinski and Brenner were now so embroiled that communications between management and record company were more often than not acrimonious. As far as Gudinski was concerned, Brenner had it in for him on a personal level; he believed that Brenner's vivid aggression was based on some bitterness he harboured from the days when Gudinski hired him to sell drinks and perform other menial jobs. Brenner felt Gudinski was ripping the band off, particularly in the area of government export grant rebates and was making sure Gudinski knew about it.

As far as Split Enz were concerned, Mushroom was off the scene and showing little interest; it would appear, however, that Mushroom's whole Split Enz focus was on trying to deal with accusations and complaints from Brenner. As far as Gudinski was concerned, Brenner was more inclined to spend his time confronting Mushroom than working with them to plan a long term recording strategy for the band.

This lack of a master plan, combined with the band's keenness to fade away from the previous six months' drudgery, allowed a vacuum to suck the momentum away. The band were exhausted and needed a break but without a blueprint in front of them, their distractions were allowed to flourish out of proportion.

By tour's end Tim, in particular, was subconsciously distancing himself from the others and thinking ahead to other activities outside the increasingly confined scope of the band. He realised that the past two years had been a personal triumph for him. In an external sense he had achieved a fair quotient of success; and at the same time realised, when confronted by the seemingly impossible task of bettering their UK and USA peaks of 1980, that his dedication to chart successes and so on was a hollow ambition. Parallel with this he had exorcised some nasty demons with his *Time and Tide* material; at the end of 1982 he found himself ready for something new.

In Melbourne, as the others eased back into a life of normality with their partners, Tim went into a writing frenzy. In a flurry he poured out a wild assortment of songs.

As well as this new material, he pulled out of his head a wad of old songs that had been unsuitable for the Split Enz scenario. Songs like *Fraction Too Much Friction* from 1979 and *Growing Pains*, which had been written the year before.

Tim's soul was still on his sleeve. In an intense, concentrated few weeks, he once again fashioned a clump of songs at the ready.

Raewyn Turner, artist

I loved 'doing the lights' for Split Enz. While other people were dealing with the real world we were on an extended childhood with no responsibilities except to our quest; and so I spent nearly eight years working in their cocoon.

The whole exercise was, in the vain years of my 20s, the perfect existence – no home, no possessions, no ties – living out of a suitcase. I was seeing the world although looking back on it, I saw very little from hotel and car windows. It was a life of ideals, fun and purity of direction. Never complicated nor muddled by possessions and the rituals of keeping and using them. Whenever I visited my family I would delight in emptying the cupboards or the book shelf and restoring each to pristine order, much to their disbelief – but satisfying my need for a sense of order. I had finished art school in 1975 and raced across the Tasman to be an artist. I made no assumptions that my career as an artist would be self-supporting and spent many weeks applying for jobs and delivering junk mail. I subsequently joined the dole queue and helped out Split Enz by switching their light show off and on at their pub shows.

By day I worked on a painting of Tim for a portrait-prize, watched the storms come in across Port Philip Bay and cut corn rows in Noel's hair, He, in turn, was hairdresser to everyone else. Noel and I often discussed the direction of visual style for the band, appropriating details from cultural uniforms and developing them Into the strange hybrid style that marked the early years of Split Enz. The band always supported whatever I wanted to do in lighting; surprisingly it was mutually agreed without discussion that I was going in the same direction as Split Enz. They were not interested in what was 'normally' done – and I too approached lighting without those expectations because I didn't know anything about it – I merely knew how I wanted it to look.

I was into the economy of design and the principle of less is more, mainly because the budget was always small. Until 1980, I didn't have the luxury of many lighting instruments, or the use of computerised lamps. I used colour contrast and projected texture for effect.

Reinventing rock 'n' roll lighting was not easy. I endured cruel comments from the male crews for the first few years assuming that their vituperation was justified because of my technical inexperience. Their sexist moans had the effect of making me more resolute to become supremely professional; to transcend their remarks and the difficulty of being their scapegoat. At that time there was only one other woman 'roadie' whom I met later on during our travels. Our common bond was that we were the first female technicians (roadies) to enter the male domain of rock 'n' roll. Another disappointing aspect was to find myself in a hotel room on the motorway, with nothing to do, nothing on TV, nothing to read, all futility; no one to phone ... nothing to look at except to study the hotel instructions again. So I started keeping diaries and drawing hotel rooms and portraits of the road crew. I had stints of painting too while the band were recording albums – but mainly I was consumed by lighting and touring and Split Enz and thus objectivity disappeared. We moved, we worked, we perfected performances, we listened to gig tapes, we judged ourselves, we succeeded while the outside world *seemed to stand still — I wanted to know how that world lived but I could never get there. After a few years I began to want a normal life and a home. I was an honorary boy for a while, that was, until Hoppy sacked me on the premise of having no girls on the road. On that same day in 1978, Robert was also sacked, and Phil re-joined, and I was promptly reinstated by the band an hour after being sacked.*

All this in the rambling guest house by the sea, standing in the cold unmoving grey fog in Burgen aan Zee, Holland. We went sightseeing on bicycles and a goat on the common ate Eddie's snotty hanky. Thus began a period of no girls except for me. It was a sad existence as I relished the company of the other girls and dearly loved to spend time with them — despite feeling detached because I was always running to the tune of the job. Hoppy was a disciple of the Rhythm of the Road and appeared to believe in the celibacy of the boys' hearts in order for them to focus on their odyssey.

Immersed in my own challenge, I was oblivious to the struggle of Tim's ambition and became disinterested in the prattle of the sine wave of successes and knockbacks.

During the redundant lull in 1978–79 I began painting again — one of these was of the band in a familiar New Zealand landscape with symbolic sheep. This painting was later used on the cover of the Frenzy album. I had been climbing a ladder trying to be a stage/lighting designer, but when I was offered work touring with other bands I couldn't bear the thought, It was but a Jacob's ladder; I decided it was time to put a folio together to obtain work as an illustrator.

1979 was a very cold winter in London and when the Enz asked me to do a six-week tour of Australia and New Zealand, I was instantly lured by the thought of sunshine and blue skies, and thus began a few more years of endless homeless disorientating touring. By then I had enough technical experience to experiment freely with projected images, effects and stage sets to complement themes. I drew and painted on film loops, sought out old gimmicky lighting, combined strobes, disco lights, chasers, Christmas tree lights, using anything and everything to create texture and movement.

Recently when I told my seven-year-old son that I was writing about my involvement with Split Enz, he said 'What do you want to do that for, it was only lighting?' – and that's what was confronting me when I opened up my compressed memories about Split Enz because it always seemed more than 'just lighting' and merely decorative. The Enz were challenging the context of contemporary music, and they had inspired me to work with light instead of paint. While the band could perform without lighting and stage sets, the lighting couldn't perform without the band. They could continue without my embellishments but I needed them for their content; I was never comfortable with the idea of my dependence in that way.

Finally, in 1982, I decided to leave. I put my gold briefcase away with a collection of hotel postcards, mending kits, numerous backstage passes, the Saint Christopher medals, and my mother's lucky black cat talisman and settled down to life in the suburbs.

16

ONE STEP UP AND TWO STEPS BACK

In December 1982, as Tim was writing furiously, as Neil and Sharon were conceiving a child, as Ed was building up a home studio, as Noel was in the studio recording *My Voice Keeps Changing On Me* and as Nigel was catching up on lost sleep, Split Enz turned 10 years old.

The band took their up-and-coming appearances at Sweetwaters and New Plymouth's Bowl of Brooklands as an opportunity to celebrate the fact. The shows were to be called *The Enz Of An Era* concerts, as a follow-up to the *Enz Of An Era* album that had been released the previous month. The album featured 14 past tracks, ranging from *Dirty Creature* to *I Got You* back to *Another Great Divide*. It had scored substantial sales and charted Top 20 on both sides of the Tasman, swinging the spotlight back on the band and the upcoming shows.

Crowther, Gillies and myself were contacted and before long the scheme was in place. It was reunion time! The band flew in to New Zealand late January and we all congregated on the hallowed stage of His Majesty's Theatre in order to refresh our memory banks.

Rob: 'Is 129 in C or G, Ed?'

Ed: *129?* ... What album was that on?'

Rob: 'Beats me, Ed.'

Tim: 'Hey, Croth ...?'

Croth: 'Yep?'

Tim: 'Try for a backwards sound on that end piece!'

The general plan of the reunion was to kick off with the current line-up and then bring on the old boys for a retrospective bash. This would entail Croth, Rob and myself coming on to perform five tracks, namely *Split Ends, Stranger Than Fiction, Woman Who Loves You, Another Great Divide* and *129*. Bob was to play some trumpet on *Dirty Creature* as a bonus, because he's ... well... that kind of guy. This of course he did with aplomb in his mouth.

On the January 30, 1983, the 35,000 Sweetwaters attendees sat still as Split Enz laid it on them. They kicked off with *Haul Away* and on the appropriate line – '*Richard and Mary drink to my journey*' – a spotlight swung to the sidestage, where Dick and Mary Finn were standing. It was a peak moment for them ... and us all. Did I see an invisible tear in the elder Finns' eyes?

The ancient mariners were then summoned to the stage; as I walked on in Noel's costume – bright yellow, skew-wiff and detailed – the sensation was surreal. Cascading in on the opening A-major chord of *Stranger Than Fiction*. I knew how to do that. The beauty of that night was, for me (and I hope them all), to be able to stand outside reality and move back in time.

However, the sense of wonderment didn't seem to be mirrored by the crowd and Tim sensed this. He pulled the plug on *Another Great Divide*, which was a pity. I was looking forward to playing it out for the last time. In contrast to my silent disappointment, Croth was just plain angry. Rob? I don't think he really cared and as we walked off, passing through the imaginary wall that had encased us, to the dark backstage area, it dawned on us that the impact had generated more curiosity than tumult. But I had drunk my fill and in hindsight, we should have performed a reunion bracket in His Majesty's Theatre.

Then 'they' – the curious onlookers from 1974 – would have come out of the woodwork to sit again on those red seats for the last time.

The *Enz Of An Era* concert at the Bowl of Brooklands in New Plymouth was destined for greatness by virtue of the crowd that came. Around 16,000 people turned up, almost breaking the previous record set by The Seekers in the 1960s. A close shave for Judith Durham's claim to fame in Taranaki!

The same show as at Sweetwaters was presented. It ran like clockwork, and we threw out the old classics. From there, the band returned to Australia, leaving behind the tranquil air of New Zealand and stepping into Melbourne where there were some decisions to be made. First up, *Time And Tide* had stalled and future recording plans had to be considered. Second, Noel had distracted the public from *Time And Tide* by releasing a cover of the country/r'n'b ditty, *My Voice Keeps Changing On Me*. He embarked on a few television chat shows and the like but the single failed to ignite. This didn't perturb Noel overly. It was all in good fun.

The decision was made to take six months off, which would allow the members to pursue various activities outside the group as a relief mechanism from the arduous months of 1981.

Neil went out and about, producing some tracks for Karen Ansell, and Eddie went working with Russell Morris and Paul Smythe. There was a general air of activity all around but little focus on the master plan for 1983 as far as Split Enz went. Nathan Brenner had been called to play a role in the United States as part of the Men At Work management and wasn't around to keep a close eye on whether or not his band of merry lads were, in fact, losing the plot.

Tim wanted to record a solo album and called a meeting of the band. He had a whole bunch of songs that Enz hadn't found suitable (such as *Fraction Too Much Friction*) and he wanted to get them out on record. This was not a serious exercise, he said, 'Just something I really want to do – a hobby.' But in his own mind it was stronger than that. He was keen to try something different outside the confines of the group, although the thought of *not* being in Split Enz was the last thing on his mind.

It appears that none of the others were particularly opposed to the idea. Eddie was also interested in the solo concept and planned to do some recording of his own. Neil did have some concerns that Tim might use up his good material on this new album and be found wanting in the future. But that was surmising – and they all drove off, not overly perturbed at this development.

With Tim's album in the pipeline, it was decided to record *Next Exit* as a one-off single which, you will recall, was written in 1978 and had been recorded as part of the Rootin' Tootin' Luton sessions. Eddie pushed for this song as he felt it deserved to see the light of day. The rest of the band saw the exercise as an interim measure and were ambivalent to varying degrees, but the project went ahead with Eddie pretty much in the producer's chair. Or so says Neil, quick to foist the blame. *Next Exit*, you see, was about to be a mistake and today no one knows quite why they let it happen.

Next Exit was released in Australia on March 28, 1983, a paltry shadow of its former self. The band had lost the grunge element of 1978 and 'clean' sounds just didn't suit the song.

It did nothing but confuse their fans. The point of the matter was that Split Enz had been evolving musically and, unable to objectively fix on future development, they presumed *Next Exit* would happily fill the gap. But the song was pegged to the seventies, and lacked the buoyancy and melodic variety of their latest stuff. *Dirty Creature* was pinned down by hooky riffs and an eerie, percussive bed; *Next Exit* relied on a tumbling, thudding rhythm section and power chords from Neil, all too pinned to the new wave era.

As well, the video clip was bordering on dicky and it failed to attract any interest. The single was not released in New Zealand; in an ignominious fashion, it slipped away. While the band weren't happy about it, there was little more than a brief moment of concern. 'Uh, oh ... a couple of flops ...,' they thought.

The good side of the *Next Exit* story was the B-side. The first track, *Two Of A Kind,* was merely pleasant. But, at last, as the single's third and final track, was *Remember When*, which had been written in 1978 and been recorded at the Music Farm over 12 months previously.

In February, shortly after putting down his *Next Exit* vocal, Tim got the okay from Mushroom to go ahead with his solo album. He put aside his Split Enz hat and headed north to Sydney's Festival Recording Studios, where eight years before he had sweated over his *Mental Notes* vocal takes. He had hired Ricky Fataar and Mark Moffatt as producers, after hearing a Renee Geyer single that featured Ricky on drums. Tim had always paid a massive amount of attention to drummers (ask Croth and Mal Green!) and his preference was always for the simple, solid, groove player. Fataar was one such stickman, and the fact that he and Moffatt were successful producers made their appointment a certainty. As far as the rest of the players went, Moffatt was on guitar and they brought in some top session people – Chris Haigon bass and Sam McNally on keyboards, as well as guests Joe Camilleri and Wilbur Wilde on brass and Venetta Fields on backing vocals. To top off this esteemed bunch, Richard Tee happened to be in town with Paul Simon; he dropped in for a session and played piano on *Fraction Too Much Friction* and Fender Rhodes on a couple of others. Tim was amazed at the man's dexterity.

From day one, Tim was blissed. His initial anticipation had seen him pretty much alone in the studio with drum machines, programmed synthesisers and so on. But with a full band in the room, the music jumped to life and he found the spontaneity uplifting. Tim had around 35 songs on offer, of which 10 or so were more than six months old and hadn't made it to the Enz repertoire. In the end it was principally the newer ones that found their way on to vinyl, although the album's lynchpin harked back to 1979: *A Fraction Too Much Friction.*

The album title looked to the future: *Escapade.*

In a lyrical sense, the material was a far cry from the dark splashes of psyche that held *Time And Tide* together. Here, Tim was in a robust mood and, while far from complacent, he had a wider focus.

After six weeks, the album was in the can and awaiting production. Tim welcomed the rest of Split Enz to Sydney for another Countdown Awards night, this time at the Capitol Theatre. During the show they performed *Next Exit* but the lyrics bore no relation to this specific occasion. In sharp contrast to the previous year when the band had registered a fat zero on the awards collection statistic sheet, they triumphed at the Capitol Theatre taking out Group of the Year (by public vote), Album of the Year (*Time And Tide*) and Songwriter of the Year for Tim. As well as the Enz hits, Tim had scored two Top 5 hits in the previous year from cover versions of his songs. Jimmy and The Boys had climbed the charts with *They Won't let My Girl-friend Talk To Me* and Jo Kennedy with *Body and Soul* from the *Starstruck* soundtrack (which also featured songs by The Swingers). It was a heady mix that swung the spotlight back on them again.

The public vote for Group of the Year was a good indication of the success of the Frenz Of The Enz fan club that was run out of Melbourne by one Peter Green. Green had started the club and it had mushroomed in membership to around 3,000 by early 1983 (it ended up with 15,000 members!). Green was adept at stimulating the hordes and the votes came flooding in. The award for *Time And Tide*, judged by music industry personnel, stands as a testament to the true worth of that record in the history books.

Three days later, Tim and Neil flew to New Zealand for their sister Judy's wedding. While there, they re-signed with Polygram Records for distribution; this time their records would be released under the 'Enz Records' banner, much as the Beatles had done with the Apple label through EMI in 1968. In an interview with *Rip It Up*, Tim provided a wider view: '(The Label) gives us the opportunity to be more or less the A&R (artist & repertoire) people ourselves ... be the ears, talent spotters. We've seen a lot of (New Zealand) bands coming up – Pop Mechanix, Blam Blam Blam, Dance Exponents –

that we've noticed emerging but haven't been able to help or do much for except encourage them. So we'll be able to say to bands, here's a deal. We'll, through our contacts, perhaps be able to arrange producers to come over here or maybe produce it ourselves. It's a whole new thing to get into.'

This pointed again to the widening perspective that was permeating the Enz. With solo albums, pet production projects, forming labels to sign kiwi bands and taking time off to retrieve some domestic normalcy, the Split Enz united sense of purpose was now well and truly weakened. As well, the wait-and-see attitude to the northern hemisphere was still hanging in the air: 'Limited touring but done with great style and impact is the answer. None of us are interested in going to America and touring for six months just to break a record. We'd rather wait for that hit single.'

I recall reading this interview in *Rip It Up* and being uncomfortable with one paragraph:

Q; 'Work should begin on the new Enz album in late June. Has much writing been done for the album?'

Tim: 'Neil's done more than I have because I've had my solo album. Neil's got heaps of songs and I wouldn't be surprised if it was his year for singles because I had a pretty good run last year. It's nice to have that opportunity to step back.'

Was this the Tim Finn I knew? Was he happy to step back?

Aware of the impending solo album, of course, and the fact that Tim had announced it as a brief affair from his marriage to the Enz, I had presumed Tim would continue to pour his energies into sustaining the high standards he had set with *Dirty Creature* and *Six Months In A Leaky Boat*. With the release of *Fraction Too Much Friction* two weeks after reading that interview, it all became very clear.

Bolstered by an extraordinary clip from Richard Lowenstein that personified the word 'cool', *Fraction Too Much Friction* walked on to every Top 40 radio station in Australasia and zoomed into the Top 10 on both sides of the Tasman. Four weeks later the *Escapade* album was released and it was there for us all to hear. This wasn't Split Enz.

This was music grounded in a different form. Based on a different premise. In many respects, the *Escapade* album had been as much an education, as far as Tim was concerned, as a creative project.

He found himself surrounded by people with strong musical roots and he was able to appreciate the soul and r'n'b legacy that those players brought to his songs. He listened to Venetta Fields as she made suggestions on harmonies; she was coming from a different place and Tim was captivated.

Consequently, while *Escapade* may have been conceived as a project free of any direct ambition on Tim's part, he had been so enthralled and excited by the sessions that he could not help but be affected. The beauty of it was there was nothing he had to prove. There was no pressure because he had Split Enz there. On release of the album he embarked on a promotional tour of Australia, during which he was obliged to talk frankly and openly about this new solo status. 'It was a labour of love if you like, we used to bandy the term "love vibration" around as a joke, but it almost became real; it was a great time. So that feeling transfers onto vinyl, you can always tell if there is a spirit to something, I was lucky in that respect. If I'd done it with machines it would have been a lot more sterile.'

In the end, *Escapade* refused to go away. It reached number one on both sides of the Tasman and sold more than 175,000 copies in Australasia. Every few months a new single would roll out and, even though they never matched the heights of *Fraction Too Much Friction*, they all received substantial radio and television play.

Seven days before the release of *Escapade*, Split Enz went into pre-production for their new album. It was June 14, 1983, and Neil was ready. Tim was there but his material was short of his usual standard. He was suffering a certain amount of guilt from the *Escapade* venture; this put pressure on him to come up with the goods.

During the months leading up to this rehearsal period, Neil had been writing furiously. It hadn't been particularly easy because, when it comes to writing songs it never is for Neil.

Perhaps an overview of Neil's general writing process is in order.

He starts to mould a riff on a guitar, perhaps, and then matches some words. He seeks out another chord that will suit the shifting melody and then starts ferreting out some more words. It's a slow process.

Another chord ... back to the riff perhaps ... or another chord. Ultimately, it is the chord progression that matters most in those early stages.

Once there is a pattern forming, he moulds the pieces into verses or choruses or whatever and eventually ends up with a basic musical bed. It's then that the major job begins – finishing off the lyrics. Neil usually doesn't know where the initial lyric thread comes from although, as time passes (we are talking years here!), the source is more recognisable. Once he has the first strand, he then spends an often inordinate amount of time finishing off the lyrics, coming back to rework them until he is happy with the form and the flow. As far as he is concerned, there is no obvious initial significance to the subject he is writing about although one is reminded, with this generalisation in mind, of the wood and the trees.

With the likes of *I Got You*, *Ships* and *Take A Walk*, this lack of conclusive focus on his subject matters could perhaps be the case. But with the songs that Neil fashioned over the first six months of 1983, in readiness for the new album and in the shadow of the *Escapade* tentacles, he found a thread of inspiration. Relating in an at times stark fashion to exactly where he and everybody else stood, Neil presented Split Enz with a collection of songs that found him standing alone. Songs that, today, he must still be very proud of.

One written outside his usual laboured method came together in a short half hour. He called it *The Devil You Know*. With *Our Day* he celebrated his impending fatherhood. With *Time And Tide*, Neil had committed himself to ensuring that Tim extract himself from his slide into despair. This had drained him, leaving him creatively exhausted while Tim rallied and, in a new found self-confidence and love for the band, poured out relief and emotions in a powerful writing spree.

Now, only 15 months later, Tim was aloft with *Escapade*, having taken the band's slackening bonds and stretched them to near

278 | STRANGER THAN FICTION

breaking point. There was an irony here: Neil, while consciously happy to assume it was just Tim playing footsy, knew full well that with the collapse of their thrust into the northern hemisphere, the worsening strained relations between Nathan Brenner and Michael Gudinski, and the failure of *Never Ceases To Amaze Me* and *Next Exit* (particularly in relation to their sustained sequence of hits from *I Got You* to *Six Months In A Leaky Boat*), Split Enz was awry.

Having always been a solid member in a democratic way, Neil was now having to come to grips with the possibility of transformations on a playing field where Tim had, inadvertently, shifted the goalposts.

He had one peculiar number that I was told by somebody (Ed methinks) to be about Brezhnev and Reagan. The title? *Bullet Brain and Cactus Head*. Two years later Neil told me that everyone thought the song was about Michael Gudinski and Nathan Brenner.

'How could they not,' I said. 'Neither Brezhnev nor Reagan had a beard!' Neil told *Rip It Up* the song came from his witnessing two men fighting in a bar.

Neil was also looking back. He found himself reflecting on his days at Te Awamutu College, when he and his mates would escape to a house beside the school grounds and meet up in the basement. The school motto was 'Kia Kaha', which translated to 'Forever Strong'. Another song, solemn toned with a gospel feel, also had a graphic, almost literal, symbolism. That was titled *Strait Old Line*.

The spelling of 'strait' is interesting. In a literal sense we are not talking about an unwavering course here, we are talking about constriction, narrow, rigorous, scrupulous, limited fortunes and hardship, if the *Shorter Oxford English Dictionary* is to be believed. Neil is telling us again (in loyalty to the promise he made himself when he was 12 years old) that no matter what lies ahead, nothing will stop him.

There is, I think, another parallel here. When Phil and Tim shifted apart by virtue of the original Australian struggle, and Tim sensed the alienation that Phil's loosening cohesion was bringing upon him, he put in words what were in his mind. Sick of holding his tongue. The circumstances were different on the surface but the same in the depths. Phil had been embroiled in a band that was charging on towards the fulfilment of his dream. But while his sights were set on taking his music to the world, he was unable to handle the setbacks; his dedication was overshadowed by pragmatic struggles. In the end, he hid behind a veneer of disinterest. As addition he became a father.

Neil, on the other hand, still had his commitments in place but was confronted with a situation whereby the whole Split Enz entity was shifting in focus. Tim's distracting solo pursuits were a prime nucleus of this swirling storyline. This produced a sharp irony as Neil was now reaching his prime as a writer, having graduated from the pop hooks of his youth to a more elegant and mature perception.

Enz was threatening to disintegrate around him. This new maturity was obvious, particularly when one takes the time to peruse his lyrics. They had come a long, long way in five short years. Neil's unguarded love song to his wife Sharon was proof of this. For once, he set out to write a specific song for her that would say it all but avoid the trite clichés of most pop love songs. With a melody that ranks in many Enz fans' heads as his most sublime, he did just that. How many people have written an almost perfect love song with the opening line 'I don't want to say "I love you"?'

Nigel was most impressed with the number when Neil brought it to pre-production rehearsals for the album and suggested that, as a match for the song's simple, pure thread, he call it *I Love You*. This was a working title for a while but in the end it was too bald for Neil. He called the song *Message To My Girl*. Neil Finn was peaking at the age of 25. (The history books show that most great writers do!)

The younger Finn was ready to present on vinyl a collection of songs that were wrapped in a vast sway of rich emotions; on July 1, 1983, Split Enz entered Paradise Studios in Sydney to do just that. On the surface, everything was in place. Hugh Padgham was back in as engineer/co-producer and everybody was set. But from the first day it slowly slid away.

Tim came to the sessions with his head reeling from the *Escapade* scenario. Having worked with Ricky Fataar and been absorbed in his style, which was rooted and simple, Tim found Noel's approach during the pre-production an uncomfortable contrast. On the first day, Ricky Fataar came along to the studio to try some tracks; Noel's confidence was blown. As far as he was concerned, this was 'bull' and 'ant' behaviour at its worst. He had suspected something was up but not actually consulted.

Aware that Ricky wouldn't be able to play drums on everything if only because the others were a bit suss about his coming down in the first place, Tim also suggested the use of drum machines. To this end he spoke to Neil and Ed, sure that this might be the answer to putting more of a 'groove' in the rhythm tracks. Neil bought it in a qualified sense and Ed went with the idea. He had been using drum machines in his home studio and was happy to try them out. He was now very focused on the production and sat next to Hugh, taking a firmer decision-making role than the others.

It didn't work. As they programmed and experimented away, time rolled by and little was achieved. In 1983, drum machines were a primitive version of what is available today and the flexibility just wasn't there. It was a foolish stage to suddenly look for this change. It's baffling that after finally reaching a good groove sensibility on the *Time And Tide* sessions, especially with *Dirty Creature*, they then appeared to lose it.

In addition the cohesive band feeling, their 'vibe', that had been so prevalent and so much a part of the success of *Time And Tide*, was negated by this 'machine' approach. Nigel, in particular, was scathing about the use of these fake drums and was not convinced they were necessary. In the end, the final tracks featured Fataar on one track only (*Message To My Girl*) as his takes on the others were considered by some to be too laid-back. Drum machines were left on a few (*No Mischief* was one) and Noel drummed on the rest. *Strait Old*

Line is one of them. Neil now says Noel should have drummed on the whole album.

But it wasn't just drum machines or their fragmented stances. It quickly dawned on them all that Tim's writing contributions were not matching the quality of Neil's. Tim's head was working away, trying to concoct new material for the album, but his heart was elsewhere, pumped with the hit singles, massive airplay and huge media attention that was still revolving around *Escapade*. A week into the Split Enz album, *Escapade* was released in America and Mushroom in Australia released its second single off the album, *Made My Day*.

Tim made it clear when he wrote a note for the Frenz Of The Enz 23rd newsletter just how he saw his position. ' ... We will be finished the NEW album in about three weeks and are hoping for a pre-Christmas release. The songs are shaping up well (Neil's anyway) and we all feel this will be a great album.'

His songs that were recorded were variable. The song titles seemed pointers. *Conflicting Emotions* and *Bon Voyage*.

Neil was frustrated and distracted. Frustrated because he knew he had a great bunch of songs and while he wasn't bothered with the *Escapade* success per se, he was disappointed that Tim had been unable to produce his usual standard of material for the current Enz project.

Distracted too because he was soon to be a father (he was flying to and fro from Sydney to Melbourne as the time drew near). By the time the album was a couple of weeks in, Neil was even more discouraged by the direction it was taking. His *Strait Old Line* ended up with a swinging, jazzy feel which was a far cry from the slow, gospel-inflected work he had presented at rehearsals. Somehow, it just changed. There were too many chiefs; it became obvious that the new album was suffering at the hands of changing minds.

There were some strange moments on the record. The oddest crops up at the start of *Conflicting Emotions*. As Tim climbs, dips, soars and sweeps in an almost 'soulful' entrée to the song, singing over and over, '*Conflicting emotions, Conflicting emotions ...*' a loud peel of laughter rings in over the top. A true incongruity that, on the face of it, seems a piss-take at Tim's expense, although he is probably responsible for it! Why is it there? The Split Enz way was to never take it all too seriously, even if the situation demanded it; here is Tim wailing *Conflicting Emotions* as a mirror to a band in atrophy, with a roll of guffaws to match?

By October, the album was completed and Neil had become father to Liam Mullane Finn on September 24. Brenner returned from the USA shortly after the album's completion and was worried by what he heard. While enjoying the aesthetic elements, he felt it was essentially uncommercial. Brenner recalls Neil as agreeing with his concept of holding-off on the release; however, in their democratic way, the band confirmed their insistence that the album go out.

This was their modus operandi. As a natural consequence of their long hard struggles together, the band had established a strong familial spirit. This was exemplified in the true democratic processes they utilised in decision making. While some were generally more vocal than others, no one member was able to dictate the final result. This philosophy ranged from practical matters to the sharing of publishing royalties. Everything.

Consequently, when the question of the album's release was raised, the majority vote was for it and that was that. Next came the decision as to which tracks should be included. In keeping with the status quo, it was deemed necessary to have a reasonable number of Tim's songs on the album even if confidence in them was low. Tim hadn't been around for much of the mixing and it seems quite possible that they could have turfed a few more of his in favour of Neil's. As it was, Neil was deemed to have too many and *Kia Kaha* was left off the album. The final tally was Neil, six; Tim, four. For the first time in many years, Eddie had nothing. Phil Judd was commissioned to paint the album cover. His work portrays the band cut off at the torsos, their heads reflected in a pool of water on the ground. Did Phil know something? The fact that Phil painted the cover stands as an interesting fact. He had painted the cover to the first proper Split Enz album, *Mental Notes*. Might he now be painting their last?

In late October, Tim put together a band and played five solo shows in Sydney and Melbourne: three in Sydney's Tivoli Theatre and two at the Venue in Melbourne. To full houses each night, Tim spun happily in the new environment, throwing out his *Escapade* material with the odd cover for good measure. The band was virtually the same that had played on *Escapade*, with Venetta Fields and Mark Williams on backing vocals.

Each was given their moment on stage. Mark Williams, in particular, shone with his solo piece in *Dock Of The Bay*. The critical reception matched that of the crowds; even those critics who had panned the album (of which there were a fair few) were smitten with Tim's performance.

Back in Melbourne, as a consequence of the *Conflicting Emotions* sessions, the doubts from Neil and Ed and, in particular, Tim, and Noel's now-deflated confidence, it had been decided to bring in a full-time drummer. Noel would return to percussion. Neil rang Rob Hirst, drummer for Midnight Oil and asked him if he knew of anyone who might be suitable for the band. Hirst suggested Paul Hester, an acquaintance of his who had proved himself a good stickman with bands like Deckchairs Overboard.

Paul was one of around 10 drummers who were auditioned by the band. The first chap to turn up offered them all some coke. The look on their faces was a noose around his neck and he ran. In the end, Hester was strung out a little by the lads who, being careful not to make a rash decision, kept him waiting.

By the third audition, he'd had enough. He pulled out a portable cassette deck and, holding it up in 'record' mode, asked them: 'Have I got the job?'

Neil recalls Hester's exemplary performance on *Dirty Creature* as his entree to the band.

His keen sense of humour and his simple style were also positive factors. As well, he had a past not dissimilar to the Finns. Hester's mother was a drummer and he recalls being dragged from his bed in the middle of the night to play drums for a roomful of boozed adults having a party. Sitting there on the stool in his pyjamas, he would whack out something from Creedence Clearwater Revival's *Cosmos Factory* album and then trot off back to bed. A regular occurrence. In exactly the same way as Tim and Neil, he was encouraged to perform and, in time, it was in his blood.

On receiving his official welcome, Paul went back to Sydney, packed his suitcase, kit and toilet bag, and drove down to Melbourne where he was put up by Tim at his Caulfield home.

Tim found this new boy on the block a refreshing addition. In his head, he could sense his impending disassociation from the band and having Paul around freed him from any direct confrontations in that regard. Hester told Tim that he had gone into Festival Studios and had the master tapes of *Escapade* played in the control room, with just Fataar's drumming coming through the monitor speakers. He listened for a long time and made a conscious effort to emulate that style. It obviously worked. As well, Paul was good for Tim: he went around the kitchen un-gluing all the honey jars, putting away the dishes that had been drying for three months, and so on.

He slowly came to run the house and Tim thought to himself: 'This is great. Someone who likes a clean kitchen!'

Paul found the Enz way a different kettle of fish to his time in Sydney bands. Neil especially impressed him with his commitment. Having always thought of rock 'n' roll as a lazy, come-what-may, follow-your-nose kind of thing, Paul found Neil's passion for hard work a real contrast.

At the end of October, Mushroom released *Strait Old Line* with a great clip courtesy of Noel. The wide, bright look to the video was thanks to a nifty lighting plan by Raewyn Turner.

The band had achieved a swirling slow motion effect by miming to the song at double speed, so that when it was reduced to normal speed the effect was essentially slow motion. Get my drift? Three weeks later, the *Conflicting Emotions* album was released. In New

Zealand, it featured a free EP in the sleeve with *Kia Kaha* on the A-side. It may not have made it on the album but, by hook or by crook, people were going to hear it!

The single had a good reaction, achieving substantial airplay – certainly more than *Next Exit*. The album was received with a generally laudatory air although there was some confusion over Tim's shortage of material. There was almost a let's-see-how-this-does backdrop in the frontal lobe of the music industry. The album entered the New Zealand charts at number five, which proved the solid core of fans.

Eventually the time came for Paul and the rest of the lads to walk on a stage together, and that moment was to be at Ballarat. Apart from the two New Zealand shows in January, it had been over a year since Split Enz as a full unit had performed live. The *Conflicting Emotions* tour of Australia and New Zealand was scheduled by Brenner with a break over Christmas for the lads to enjoy the New Zealand tranquility – by now a regular feature of the Yuletide.

Mushroom planned an extravaganza at Ballarat, and drove a hefty contingent of press, media and television people up for the show. A special function was held backstage, where the band were handed presentation discs to celebrate sales of more than a million records in Australia over their career. The show itself had a few hitches technically; Noel produced the 'Russian' cossies for the first time, the sound out front was muddy, Eddie had a hunch they were too rusty and Hester was nervous. In between songs, he would whack the snare or tom to alleviate his knocking knees. Ignorant of the bad sound and pleased with the response, the band left the stage in good spirits.

Tim walked beside Paul and said: 'That was good, Paul; you played well. But don't ever ever hit the drums between songs again!' He never did. At home Hester may have been the rooster in the kitchen, but on the road the roles were reversed.

The next night on the nationally broadcast music show *Countdown*, host Molly Meldrum slagged the Ballarat show. Neil wasn't happy when Meldrum drew comparisons between that show and Tim's recent solo concerts. As far as Neil was concerned, this was a swipe at him.

By virtue of the *Conflicting Emotions* album featuring his work so strongly, the Split Enz focus was now on the younger Finn and he could sense it. Whatever Tim's activity in the Enz environment, the Australian public were still considering him a solo artist.

The rest of the dates through to the middle of December were a major improvement production-wise on the Ballarat show and the houses were good. But the Countdown put-down had had an effect and there was a murmuring in the Australian music industry that Enz were on shaky ground.

This didn't relate to the fortunes of the second single, however; *Message To My Girl* received massive airplay into the New Year and peaked at number 11 on the Australian national chart. The film clip was shot in November in a disused Melbourne warehouse and was virtually a one-take clip. Make that two classics in a row from the House of Crombie.

The band wrapped up their 1983 time in Australia with a concert at the Myers Music Bowl in Melbourne, which ran under the title *Thank God It's Over*. Another rather bold statement in the circumstances. Very Enz.

In the third week of December, they flew to Auckland where they disappeared into the undergrowth before surfacing again on the 30th in preparation for the big New Year's Eve concert at Mount Smart Stadium with a solid support line-up in Big Sideways, Herbs and Coconut Rough. This show was to kick off the New Zealand leg of the *Conflicting Emotions* tour with their biggest Auckland concert yet, but wet weather put paid to that. A smallish crowd of only around 3,000 turned up but the reception, despite the wintry feel, was full-on.

During *My Mistake*, Tim broke into *Fraction Too Much Friction* in another moment of Enz irony: although to quote Mark Everton in *Rip It Up*, 'there was no hint of parody.'

To continue Everton's response to the show: ' ... Tim gives less away each time we see him. The genial host mask doesn't slip tonight. Are we talking about emotion here? Where's the vulnerability? ... Sometimes I want to take him seriously. I wish sometimes he'd just stand there and sing.'

As January rolled along the tour wound through New Zealand, with a huge outdoor show in Te Awamutu as part of the town's centenary. Although the Finn family had been gone three years, the town was still dear to the brothers and the Finns are legendary there.

The town Mayor introduced the band: 'They've had success all over the world but they've never forgotten where they came from ...'

On cue, Tim (from behind the stage) opened the performance with *Haul Away*. The life story. During *Kia Kaha* a local Maori dance party came on to recreate the haka (which is on the recorded version); Tim rallied in his front-of-stage role, relishing the opportunity to wrap up all his old Te Awamutu memories in a transcendent one-night stand.

The tour continued on its way, the band drawing huge crowds as usual. This was the upside of the New Zealand situation. While the singles were now failing to chart to any great extent (*Strait Old Line* peaked at 15: *Message To My Girl* to 28), the airplay was always near to saturation and the concerts attracted huge crowds.

In a live sense the band was still peaking, with the Auckland show the only disappointment.

At the end of the tour, Neil was interviewed by *Rip It Up*: 'I think it's a crunch year actually. The band's at a crucial stage of its career. We've been going for a long time and we need new challenges and we need to arrive somewhere definite ... Joining Split Enz means I've learnt a lot of lessons that probably would have taken me years to learn otherwise. I wonder if it would be good for me to do something else, to start something with my own stamp.'

Split Enz headed into 1984 a very changed unit from that which had walked tall only 18 months before, high on the global acclaim for their *Time And Tide* album. The past year had seen stagnation, and distractions. *Escapade*, the many months off, the *Conflicting Emotions* recording fiasco, and the management/record company antagonism had all contributed to a messy situation. Brenner was now insisting that all correspondence between himself and Mushroom be in the form of letters or faxes and the files were inches thick. The usual joint effort that record companies and managers hope to achieve for their artists was not a reality in the case of Split Enz. Split Enz were gradually going into the Mushroom too-hard basket, and meetings between the label and the band members never happened. And Brenner seemed powerless to hold back the group's internal decay.

1984 was shaping up as a make-or-break year and it was looking like a lot of things had to change, revert or transform if they were going to have half a chance of climbing back to the top.

17

DEATH'S DREAM KINGDOM

In the last week of January, Split Enz returned to Melbourne for a week's rest before the start of their next Australian dates, the *Kia Kaha* tour, which was scheduled to cover all the main centres including Perth. Kick-off date was February 1.

They had no plans to play further afield as A&M had turned down the release of *Conflicting Emotions* in the States and the UK. Despite this ambivalence from their parent territories, Canada and Holland, the two stalwarts, were gearing up for a spring release.

While in Melbourne, Tim was asked if he would write the theme music for and take a bit role in a movie that was being shot in April in Sydney. The director was Dusan Makavejev; the movie was *The Coca Cola Kid* and would be starring Eric Roberts and Greta Scacchi (pronounced *Skakkee* everybody – as in wacky!). He knew about Scacchi having seen *Heat And Dust*, and she was his image of perfect beauty (and everyone else's it seemed). He felt an exciting anticipation. Paul Hester became aware of Tim's new focus and teased him on the subject.

Eight weeks later, Tim flew to Sydney to start work on the movie and found Scacchi arriving at the same time. They agreed to meet again that same night. Scacchi had a dinner engagement with Makavejev and his wife, and she invited Tim to join them. Eighteen months later, Scacchi talked to me about it: 'Dinner with Makavejev was such a success. Makavejev's lowest common denominator is sex. He reduces everything to it and wallows in it. And he and his wife were playing games ... intrigues ... and Tim was so bright.

'He managed to fool them ... always one step ahead. But he had this terrible habit of staring at me. Gazing. At the end of the night I thought – no way! But the next night was different.'

Paul Hester flew up from Melbourne and relished in his mate's new partnership, laughing at their failed attempts to keep it subtle. During one break in shooting they both disappeared and came back a while later separately, as if nothing had happened. Tim was sporting a clown's mouth with lipstick smeared around; Greta's lips were clean – both oblivious that everyone was aware.

Shortly after his work on *The Coca Cola Kid*, Tim flew to Europe to promote *Escapade* and play a few shows. Holland had been very successful, with *Fraction Too Much Friction* reaching No 2 and the album Top 10. There was plenty of attention waiting to be showered on the lad.

While he was over there, the rest of the Enz played three shows at the Club in Melbourne under the moniker *When The Cat's Away*. They had Sam Hunt in support who riled a few of the attendant lesbian feminists with his wild style! Sans Tim, they played a variety of Enz tracks, a stash of odd covers, such as *Something In The Air*, as well as a long epic they had written the year before as an opus akin to the likes of *Nightmare Stampede*. It was entitled *Aotearoa – Land Of The Long White Cloud*. They had only performed it once (at the Founders Theatre in Hamilton) and they played it again – for the last time.

While in Europe, Tim rang, wrote and wired Greta as she worked to finish the film.

Makavejev had turned Frank Moorhouse's witty, satirical script into a load of garbage and Greta's part had become reduced to a joke.

It became a struggle for her and when she was later to see the film in its entirety she felt 'sick'. By the time she flew back to the UK, Tim had left for Melbourne and they waved at each other over the North Pole.

It was awards time again in Melbourne and Split Enz were in the final nominations for Group of the Year, which you will recall they had won the year before. They took their seats in a row, Tim sitting next to Neil. Split Enz didn't win. But Tim, as a solo artist, won Male Performer of the Year, Songwriter of the Year, Album of the Year, the clip for *Fraction Too Much Friction* won Video of the Year, and Fataar and Moffatt took Producers of the Year. Performing *In A Minor Key* during the ceremony, Tim was in control. He was singing live to a mimed piano part when the tape suddenly stopped. In a moment of extraordinary 'cool', in front of a national television audience, he said 'Let's wind it back' and told a few jokes while the tape was corrected, His eyes were open and the sweat dried from his palms. He then sang the song in toto and left the stage. The night was his.

S am Hunt, poet

Around 1983, I was a guest co-host (with Karyn Hay) on her television programme, Radio With Pictures. *I did an interview with Tim Finn. His single had just come out – we used to call it A* Fraction Too Much Traction; *or was it A* Diction Too Much Friction? *Well, I'd never interviewed anybody before. Tim was great! We recorded it in a Wellington pub, shared (among other things) experiences of Catholic secondary schools. The next year (or thereabouts), Tim and I met up again in Melbourne. We were both flying to Sydney and drove out to the airport together. We ended up drinking and talking so much we missed the plane. Back to the bar. More drink. When we finally got to Sydney, we found Greta Scacchi arriving at the same time, also from Melbourne, but on another flight. The rest, I guess, is history ...*

• • •

Underneath this cover of success, however, was a nervous, uncomfortable human being. In essence, this whole showering of accolades on Tim found him, sitting next to Neil and the other Enz lads, racked with guilt. He felt uptight. It was exacerbated after the show when he was surrounded by well-wishers. His stomach knotted; he had a traitor's heart, which prevented him from enjoying the glory.

A week later, the band gathered at his Caulfield home to kick off new rehearsals. It was clear immediately that nothing was there. They ferreted around for some direction in a dark room, devoid of any momentum; Tim avoided talk of the band's future although he did take part in discussions on the future album. He was insisting that a big-name producer be hired for the project or else they wouldn't be in the picture.

Unfortunately, with *Conflicting Emotions* failing to even be released in the major world territories, the likelihood of securing a 'name' producer was remote. Tim's concentration on the producer angle was his way of easing himself free of the situation. With the band unable to meet his request, he was able to give himself options. He was also aware that some members of the band were more intent on doing Neil's material then his own, and this made him even more detached, Neil recalls those days as 'dire'. There was a general air of 'What are we going to do?' The thought that Tim may as well flag it away was in certain members' minds.

This was logic at play. Tim, for the first time in his life, was obsessed with a woman. She was 12,000 miles away and he wanted to be with her. This was matched with his waning commitment to the Enz. A commitment that, over the years, had thrived on tension, ambition, frustrations, and a quest for goals based on his childhood premise of never-give-up.

With his cathartic *Time And Tide* album firmly in the history books and the subsequent shakedown of his obsession with success in the northern hemisphere, his dedication was now wasting away as he found less and less to strive for in the framework of Split Enz.

In many ways, it was as a consequence of his *Time And Tide* period, where through a remarkable internal chemistry with the band he had found a belief in himself that surpassed his ambitions for global success. He was unable to persevere through this time of indecision and dwindling resources. Greta's entrance had knocked him for six and with the sliding successes of the Split Enz records and his own solo fortunes still solid (*Escapade* had been Top 20 for seven months!) he was able to make a certain decision when, at last, he came to that fork in the road.

On June 16, 1984, Tim made his move and rang each member of the group to tell them he was leaving Split Enz.

He rang Neil first and Neil was not surprised. Tim suggested Neil form a band with Paul and try something new; Neil, reacting to Tim's suggestion, said he would continue with Split Enz. He wanted to get another album recorded. They all did. There was a general response – 'It will be better, now' – and plans were made with regard to the new album.

Eddie and Nigel were not overly concerned as they were now convinced that Neil's songs were good enough to carry the whole Enz musical front. They hadn't been overly taken with the *Escapade* album on a musical level and the *Conflicting Emotions* sessions had confirmed their shift to Neil's material.

Meanwhile, as Tim made plans to fly to Europe and meet up with Greta, a press release went out from the Mushroom office proclaiming Tim's exit. The next few days, the press was full of it. In New Zealand, the *New Zealand Herald* made comment on the editorial page; the first time a New Zealand rock 'n' roller had ever graced that column:

'For pop music in this part of the world, Tim Finn's departure from Split Enz is equal to the upheaval the Beatles would have suffered if John Lennon had deserted them 20 years ago. The Liverpudlians were at their peak then; Split Enz have been the No 1 group in New Zealand and Australia for the past several years ... Finn, born in Te Awamutu, founded the group in the early seventies and hauled it up the dizzy heights of commercial success to the top of the charts ... Now Finn – lead singer, lyricist and lurex light – is leaving the group to pursue a solo career. He will be missed as a Split End, but he will remain one of New Zealand's most popular sons.'

As Tim flew off to London, Split Enz set about preparations for a new album with demo sessions at Eddie's home. Various bits and pieces were tried out. One of them was a chorus that Neil brought along. Its title was *Something So Strong*.

By now, Neil had realised the full weight of Tim's decision. While he was not perturbed by the changing musical perspective, change was afoot and he found himself thinking: 'I'm now going to be fronting this band that's been defined by Tim's presence for the last 10 years and all I'm going to get are people comparing it to the old Split Enz.' This found him very uncomfortable. He stewed for a fair few days, the options cropping up like ducks at a shooting gallery. This was (is) Neil's way.

In contrast to the quick left-turns Tim throws into his life, Neil plays with options as if dealing a poker hand, waiting for the full house or the royal flush. It was in this turbulent state of mind that he realised the demo sessions weren't working. There, the reality was clear. He found the work they were doing to be all too familiar. Here was a band with a new focus and the chance to grapple with a new direction but Neil couldn't see it coming; he couldn't find the new ground and he became quickly frustrated ... and convinced.

Three weeks after Tim announced his departure, Neil called a meeting at Eddie's and told them all he was planning to leave. A formal meeting was then arranged at Nathan Brenner's office a few days later. There the fate of Split Enz was sealed, as Neil confirmed his intention to quit.

Discussions ensued as to what this would entail. It was decided to wrap up the whole affair with a major Australasian tour, which would go under the title *Enz With A Bang*, and they would record some of the newer material for an album. They had been rehearsing the stuff so they may as well commit it to vinyl.

Gudinski suggested they bring Tim back for the final album but they weren't interested – Tim was now gone. They did think Tim should return for the tour and plans were made to contact him.

In essence, Noel, Nigel, and Eddie would rather Enz had sustained. Nigel was particularly frustrated as he felt that he had spent years working with these people, building up an internal respect for each other and so on, only to have it thrown away. In a general sense though, they were all ready for the change and didn't think of it as a definitive 'end'. Nathan could still manage them in whatever role they moved into and there would still be the happy family feel.

It made sense to them.

As Neil drove away from Brenner's home, he was sideswiped by a speeding car driven by a drunk woman. His vehicle came to rest at the side of the road and he was dazed. Two Greek men came to his aid and they waited for the police to arrive. As Neil stood there flustered and breathless, Noel drove slowly past in his 1949 Triumph Renown, edging past the wrecked cars. Neil said to the man beside him, 'I know that guy ... Noel!' Noel drove on unaware that Neil was there. A short while later, Nigel drove past in his 1954 Fiat stationwagon. Nigel cruised past slowly, unaware of Neil. Neil said to the man next to him, 'Hey, there's Nigel ... Nigel!' A minute later Eddie drove past in his Morris Major. Again Neil exclaimed 'Hey, it's Ed ...'; as with the others, Eddie was oblivious and drove on. The two Greeks looked at Neil as if he was a deluded madman.

On July 25, a press reception was held in the Hilton Hotel, Melbourne, to announce that Split Enz were calling it a day. In a rather macabre setting, the five of them – Neil, Noel, Nigel, Paul, and Ed – lined up in front of the assembled hordes. A life-size cut-out of Tim was placed in the one empty chair. Questions were thrown from the floor and answers parleyed around.

Ed: 'In the end (Tim) had no enthusiasm for the band. We found we were better at playing Neil's songs.'

Neil: 'It's as amicable a split as it can possibly be. There were a few tensions but nothing beyond those of a normal group.'

On the phone to *Rip It Up* the next day, Neil was asked if Tim's departure prompted the end:

'Because of the timing of the two announcements, it might go down in history as that being the reason for breaking up but it wasn't really. Tim's leaving was something he could have done two years ago before he did *Escapade* but, because of strong ties with the band and that, we struggled on. But from that point his involvement with us became a bit plagued with problems – partly because of the time he took on his album but also because the songs he was writing were growing further away from what we wanted to play, so there was a bit of conflict. Not conflict in a personal sense, I want to stress that. But just musically.

'So at the point Tim left we were hoping he was going to really, so we could get on with being a more united band and we also thought it would do us good musically. But for quite a long time I had been thinking about the fact that I had been in Split Enz for seven years, since I was 19, and I've never played in another band barring two gigs as After Hours. And I guess I'd formed my own reasons for wanting to call it a day – so the two events happened almost simultaneously but they're not as connected as a lot of people probably think they are ... We're still very ambitious, particularly me as far as another band goes. There'll be plenty more heard from us but now we'll have the freedom to do a lot of things that being in a band had meant we haven't been able to.'

Neil wrote a note for the Frenz Of The Enz club:

'This is not a farewell letter, nor is it a message of gloom. Yes, the band is calling it a day, there comes a time in everyone's life when a change is for the best. Such is the case now for us. We have all shared the last few years and packed them full of good memories to last a lifetime. The farewell tour will be a great opportunity to see you again and celebrate the great times we've had.

'Who knows, Paul may even streak again (if the money's right, of course). It won't be easy but we might even convince Crombie to break out the old spoons one more time. Then there's Tim's press-ups, Eddie's pout, Nigel's fish impersonations and I might even fall over once or twice if the mood's right – all manner of ridiculous exploits to relive!

'Contrary to what you might hear from the scandal mongering media or from your local gossip, all of us including Tim are and always will be great friends. We all have plans for new projects. I will more than likely form another band in the near future but whatever happens, you will be hearing plenty more from us and that's for sure. We are very excited about what the future holds in store. We'll be giving it heaps – make sure you do the same.

'Thanks a million for your support over the years – it has meant so much to us. See you on tour and remember; don't be sad, the best is yet to come, Yours forever in Frenzship ... Neil.'

While Tim was in London, he recorded the song he had written for *The Coca Cola Kid*. It was entitled *Home For My Heart* and was produced by Phil Manzanera at his Gallery Studios.

He then met up with Greta and they both crossed the channel to Italy, where he dived deeply into another world and had the time of his life. In a hazy back street of a Tuscan village with peeling church bells, the incoherent bubble of Italian voices, and cypress trees swishing outside an open window, Tim lay between linen Italian sheets with this wonderful creature beside him. Greta's father, Lucca, was pure Italian and Tim found him captivating – a wild, exhausting character. And then there were the directors, writers, actors, and so on.

In September, it came to an abrupt end. He had to shuffle it all to the back of his head as he flew south to Australia to meet up with his old cohorts and commence rehearsals for the *Enz With A Bang* tour.

While Tim had been biding his time with a heady mix of sex and all things non-musical, Split Enz as they now stood had been recording tracks for a final EP. The sessions were held at Armstrongs (now shortened to AAII) in Melbourne with Jim Barton, the in-house engineer, engineering and co-producing. Eddie was pretty much the band's studio spokesperson. The sessions were a mixture of old and new. In the end, it was decided to bring some of the old stuff recorded at the *Next Exit* sessions out of the woodwork and make the record a full-length album. Noel reworked his *Ninnie Knees Up* track, which had been released as the B-side to *My Voice Keeps Changing On Me*. Eddie had an instrumental, *The Lost Cat*, and Nigel's *Adz* was included. Paul had a wild, shuffling thing called *This Is Massive*, which surprised a few people. 'This boy can sing!'

But, as with *Conflicting Emotions*, Neil carried the album. He brought in a varied selection; not all of them were new. The wonderful *Kia Kaha* was hauled from the vaults and confirmed a place; *Late In Rome* was re-recorded but passed in.

Not so with Neil's reworked version of the song he wrote in 1977 entitled *Fallout With The Lads*, which had been recorded in the After Hours demos. Neil thought that it was time to bring some of the fringe material into the light of day, and this was one of them. He had pulled it out of his memory bank and strummed it one day, thinking to himself, 'Shit, did I write that?' Impressed with the chord sequence that his formative brain had pieced together all those years before, he wrote a new lyric and added a chorus. The original was only a minute long. At rehearsal, Nigel was particularly impressed with the final version and championed it on to the record. The great sax solo is by Wilbur Wilde.

As well, Neil had a demo of a 'thing' he had put down at home. It was a few chords with a bunch of lyrics that he committed to tape just to see if it had life. When he took it to Eddie, Ed offered a melody he had written as a suitable merge piece. The end result was called *Years Go By*. Indeed they had.

Aside: If you think the lead solo in that song is exemplary then take note that it is one of which Neil is particularly proud. The other solo of which he is fond is on *How Can I Resist Her* from *True Colours*.

The track that cropped up as the obvious lead-off single was

Neil's and it drips with the spirit of change. As an epitaph to friends on the impending final moment, the song speaks without any maudlin airs or bitter tones. It was, and still is, a worthy paean to the old world from someone striding headlong into the new. Who needs a press release when you've got a title like this? *I Walk Away*.

By mid-September the album was completed and entitled *See Ya Round*. Noel conceived a cover on the 'round' principle and it was scheduled for release in the first week of November. *I Walk Away* was scheduled for early October. The video clip was shot in Melbourne and has a convivial air about it. Noel's conception was subtle and the soft lighting and shifting emphasis worked well. Dressed in black, reminiscent of the *One Step Ahead* video, the band put in a stirring almost moving performance without any hint of self-pity, resignation or defeat. The only Split Enz clip without Tim, *I Walk Away* finds Neil even 'looking' different. The picture that was painting a thousand words, yes?

With the news of the band's demise still ringing in everyone's ears, the album failed to make much of an impact in Australia. In New Zealand it was more promising. The news of the break-up had created huge coverage and the album peaked at number five. It only remained in the charts, however, for 10 weeks. By now, Gudinski had had enough of Brenner's deal with Polygram Records and the album was released on the Mushroom label through Festival Records. Months before, Brenner and Gudinski had ended up on the steps of a Melbourne courthouse, as writs flew left right and centre. The Enz Management/Mushroom Records affair had deteriorated to such an extent that had the band not folded, their support structure might well have suffocated them to death anyway. But that is another story, another wild array of rights and wrongs.

In yet another ironic setting, the external struggles never really touched the band. Split Enz were oblivious to most of the clashes, contests and quarrels that surrounded them.

While waiting for Tim to return from Europe, Neil and Paul started planning a new group.

Neil was intent on a 'guitar' band and they put out the word for a bass-player and second guitarist. They spent some hours mucking around with odd bits and pieces – just drums and guitar – and they would make tapes. They talked about the future. Who, where, why, what? They played with the odd musician now and then but no one seemed ideal.

In the last week of September, Tim was back with the lads and rehearsals kicked off for the tour, which was to be promoted by Enz Management. Enz Management was Nathan Brenner, Simon Zaicz (long serving tour manager) and Grant Thomas (as tour accountant), who had joined the ranks from being tour manager for Ian Magan in New Zealand. Brenner had suggested that instead of having third-party promoters handle the tour, 'we' would be the promoters. The band thought that made sense although some of them weren't quite sure who 'we' were. The tour was booked into major venues and from the word go looked like being a monster. The tour of New Zealand was put in place by Ian Magan and was scheduled to wind up at Auckland's Logan Campbell Centre, a fitting city for the band's final concert. It did start there after all.

With the wheels in motion, the end in sight and no responsibilities to weigh them down, Split Enz kicked off their *Enz With A Bang* tour at the Canberra Sports Centre and never looked back. Sharon and Greta travelled with them, the crowds flocked to see them and the reception was enormous. From Perth to Townsville, Hobart to Lismore, it ran like clockwork and the old tricks came back into play. Noel was whacking his spoons and cutting his teeth on crunching guitar solos. Tim was flying high with his adrenalin press-ups, and Neil would skip and dart across the stage. There was the odd moment when the broad view and the uncertain future would sneak in and slap one of them in the face, but it wasn't often.

Tim spoke to the *New Zealand Times* from Brisbane: 'We're having a lot of fun, actually; we're being quite adolescent about the whole thing. We've never been so close, ironically.

'We've found over the last few days that instead of us all going down to the soundcheck in two or three different cars, we all tend to jump into one car, with six people all squashed in. It's just happened coincidentally ... We all drift around the hotel at night and end up in one room, just talking and joking about old times.'

At the third Melbourne Festival Hall Show, Neil was having technical problems with his gear. He couldn't find the resilience to shake it off and his emotions surfaced to play havoc with him. He flew off on a tangent, played a heavy metal solo on *I Hope I Never* and then decided to do a stage dive. He'd seen someone do it on television the night before and thought 'Fuck it ... anything to make the gig better!'

As he threw himself off the stage in anticipation of the crowd holding him aloft, the sea of faces parted and he crashed onto the floor. Neil recalls lying there with a mish-mash of teenage girls removing his shoes, socks, shirt, tie, etc. He looked up to find Frenz Of The Enz boss, Peter Green, standing over him and exclaiming: 'Just you wait until Sharon hears about this!'

Greg Taylor from *RAM* magazine takes up the story:

'Neil Finn, come on down!' intones Big Brother as the Wild One is eventually hoisted back on stage looking faintly seasick. 'That was the most intense experience of my life,' announces Neil, breathlessly. 'I've waited twelve years for that.'

'The guitar transmitter never fully recovers and Neil keeps breaking strings; but the mood has been established. Taking chances, revving up, kicking the finely wrought sensitivity that is Split Enz out the window. At last the twin percussion becomes more than decoration: Noel Crombie and Paul Hester are going for it like bats out of Burundi – and the night ends in screaming triumph as the audience invades the stage.'

Between the main set and the encore, Neil found himself back-stage crying.

At the after-show function at the Tropicana, Neil hit the tequila slammers and quickly sloped off into a drunken stupor, In this rather vulnerable condition, a young chap came up to him and said he wanted to try out as bassist for the band that Neil was putting together with Paul. His name was Nick Seymour. Neil said, 'Yeah, sure ... anything ...' Seymour drove Neil home, as Sharon had by now left him to it. Near the end of the night she had asked him what he was drinking. 'Orange juice, Sharon.' Smelling the vodka from five feet, she had plucked the car keys from his pocket. As Neil waddled in the direction of his home he thought to himself, 'I wonder if I can get to the fence?'

The next night, they all gathered at a Japanese restaurant for a media dinner with *RAM* magazine. They were reminiscing and the interviewer, Greg Taylor, was trying to focus on the Split Enz essence:

'Late in the evening, as the last cups of green tea and Japanese beers are drained, I'm still trying to fabricate that handle, that essence of Edwardian drawing-room charm and manic clowning that clothed some fine romance ...'

Tim: 'Yeah, it's a corny thing, but I think it was projected as a naiveté, an innocence ...'

Neil: 'It's definitely a friendly image – it's not the Tatts or anything.'

Tim: 'An eccentric uncle maybe? The uncle who was a bit potty: unpredictable but definitely warm.'

Neil: 'We've been a lot of things to a lot of people ... In the early days it was kind of Credibility/No Success, then we had Success/Moderate Credibility ... Now it's sort of like ... I don't know what it is.'

Tim: 'It's finished, Neil.'

Each city in New Zealand welcomed the band with open arms, knowing that this was the last time they would be able to do so. By now, the lads were red hot on stage, wringing every last drop of substance out of their now vast catalogue of popular songs. To capitalise on any ironic twists they went back in time for some of the material. *Time For A Change* was brought out and dusted. The first show was in the Wellington Town Hall and the following day Wellington's *Evening Post* printed an editorial:

'Only Tim Finn remains from an original group that was totally unconventional when it started twelve years ago. Now the rest of the world has caught up as the band slowed down. But Split Enz has managed through several changes to remain a witty and engaging group of counter culture commentators, occasionally capable of Beatle quality irony ...

'An Australian critic once observed of the original band: "Each member is a virtuoso in his own right. I have often thought the technical excellence of New Zealand music is because there is nothing else to do in that Godforsaken hole but practise, practise, practise ... Be that as it may, that technical excellence set a standard for young performers. While an older generation will always associate Split Enz with ear plugs, the group has done something to increase the sum of human happiness for hundreds of thousands of young New Zealanders. As the group members go their separate ways great goodwill goes with them".'

The same night, the band turned up at the Michael Fowler Centre as finalists on the Top International Performer category of the 1984 New Zealand Music Awards. The other two finalists were Dragon and Tim Finn. The award was presented by Prime Minister David Lange and he read the winner's name out loud and clear to the watching nation: 'Tim Finn.'

I was in the audience and thought, 'Sheeeeeit!' Tim was taken aback. Sure, his *Escapade* album had done well in Australia and Holland. But here he was back in the ranks, halfway through a huge tour and relishing the chance to celebrate Split Enz' grand wealth of musical works in the great 'final gesture', and he was still being hauled out as the more worthy entity.

In many respects, it dampened the occasion and as the band shuffled on to perform *Kia Kaha* there was an uncomfortable air in the room. Here was the music industry's chance in front of a national television audience to see them off in style and it hadn't happened.

Neil's song to his old classmates sounded rich and elegant, and I turned it around in my head. I took the liberty of interpreting the lyrics in my own way – Neil was waving goodbye to his merry band. Wishing them well and then turning his head around to face some cloudy horizon ahead. Unperturbed.

The following day they were off across Cook Strait to Nelson and another ecstatic response. They were in the swing of it, enjoying each other's company and lapping up the attention that was lavished on them at every turn.

The pressures were gone; they had nothing to prove. On stage, off stage, they looked each other in the eye and managed to assuage any acrimony that had crept in over the past 12 months. It had to be that way. We are talking about a bunch of people here that had lived, breathed, played, sang, strummed, walked, flown, driven, slept, rooted, argued, water-pistoled, shenaniganed, farted, eaten, partied, and cried together for many years. They were grown men and, in the final moments, knew the bonds they had and respected them. This was their own last chance as much as it was the public's, and they weren't going to spoil it for themselves or anyone.

The rest of the tour was sold out and came to rest in the sunny climes of Auckland. The Logan Campbell had filled two nights so quickly that Ian Magan put in another two for the 3rd and 4th December. They too sold out immediately.

Neil and Paul took the opportunity to audition Bones Hillman on bass one afternoon before soundcheck. Bones had lain low since the demise of The Swingers and was a little rusty, although he was keen. As the rest of the Enz guys walked in for the soundcheck they found Neil, Paul and Bones bashing away on the stage and it dawned on them. Neil was up and away. The ant was off.

With an unprecedented four nights of sold out Logan Campbell shows ahead of them, this was shaping up to be some doozy farewell ... and it was. I was there for the last night.

Suited in wild colours and hop, skip, jumping, lurching and leaping abounding the stage, Split Enz gave their home town a warm, luscious, emotional send-off. Neil's final effort in the single stakes – *I Walk Away* – kicked off the proceedings and struck an immediate chord. I think it was C major. Hester was now inextricably immersed in the Enz spirit and his performance out front on *This Is Massive* was masterful. Nigel poured thick molasses bass all over our ears. Tim was springing around, his frenetic stage persona of the seventies a shadow on the back wall. He was now level on the stage with the rest of them and they looked, sounded, smelt like a unit ... a one-piece shot of exalting musical superiority.

Tim sat at the piano and tinkled a few notes in E major, a sure sign he was heading to *Time For A Change*. He spoke: 'This song is dedicated to all the past members of the band that are here tonight. They know who they are.' And he started to sing.

Lyrics from the 19-year-old head of Phil Judd. It was uplifting. I flew around the hall for a while and slid out the door, sailing out over the city. The Wynyard Tavern was murmuring with a few hither-and-thither conversations; Levys Saloon was thundering to the sound of 100 space-invader machines which had long replaced the Video Table Tennis ones. A quick right-turn and it was down to the beach at Kohimarama where the footprints still stood, etched under a thousand tides. Like every note etched in my head, their heads ... a nation full of heads still oscillating to some, a few (all?) of Tim, Neil and Phil's words and melodies. Eddie's notes. Noel's magic vision. The lot of them. Putting on the headphones – standing in a line.

Charlie brought a huge response in its timeless allure. Tim's vocal precisely in tune and Ed's cascading piano frills drowning us all. Pouring out of the speakers like beads of emotion. *The Woman Who Loves You* brought Noel out for his final spoons love affair with the public. Once again his legs buckled over, flew out to right and left, his head statuesque and grim. Unique.

The final encore was *Hard Act To Follow*. Tim's sweat flew all over the front row and Neil squashed his distortion pedal. As the final chord reverberated around they came to the front of the stage and lined up. They'd had a good show. Who would follow them?

As they wandered away to the waiting blackness sidestage, Eddie paused and struck a piano note. Neil noticed this and came back and punched out another one. As the younger Finn then left the stage, Eddie ran back and quickly pushed down a key. I think it was an E flat. It sang out over the sustained applause and stamping feet. I caught it as it went by and put it in my pocket ... the very last note ever played by Split Enz. And it was Ed ... it HAD to be Ed, that played it.

I went home and put Eddie's note in my bottom drawer, beside the Stebbings demo tape. I still have both of them.

Back in Australia, the band met at Nathan Brenner's office to sort out the tour accounts.

The tour had been extraordinarily successful; they were keen to get their superannuation and get on to the next stage of their musical conquests. The windfall was not, however, to their liking.

Brenner, as both promoter of the *Enz With A Bang* tour (along with Grant Thomas and Simon Zaicz) and group manager, ended up with a substantially larger sum than the individual band members – far more than they had anticipated. As far as Brenner was concerned he was entitled to his 15% share of gross as manager and 15% share of net as promoter. As far as Enz were concerned, they were all promoters together and Brenner's definition of 'gross' in a management sense was greedy. Brenner stood firm, unhappy with the band's claim of his taking more than his share. While Brenner had not taken his commission at certain stages in his time with them (particularly from record advances), it was felt by most of the lads that his take from the final tour was overkill. They left intent on never having anything to do with him again. Tim was the odd one out. About to fly to Europe, he adopted his usual better-the-devil-you-know approach and later re-signed with Brenner. That contract led to more strife for Tim when he dropped Brenner about a year later.

As Neil walked away from the meeting, he said to Paul Hester: 'You and me, Paul ... We'll form this band and do it together. Just you and me.' He made a promise to himself never to sign another management contract and he hasn't to this day. While December 1984 saw the end of Split Enz as a performing unit, December 1985 saw the final lid put on their recording career. The Melbourne Festival Hall and Auckland Logan Campbell Centre shows from the *Enz With A Bang* tour had been recorded and a double live album was put into production through 1985. It took a while to come together what with mixing, cover art and the problem of trying to decide which tracks to put on, but in the end it was ready and released in early December. It was entitled *The Living Enz*.

By now, I had exited my role as general manager of the New Zealand branch of Mushroom Records and was readying myself for a few years in London. I was keeping creditors at bay by writing a record review column for the *New Zealand Herald* and out of the blue I received the Enz album in the mail. Ignoring the arms-length distance I was supposed to have in that role, I absorbed the record and wrote a review for the paper, which was printed.

'Most New Zealanders who have been motivated to witness live music have at some time or other been to a Split Enz concert ... From the first performance in a coffee bar in December 1972 to its final concert at the Logan Campbell Centre in December 1984, Split Enz toured New Zealand 13 times (give or take the odd burst in the early days), playing to more than 200,000 people (excluding the Sweetwaters and Nambassa festivals). Since leaving the band in 1977, I have seen them perform on all but one of their tours and the overriding factor has been their consistency. The costumes, stage sets, choice of songs and gimmicks have always provided colour to varying degrees – but the band's unwavering high standard of musical performance has never been less than excellent. That is why very, very few people have ever left a Split Enz concert unsatisfied. At the very least, people got a musical hammering that could not fail to impress.

'In many respects, Split Enz broke the rules. Its democratic musical process avoided the usual pitfalls of over-indulgence and the internal rapport was so acute that the band could sway the most blasé listener with its combined sense of fun ... and sense of purpose.

Spurred by Tim Finn and Noel Crombie who were chiefly responsible for the band's initial dedication to "excellence on stage"', Enz
members never forgot their dictum – "the people have paid for this –
we are here to entertain."

'Whether it was wholesale laughter as Crombie played his
spoons, banging heads to the raucous *I See Red* or shutting eyes to
Tim's plaintive *I Hope I Never*, the audience displayed a wide spectrum of emotions throughout any performance – proof of the musical
power and entertaining glory that was once theirs ...

'The only sad thing about this record is that it is the end – the last
album for the band that in 1980 surged to the top and, while
retaining its unique musicality and integrity, won over a whole
nation. In April 1976, Roger Jarrett, then editor of New Zealand rock
magazine *Hot Licks*, wrote a review of the band's concert at His
Majesty's Theatre and took the opportunity to farewell the group on
its trip to Britain. He signed off with: "Thanks for the vision, thanks
for the trouble and thanks for the time."

'To Tim, Eddie, Noel, Neil, Nigel etc., I can only say 'Hear, hear!'

At the time of the release of the album, over a year since the band
had last performed, Noel was interviewed by Colin Hogg for the
Auckland Star.

Noel put the entire Split Enz quintessence in one simple, direct
and perfect sentence. He said: 'We are all still inextricably entangled
– Split Enz isn't just something you can walk away from.'

18

POSTSCRIPT

Neil Finn formed Crowded House in 1985 with Paul Hester and Nick Seymour. Through a string of hard yakka and fortuitous moments they recorded an album in Los Angeles. A single from that album *Don't Dream It's Over* took Crowded House to number 2 on the US singles charts. That catapulted them into outer space.

These days Neil, Sharon and at odd times their sons, Liam and Elroy, live in Auckland and keep various musical projects alive as well as own the Roundhead recording studio. And further to that – Wikipedia.

In 2018, Neil joined Fleetwood Mac as a singer/guitarist. The band perform *Don't Dream It's Over* in their sets. That's cool.

Many things happened to **Tim Finn** after December 1984. The coolest one bodes a telling. In some year – probably the early 1990s – he met Hayley Mills. It was in LA and Tim was there with Greta Scacchi who had a global reputation as a film actress. Hayley was introduced to Tim and they chatted and then the night was over. Some months later Tim and Greta were somewhere and Hayley Mills happened to be there too. She walked up to him and said 'Hi,

Tim'. When he told me this I wanted to kill him. All the other things he's done? Wikipedia has it all.

Phil Judd has maintained a songwriting focus from his home in Melbourne where he has a recording studio and brings tracks out into world. He has built a substantial fan base who are loyal and supportive. As well, his painting skills come to the fore on a fairly regular and irregular basis.

As with the Finn brothers, Wikipedia covers the post-Split Enz life very well.

DEDICATION

For Von and Jerry

PUBLISHER'S NOTE

If you have enjoyed this book by Mike Chunn, we would appreciate it if you could write an online review at whichever online retail site you bought it.

The first digital edition of *Stranger Than Fiction* was published in 2013 after Mike revised his manuscript for the best-selling printed book of the same name, first published by GP Publications Ltd (New Zealand) in 1992. This edition was updated in 2019.

Also published by Hurricane Press

I'm With The Band, *by Mike Chunn, Jeremy Chunn and Barney Chunn*
Whether you want to make a living from music or play for fun, this is the essential guide to the New Zealand music industry.

I'm With The Band explains everything you need to know from recording demos to signing contracts, from hiring a manager to protecting your music.

Key figures in the New Zealand industry — names like Neil Finn

— share their inside knowledge and experiences to help everyone from the hobby band to the performer on the brink of discovery.

The talented Chunn family, led by Split Enz founding member Mike, combines to provide this unique insight into what it takes to forge a career in popular music.

The Chunn family are New Zealand music royalty — Mike is a founding member of Split Enz and Citizen Band, and has managed Sony Music Publishing, Mushroom Records and APRA and established the music charity Play It Strange.

Jeremy Chunn has played in bands in New Zealand, Australia and Europe. A journalist, he has written about music for Rolling Stone and other magazines.

Barney Chunn writes about music and performs original music with his band, The Tricks.

Reviews include:

'This book is the real deal. I wish I had the chance to read it at the start of my career.' — Dave Gibson, vocalist for Elemeno P.

'Gives advice on every part of the musical process.' — *Salient Magazine.*

LIVE: Gigs that rocked New Zealand, *by Bruce Jarvis and Josh Easby*

* *with contributions by Mike Chunn*

Whether they played to a few hundred in a back bar or to 80,000 fans in a stadium, many of the world's biggest music stars have performed in New Zealand.

This beautiful coffee table book celebrates 50 years of tours, concerts and one-off shows performed in New Zealand by our favourite acts.

From Johnny Cash in 1959 to today's artists, this large format high quality book revives memories of shows that created history — The Beatles, Rolling Stones, Led Zeppelin, Bob Marley, Bob Dylan, David Bowie, Split Enz, Elton John and many more.

Weighing more than 2kg, the 288–page hardback book is

arguably the boldest music book publishing project ever attempted in this country.

More than 50 photographers and 20 of the country's best music writers have collaborated to bring together this amazing collection of images and stories about the best concerts in New Zealand over the past 50 years.

Photographers include Bruce Jarvis, Kent Blechynden, Murray Cammick, Garry Brandon and other concert specialists. We've also had access to private and public collections, including those at the Alexander Turnbull Library and at major newspapers.

Writers include Josh Easby, Phil Gifford, Russell Baillie, Graham Reid, Garth Cartwright, Bryan Staff and Murray Cammick, with contributions from musicians like Mike Chunn (Split Enz), Midge Marsden and Chris Parry (Music Hall of Fame inductee).

The reviewers have enthused about the book:

'A volume that will have your ears ringing for days.' — Russell Baillie, Entertainment Editor, *New Zealand Herald*

'Spectacular ... bloody brilliant, loved I!' — book blogger Graham Beattie

'This book is on a grand scale.' — Tom Cardy, Entertainment Editor, *Dominion Post*

'Some of the images belong in the rock photo hall of fame.' — Chris Bourke, author of Blue Smoke, writing in *The Listener*

'This coffee–table page–turner captures the magic.' — Graham Reid, music writer, author and editor Elsewhere.co.nz

'Brings them all back like a Beatle singing Yesterday.' — Tommy Kapai, *Bay of Plenty Times*

'Superb.' — Grant Harding, *Hawkes Bay Today*

'Dynamic photographs and memories.' — *Kia Ora Magazine*

'A stunning book, both visually and in its content.' — Jillian Allison-Aitken, *Southland Times*

'Awesome.' — Sir'Vere, *Rip It Up*

'Epic in its scope.' — Piers Fuller, *Wairarapa News*

'Looks great - an amazing compilation.' — Neville Aitchison, *Employment Today*

Radio announcers love the book:

'Fabulous!' — Danny Watson, *NewstalkZB*

'Outstanding!' — Dean Young, *Radio Hauraki*

'Fantastic!' — Maggie Barry, *Radio Live*

'Amazing!' — Brendon Weatherley, *Classic Hits Taupo*

'Awesome!' — Toast, *More FM Waikato*

'Really amazing!' — Richard Dryden, *Classic Hits Manawatu*

'Stunning!' — Robert Scott, *The Breeze*

'Magnificent!' — Noelle McCarthy, *National Radio*

'Fantastic!' — Tim Gruar, *Groove Wellington*

'Brilliant!' — Charlotte Ryan, *bfm Auckland*

'One of the best books to land on my desk for a long, long time. I love it.' — Kerrie-Maree Adams, *KMTV*

'I can confirm you have a hit on your hands.' — Murray Lindsay, *Classic Hits* National Network

HURRICANE PRESS

How to find us
www.hurricane-press.com

PO Box 568, Cambridge, New Zealand 3450

Printed in Great Britain
by Amazon